From Personality to Virtue

"You know my methods. Apply them." — Sherlock Holmes

From Personality to Virtue

Essays on the Philosophy of Character

"LITTLE THINGS AFFECT LITTLE MINDS."
— BENJAMIN DISRAELI

EDITED BY
Alberto Masala and
Jonathan Webber

UNIVERSITY PRESS

Great Clarendon Street, Oxford, OX2 6DP,
United Kingdom

Oxford University Press is a department of the University of Oxford.
It furthers the University's objective of excellence in research, scholarship,
and education by publishing worldwide. Oxford is a registered trade mark of
Oxford University Press in the UK and in certain other countries

© the several contributors 2016

The moral rights of the authors have been asserted

First Edition published in 2016
Impression: 1

All rights reserved. No part of this publication may be reproduced, stored in
a retrieval system, or transmitted, in any form or by any means, without the
prior permission in writing of Oxford University Press, or as expressly permitted
by law, by licence or under terms agreed with the appropriate reprographics
rights organization. Enquiries concerning reproduction outside the scope of the
above should be sent to the Rights Department, Oxford University Press, at the
address above

You must not circulate this work in any other form
and you must impose this same condition on any acquirer

Published in the United States of America by Oxford University Press
198 Madison Avenue, New York, NY 10016, United States of America

British Library Cataloguing in Publication Data
Data available

Library of Congress Control Number: 2015945724

ISBN 978-0-19-874681-2

Printed in Great Britain by
Clays Ltd, St Ives plc

Links to third party websites are provided by Oxford in good faith and
for information only. Oxford disclaims any responsibility for the materials
contained in any third party website referenced in this work.

Contents

List of Contributors   vii

Introduction   1
Alberto Masala and Jonathan Webber

1. Character, Punishment, and the Liberal Order   9
   Jonathan Jacobs

2. Virtue Ethics and Criminal Punishment   35
   Katrina L. Sifferd

3. Character, Will, and Agency   62
   Roman Altshuler

4. Practical Necessity and Personality   81
   Katharina Bauer

5. Implicit Bias, Character, and Control   106
   Jules Holroyd and Daniel Kelly

6. Instilling Virtue   134
   Jonathan Webber

7. Does the CAPS Model Improve Our Understanding of Personality and Character?   155
   Christian B. Miller

8. Friendship and the Structure of Trust   186
   Mark Alfano

9. The Psychology of Virtue Education   207
   Nafsika Athanassoulis

10. Mastering Wisdom   229
    Alberto Masala

Index   255

List of Contributors

MARK ALFANO is Associate Professor, Delft University of Technology. Since completing his doctorate at City University of New York in 2011, he has been Distinguished Guest Fellow at Notre Dame Institute for Advanced Study and Postdoctoral Research Associate at the Woodrow Wilson School and Center for Human Values at Princeton University. He has published numerous articles on the situationist challenge to virtue ethics, on extending this challenge to virtue epistemology, and on experimental philosophy of intentional action. His book *Character as Moral Fiction* was published by Cambridge University Press in 2013.

ROMAN ALTSHULER is currently Assistant Professor of Philosophy at Kutztown University, having completed his PhD at SUNY Stony Brook in 2010. His research interests centre on philosophy of agency, with special interests in free will, moral responsibility, and moral psychology. He also works on several figures in the history of philosophy, especially Kant and Heidegger, in relation to discussions of agency. He has published on action and ethics, and is currently working on papers on narrative identity and constitutivism, along with editing a collection on philosophy of action.

NAFSIKA ATHANASSOULIS is an independent researcher who has previously held lectureships at Keele University and the University of Leeds. Her monograph *Morality, Moral Luck and Responsibility* was published by Palgrave in 2005. She has published papers on medical ethics and research ethics in *Ethical Theory and Moral Practice*, *Journal of Value Inquiry*, and *Cambridge Quarterly of Healthcare Ethics*. Her response to the situationist critique of virtue ethics is one of the most cited in this literature. She is currently working on papers on virtue ethics and formal education.

KATHARINA BAUER is Lecturer in Philosophy at the University of Dortmund and Postdoctoral Research Fellow at the Ruhr-Universität Bochum. Her areas of specialization are theories of practical necessity, theories of personal identity and character, contemporary French philosophy (existentialism, phenomenology, and post-structuralism), and the relation between philosophy and literature.

JULES HOLROYD is Vice-Chancellor's Fellow in Philosophy at the University of Sheffield. Her research concerns the intersection of moral psychology and political philosophy. She has published papers on autonomy, responsibility, and punishment in *Ethical Theory and Moral Practice*, *Journal of Moral Philosophy*, *Journal of Social Philosophy*, *Philosophical Papers*, and *Social Theory and Practice* and is currently directing a major Leverhulme-funded research project on responsibility for implicit bias.

JONATHAN JACOBS is Director of the Institute for Criminal Justice Ethics, and Professor and Chair of Philosophy at John Jay College, City University of New York. He works on criminal justice and philosophy of law, as well as moral psychology and metaethics. He has received grants from the National Endowment for the Humanities, the Earhart Foundation, and the Littauer Foundation. His books include *Virtue and Self-Knowledge* (Prentice-Hall, 1989), *Practical Realism and Moral Psychology* (Georgetown University Press, 1995), *Choosing Character: Responsibility for Virtue and Vice* (Cornell University Press, 2001), and *Aristotle's Virtues* (Peter Lang, 2004).

DANIEL KELLY is Associate Professor of Philosophy at Purdue University. His monograph *Yuck! The Nature and Moral Significance of Disgust* was published by MIT Press in 2001. He has published papers on empirically informed moral psychology in *Brain and Behavioural Sciences*, *Cognition*, *Mind and Language*, and *Journal of Social Philosophy*. He has previously co-authored papers with Dan Fessler, Edouard Machery, and Stephen Stich.

ALBERTO MASALA is postdoctoral researcher at the Sciences, Normes, Décision research centre of the Sorbonne. His doctoral thesis was on the prospects for naturalizing virtue ethics, and his paper 'Excellence et spécialisation morale' was recently published in *La morale humaine et les sciences*. He is also currently director of a project at the education research centre Compas that aims to develop tools for training wise judgement.

CHRISTIAN B. MILLER is Associate Professor of Philosophy at Wake Forest University. He is the author of over thirty articles in metaethics, moral psychology, moral character, action theory, and philosophy of religion. His two books on character, *Moral Character: An Empirical Theory* and *Character and Moral Psychology*, have recently been published by OUP. He is Director of The Character Project, which is funded by a $4.2 million grant from the John Templeton Foundation.

KATRINA L. SIFFERD is Associate Professor of Philosophy at Elmhurst College. Before becoming a philosopher, Katrina earned a Juris Doctorate and worked as a senior research analyst on criminal justice projects for the National Institute of Justice. She has published many papers on neuroscience, moral psychology, and legal theory, including in *Consciousness and Cognition* and *Law and Philosophy*.

JONATHAN WEBBER is Reader in Philosophy at Cardiff University. He has published empirically grounded articles on philosophical moral psychology in *Ethical Theory and Moral Practice, European Journal of Philosophy, Journal of Moral Philosophy, Mind, Philosophical Quarterly,* and elsewhere. He is also the author of *The Existentialism of Jean-Paul Sartre* (Routledge, 2009) and *Rethinking Existentialism* (OUP, forthcoming), which bring insights from phenomenology and existentialism to debates in moral psychology.

Introduction

Alberto Masala and Jonathan Webber

Character plays a central role in our everyday understanding of one another and of ourselves. It informs the expectations that ground our plans and projects, our moral responses to actual behaviour and possible courses of action, and our political decisions concerning formal education, criminal punishment, and other aspects of social organization. The very idea that people have persisting, though not entirely fixed, character traits that explain their behaviour is woven throughout the fabric of our culture. The recent philosophical suggestion that we should abandon or radically reform this idea in the light of the situationist tradition of experiments in social psychology has not been accompanied by any serious consideration of the extent of the reforms that we would have to make if we did so. This is perhaps because the prospect of even beginning to map those reforms is sufficiently daunting to encourage us to reconsider whether this is indeed the correct response to those experiments.

This situationist critique of character has, however, succeeded in awakening philosophers from the dogmatic assumption that an idea of character developed purely through philosophical reflection captures the psychology of human motivation sufficiently to justify the moral and political recommendations that might be grounded in it. What began as a debate about whether the situationist experiments are compatible with virtue ethics has thus broadened into a discussion of how the findings of contemporary empirical psychology should shape the conception of character employed in philosophical thought. At the same time, interest has been growing among empirical psychologists in the conceptual frameworks that philosophers employ to integrate experimental findings and in the ethical and political considerations that philosophers have argued should constrain our attempts to influence one another's characters and motivations.

This volume of essays is intended to consolidate and extend this growing rapprochement between philosophers and psychologists working on the nature and evaluation of human motivation. Eleven philosophers have contributed papers that together advance the current debates over the nature and extent of character traits and their moral and political significance. These essays are informed by work in empirical psychology, but are not simply responsive to it. Instead they are intended as contributions to the integrative development of that work as well as to the philosophical debates they address more directly. Indeed, one of the common themes of these essays is precisely this issue of the relation between empirical studies of motivation, philosophical treatments of character, and the inspiration for both in Aristotle's subtle and sophisticated treatment of character and motivation.

A second underlying theme is a concern with the relation between an individual's character and their social context. Although situationist experiments often indicate the dependence of motivation on the specifically social dimension of the situation, this aspect has played only a minor role in the recent debate over their relevance to the ethics of character. The essays in this volume place great emphasis on the role of an individual's social and political context in forming their character, generally seeking to accommodate the insights of the situationist tradition within what remains recognizably a theory of personal character. Put another way, these essays emphasize the Aristotelian idea of the individual as a social animal rather than subordinating it to the equally Aristotelian idea of a rational animal.

The essays differ from many purely psychological studies of personality in emphasizing the dynamic nature of this aspect of motivation. Personality psychology generally takes static snapshots of traits by comparing individuals in a particular scenario and delegates the study of individual change to the psychology of child development. This is perhaps indirectly due to Gordon Allport's influential claim that personality psychology should operate entirely independently of ethical concerns. 'Character is personality evaluated, and personality is character devaluated,' he wrote, in a passage that has come to define the field, so 'character is an unnecessary concept for psychology' (1937: 52). As a resolutely ethical concept, character is intimately bound up with ideas of personal improvement and moral deterioration in adult life as much as in childhood and adolescence. By denying this ethical perspective to personality psychology, Allport may have removed the impetus to studying the waxing and waning of particular traits in adult life.

In this regard, character differs not only from the psychological idea of personality but also from the ethical idea of virtue. Many philosophers emphasize the claim that virtues are traits that require continual ethical work to maintain, rather than being states that continue under their own inertia once established. Independently of this point, philosophers disagree over whether the term 'virtue' should be reserved just for those ideal ethical traits that cannot be improved upon or whether it can also be applied to more achievable approximations of those ideals. Philosophers do tend to agree, however, implicitly or explicitly, that an ethical virtue can be fully understood in terms of the motivations and behaviour of the person who possesses it at a particular time. The dynamism of moral development inherent in the idea of character is not usually considered essential to ethical virtue itself.

The growing philosophical investigation of the idea of individual character therefore has the potential to transform both the consideration of personality and motivation in empirical psychology and the conception of virtue employed in philosophy. The essays in this volume are intended to contribute to this development through their analysis of the social aspect of character in the context of its dynamic aspect, particularly as this is played out through the contribution of reasoning to character development. They are also intended to draw from this investigation practical lessons for educational and penal theory as well as for personal ethics.

Jonathan Jacobs opens the central discussion with a careful analysis of the idea of character and some of its implications for criminal punishment within a liberal political system. Although liberalism is often taken to include the idea that the state should not aim to shape the character or preferences of the people, Jacobs points out that the very existence of a liberal polity rests on certain character traits being widespread among the population. He then develops a critique of penal policy and practice in the USA on the basis of these thoughts. He argues that the conditions in which many prisoners are incarcerated are not conducive to the development of the kinds of character traits on which the liberal polity depends. Moreover, he argues, some prisons are fostering the development of the kinds of character traits that will lead to repeat offending and which are generally inimical to the functioning of liberal society.

Katrina Sifferd augments this political argument with the more directly ethical concern that although the liberal state should not aim positively to foster virtuous character traits, nevertheless it ought not preclude or hinder any citizen's development towards virtue through their own decisions and actions. What is more, she argues, the state should not treat criminal offenders any differently from other citizens in this regard. Sifferd then critiques two current forms of judicial punishment on this basis. The use of isolation from human contact is an extreme external constraint on the individual's potential for development through personal relationships, mundane decision-making, and education and training. Chemical castration sets internal constraints on the prospects of developing character traits that subsume and shape one's sexual desires. Sifferd concludes that these practices are politically unjustifiable in a liberal context.

Roman Altshuler focuses on the question of exactly how character is related to reasoning and deciding, or the will. He points out that most philosophers working on motivation focus on either character or the will, but seldom employ both concepts. This is because, he argues, employing both seems to raise a dilemma. Either one's account is fragmented between actions with one kind of motivation and actions with the other, or it claims every action to have two motivations each of which is individually sufficient. Altshuler argues that there are strong theoretical reasons not to resist this dilemma by casting motivation as combining character and will. Some purposes in explaining action are best served by the language of character, others by the language of the will, he argues, and neither of these can be reduced to or eliminated in favour of the other.

Katharina Bauer addresses the relation between character and the will through the social practice of making ethical demands of someone's decisions and actions. She argues that one's character can be revealed in personal necessities that one cannot reasonably be expected to abandon. Expressions of personal necessity are insights into the structure of an individual's personality. And they are distinctive features of ground projects and convictions, which are essential for somebody's self-conception. As such, Bauer argues, they are demands that some limitation on the behaviour that one sees as possible for oneself should be respected. Nevertheless, whether such a demand ought to be met is itself an ethical question. The correct response can be a demand to reform that personality. Bauer concludes that the ethics of character rests on the tension between seeing each person as an individual and as a member of the collective, between the ideals of authenticity, autonomy, and morality.

Jules Holroyd and Dan Kelly approach the question of the extent of character from a different angle. Since character is an ethical concept as well as an explanatory one, they argue, it can cover only those cognitive and behavioural dispositions for which the agent can justifiably be held responsible. This raises the question of whether we should consider the phenomenon of implicit bias, where behaviour is influenced by a disposition that the agent is typically unaware of having and might disapprove of, to be an aspect of the individual's character and thus within the scope of personal responsibility. Although control over a disposition is necessary for it to form part of character, Holroyd and Kelly argue, this control need not be direct or immediate. One can control the dispositions underlying implicit bias through manipulating the social and cognitive environment in which they are embedded. This ecological control, they conclude, is sufficient for classifying these biases as aspects of character for which we are responsible.

Jonathan Webber continues this discussion of the relation between character and implicit bias. His question concerns how we should understand the idea of improving one's own behavioural dispositions. The standard view is that we have stable moral beliefs but might need to train our dispositions to bring them into line with these beliefs. An alternative account denies that our moral judgements reflect stable beliefs and argues that we should ground these judgements in careful deliberation. Webber argues that there is strong empirical reason to reject both views in favour of the idea that the same stable evaluative attitude can result in consistent judgement and behaviour, but that in the absence of such an attitude both judgement and behaviour will vary with situational details. He concludes that moral improvement is a matter of instilling in oneself the right strong evaluative attitudes, which he aligns with the Aristotelian idea of habituating ethical virtue.

Christian Miller then turns the discussion directly onto the detail and development of the cognitive-affective system theory of personality, which Webber draws on in his argument and which can be seen as an empirically grounded context for many of the ideas expounded in this volume. He shows that this theory confirms some of the central tenets of the common-sense idea of character. Since it rests on considerable empirical support and accommodates the findings of situationist experiments in its structure, this is evidence that those experiments do not require us to abandon the idea of character. Nevertheless, he argues, the theory does not offer any significant theoretical advance over that common-sense idea. Its strength lies not in its own articulation of personality, according to Miller, but in the evidence it musters for using this theory, whether described in common-sense vocabulary or in technical jargon, as a framework for research into motivation and personal traits. Miller closes with some suggestions for the directions in which that research should develop.

Mark Alfano questions an assumption made by the other papers in this volume. He explores the idea that aspects of an individual's social situations form constitutive parts of some virtues, not merely the causal background against which virtues are developed. He develops his idea of 'factitious' virtue, which mimics virtue as classically understood without possessing the classic internal structure of virtue, through a consideration of trustworthiness. To be factitiously trustworthy, he argues, it is sufficient that one is relied upon and wants to live up to the image of oneself implicit in that reliance. One does not need to possess already any qualities implied by that initial reliance. Alfano concludes that this kind of trustworthiness, which may be far more common than the ideal trustworthiness it mimics, is structurally analogous to friendship and suggests that this might provide a model for factitious forms of other virtues, such as courage or generosity.

Nafsika Athanassoulis considers the implications of the situationist tradition in experimental social psychology for the idea that education should aim to form the ethical character of the students. Drawing on comparative analysis of the varieties of situationist experiment, Athanassoulis argues that educators can shape ongoing character traits through providing students with carefully structured situational challenges, imparting information about the kinds of situational pressures that can undermine one's ethical aims, and then discussing the students' responses in a spirit of collaborative ethical inquiry. The primary role of the educator in this process is neither to inform nor to explain, but instead to model virtuous behaviour and self-critical reflection. It has been a mistake to think that experimental psychology conflicts with the traditional Aristotelian idea of educating for ethical virtues, Athanassoulis concludes, since it rather provides practical insights into precisely how this is best achieved.

Alberto Masala concludes the volume by arguing that these debates have been mistaken to focus on whether and when behaviour consistently manifests endorsed values across variations in situations. This emphasis on performance has modelled ethical virtue on mere competence, but we should rather think of it as a form of mastery. Masala argues that there are important psychological differences between these two kinds of skill. If we model virtue on competence, then we recognize that it is rare and difficult to achieve, so we are less motivated to improve. Instead, we should see the ethical task as the continual improvement and sophistication of our practical understanding through reflective engagement with the problems that life raises for us. Masala concludes that contemporary education has become overly concerned with the easily measurable outcome of competence, where what is needed to foster better citizens is an education that propagates the psychological structures of mastery, or what virtue ethicists have traditionally called practical wisdom.

These essays vary considerably in argumentative technique and rhetorical presentation. In this regard, they reflect the broadening of influences and methodologies that characterizes the contemporary development of anglophone academic philosophy. This intellectual context has a geographical aspect: the authors of these papers are spread fairly evenly between Europe and North America. As well as contributing to the growing collaboration between philosophers and psychologists in this area, this volume evidences the fading of the once bright line between analytic and Continental philosophers. Academic philosophy has recently been regrouping either side of a new dividing line, which separates work that is deeply engaged with empirical research from work that is not. This volume is intended to support the idea that integrating insights from both analytic and Continental philosophy with the ongoing empirical research into the psychology of motivation and moral judgement is essential to meeting the challenge laid down by Elizabeth Anscombe (1958) to ground ethics firmly in a sound understanding of the mind.

Works Cited

Allport, Gordon. 1937. *Personality: A Psychological Interpretation.* New York: Holt.

Anscombe, G. E. M. 1958. Modern Moral Philosophy. *Philosophy* 33 (124): 1–19.

1 The concept of

Character, Punishment, and the Liberal Order

Jonathan Jacobs

This paper explores an intersection of moral psychology, ethics, and political principle. It defends the claim that the concept *character* has significant explanatory import, especially in ethical contexts. Failing to recognize the significance of considerations of character, understood as comprising enduring features of persons, would be costly to our conceptualizations and explanations of important aspects of persons and actions. Those considerations figure appropriately in our understanding of aspiration, regret, self-regard, expectations of our selves and others, and additional, significant features of our lives, choices, reactions, and undertakings. Making the case for this view and its discernibly Aristotelian resonances will include examination of the role of considerations concerning character in the context of criminal sanction in a liberal polity. This is, I believe, a timely, important, and especially effective context for highlighting the explanatory and ethical significance of character.

The discussion is not a study of the role of considerations about character in particular court cases or in sentencing. Instead, it considers respects in which the concept *character* is relevant to our understanding of some of the most important issues concerning legal punishment in a liberal polity. I focus on the liberal political order because the issues discussed have some real urgency in the US and the UK, each with a broadly liberal political culture, and each wrestling with challenges concerning the forms, aims, and justification of legal punishment. That is an important matter in its own right yet, in addition, examining it will reveal significant ramifications for our broader understanding of civil society and the rule of law. Those ramifications only heighten the significance of considerations concerning character in our understanding of significant explanatory and normative contexts.

1.1

One of the chief features of a liberal political order, in several influential conceptions, is that it is restrained with regard to legal moralism. A liberal order does not impose or enforce a specific conception of a well-led life, of what persons should regard as good or worthwhile or what states of character they are to have. To be sure, there are multiple conceptions of liberalism and the liberal tradition includes diverse currents of thought. Still, even given that diversity, it is fair to say that many who endorse liberalism regard the enforcement of morality or the imposition of life plans in a comprehensive manner as illiberal. For example, William Galston writes:

A liberal polity guided (as I believe it should be) by a commitment to moral and political pluralism will be parsimonious in specifying binding public principles and cautious about employing such principles to intervene in the internal affairs of civil associations. It will, rather, pursue a policy of *maximum feasible accommodation*, limited only by the core requirements of individual security and civic unity. (2002, 20)

Yet, at the same time, sustaining a liberal order depends upon broad agreement on several fundamental values and principles. A stable, widely endorsed framework of institutions and laws within which people can exercise extensive liberties is required to preserve a liberal order. Complete neutrality is neither necessary nor practicable. The very notion of the liberal state's restraint reflects commitment to specific, significant values. They shape political institutions and the rule of law, even if there are contested issues concerning the realization of those values. Still, the liberal order's values leave wider, rather than narrower scope for persons to have diverse commitments, interests, and aims. Indeed, it is likely within a liberal polity that there will be, at least to some extent, disagreement over precisely what form it should take and what policies it should implement.

The distinctive commitments characteristic of liberalism, such as the fundamental importance of individuals' rights and liberties, require endorsement of values shaping the normative architecture within which pluralism is possible. In addition, that endorsement depends upon persons having certain general dispositions and attitudes; without them, a liberal political/legal order is in a precarious condition. Among the most important dispositions is the willingness of persons and groups to be restrained in regard to imposing their values upon others, whether by formal political means or otherwise. The *state* is to be restrained, and it is also important that *individuals* exhibit restraint with regard to beliefs, practices, and perspectives they may, in fact, find objectionable. A willingness to tolerate things one finds obnoxious or objectionable in some respects is needed. A willingness to discriminate between what one does not like about the conduct or way of life of others and what actually causes harm is needed. The success of a liberal order depends upon the maintenance of a certain kind of political culture *and* formal institutional arrangements.

Especially if society is diverse and pluralistic rather than largely homogeneous (ethnically, religiously, culturally, and so forth) a liberal polity depends upon persons being tolerant and accommodative, even in ways that might test their commitment to liberal principles. A liberal polity depends upon people recognizing, in an enduring, effective way, that at least some of one's values cannot be presumed to be correct for everyone, and that others have the right to act and live in ways one does not approve. This can be a source of friction and tension between different groups but it can also be a source of salutary interaction and interpenetration of the values of different traditions and perspectives.

While official legislative acts of the state and jurisprudential rulings of the courts are crucial elements of restrained legal moralism, it is also important that in their daily participation in the multiple contexts of civil society people refrain from pressuring others to conform and from placing impediments in the way of people acting in ways that reflect their own valuative commitments. Willingness to interact with others in ways that respect their equality is required. Influence, obstacles, and pressure can take many different forms distinct from official government acts and judicial rulings. We will see (section 1.5) the significance of this consideration with regard to persons who re-enter civil society after being released from prison.

1.2

What is the significance of the concept *character* in elucidating some of the most important, complex challenges concerning punishment in a liberal order? A brief summary of the main issue is this: while there is an important sense in which an individual's character is not properly a direct concern of the liberal state, criminal sanction, at least in forms in which it is practiced in the US (and some other liberal democracies) has a significant impact *on* offenders' characters in ways that are antithetical to the principles of the liberal political/legal order. That is the core issue of the present discussion. If this is true for large numbers of offenders and not just an anomalous, occasional circumstance, then it is a basis for regarding the legitimacy of at least some significant policies and practices of criminal justice as doubtful. Considerations concerning character have an important role in diagnosing the issue conceptually and normatively.

While criminal law is generally directed at punishing conduct rather than character, criminal sanction often has an impact on character in morally significant respects. The central concern of the present discussion is that current carceral practices damage large numbers of prisoners in ways that render them less able or even unable to re-enter civil society successfully. Many prisoners are harmed and worsened by the conditions to which they are subject. That is an important respect in which punishment exceeds what would be *just desert* and in which it also does damage to civil society.

By 'civil society' I mean the overall complex of contexts, settings, and departments of life in which persons engage in voluntary activity, voluntary association, and participate in all variety of institutions and activities.[1] These can include institutions and activities having to do with economic life, education, philanthropy, leisure and cultural life, religious life, and so forth. The significance of the way that civil society is damaged is to be understood in the following terms: Liberal principles shape and preserve a political/legal order within which there is scope for open, pluralistic civil society. Participation in such civil society can provide people with reasons to want to preserve the liberal order, on

---

[1] My conception of civil society is influenced by views developed by Edward Shils, especially his *The Virtue of Civility* (1997).

account of enjoying liberty and the multiple ways it matters to their lives. That relation of mutual reinforcement is highly important. In addition to the institutions and policies the liberal order involves, features of people's character have a key role in shaping (or weakening) it. If civil society is diminished, either by a shrinking of the scope for it or by incivility becoming prevalent, the concern to preserve a liberal order can also be weakened.

A chief concern here is to explicate how considerations concerning character help us understand how and why current carceral practice damages individuals and society. Nevertheless, the damage that is done is not a basis for concluding that the state should encourage certain virtues through enacting specific policies that have that as their specific aim. The damage in question can be limited without erring on the side of illiberal imposition on people's lives. There is an important difference between the state preserving conditions in which agents can acquire virtues and the state making the encouragement of virtue a specific aim of policy. It may be difficult to draw a clear, bright line marking the difference but the latter is more susceptible to involving illiberal interference in people's lives and in civil society.

The damage done to incarcerated persons is on a scale that impacts civil society overall. A key aspect of that impact is the effect on what I shall call a 'civil disposition.' By that I mean the overall ensemble of habits, attitudes, and motivational patterns crucial to the health and civility of society under a liberal rule of law. It is not necessary that members of a civil society under a liberal rule of law should have a notable or outstanding level of ethical virtue or even a high degree of civic virtue. That would of course be welcome and such persons are to be admired and appreciated. But it is implausible to expect people in general to exhibit more than a modest degree of virtue. The civility of civil society depends most fundamentally upon willingness to respect the rights and liberties of others, refraining from harming persons, toleration of differences, and willingness to trust others while also being trustworthy. That willingness is no small thing but attaining and maintaining it does not depend upon a high degree of virtue.

The relationship of mutual reinforcement (or weakening) between civil society and the liberal order reflects the significance of moral-psychological phenomena to the practical realization of the principles and values of a liberal order. If civil society is compromised by a lack of civil disposition there are untoward results for the liberal order. We will see that there is empirical evidence of how incarceration worsens people in ways that weaken or undermine a civil disposition and, thus, civil society.

The type of civil society made possible by a liberal political/legal order both *enables* and *requires* individuals to interact in a potentially vast and open-ended variety of exchanges, cooperation, mutual reliance, and contract, all of them more or less dependent upon expectations of good faith. Trust and trustworthiness are among the conditions enabling persons to pursue their interests, commitments, and concerns independent of imperatives coming from the state. Though one's character is not a direct concern of the state the liberal polity *depends upon* the great majority of persons having a civil disposition. A civil disposition can be supported by reliably continent—rather than firmly virtuous—character, and such a disposition makes the complex metabolism of civil society possible.

There is an important sense in which no one is 'in charge' of the metabolism of civil society in a liberal polity, though it is informed by rules, principles, and attitudes people endorse or at least accept. A civil disposition obviates the need to always examine other persons' bona fides, doing a sort of credit check of civility prior to interactions, exchanges, and cooperation. There are numerous contexts in which formal checking of certain specific types is appropriate or necessary. Nevertheless, in a great many cases, it is not, and the spontaneity of civil society depends, to a large extent, on that fact.

1.3

We can now examine more closely some of the ways that character figures in the nexus of the liberal order, civil society, and criminal sanction. By *character* I mean relatively stable dispositions that guide choice, and shape reactions, attitudes, and motives. One's character is not a fixed set of dispositions if by 'fixed' we mean (i) the person has them without there being a role for voluntariness in coming to have them, or if we mean (ii) they are unsusceptible to change, or (iii) they are exhibited in action in a completely uniform way across different contexts. Those notions of fixity ignore the respects in which reasoning and judgment are involved in many expressions of character, and they make no allowance for the respects in which aspiration can be important to how one sees one's own character and might seek to develop or change it. The different elements figuring in the shaping of one's character include features of natural temperament and the specific ways one's capacities for reasoning and voluntary activity have become disposed *through their exercise*.

Our decisions, responses, ways of weighing considerations in deliberation—these make a difference to what dispositions we acquire and how firmly. Of course, the examples set by others and the ways in which the people by whom we are surrounded encourage certain behaviors and discourage others are central to the habituation we undergo. It is extremely difficult to disentangle the degree to which character is the result of natural endowment, the degree to which it is the result of a person's voluntary activity, and the degree to which habituation by others has shaped it. Generally, in being habituated a person is still acting voluntarily; most seven-year-olds are not coerced or threatened with violence in learning to say 'thank you' for a holiday gift. Habituation should not be thought of as excluding voluntariness, as mechanical, unresponsive to what the 'recipient' chooses to make of those influences. And with maturity the recipient is increasingly capable of being actively involved and not merely a patient.

Aristotle plausibly highlighted the fact that we do not have fine-tuned control of the ways in which what we *do* makes a difference to what we are *like*. Still, he held that it is appropriate to regard persons as responsible for their characters because we know that what we do *makes a difference* to what we are *like* (see *Nicomachean Ethics* book III chapter 5). That fact about the formation of states of character is accessible to just about anyone who gives thought to how their own experiences, actions, and motives impact their attitudes, habits, and concerns. Aristotle remarked that only an insensible person would not be aware that choices and actions shape character (1114a 10–20). It is reasonable to expect people to be aware of that. One would have to be extraordinarily inattentive not to recognize that fact, and the inattention itself may be voluntary. Also, awareness that what we do voluntarily can have an impact that perhaps we did not *intend* is not a reason for concluding that we are not responsible, in part, for our characters.

Moreover, especially with respect to virtues, one does not just *find* that he or she has a given state of character by accident. Natural temperament surely matters but acquiring a virtue requires certain kinds of attention,

16 JONATHAN JACOBS

awareness of diverse valuative considerations and their weights, and various sorts of self-awareness and self-control. It requires reasoning in certain ways rather than others and judgment and decision based upon recognizing facts as considerations with specific sorts of significance. That our actions can make a difference to our dispositions is one of the things we need to understand if we are to have a decent prospect of acquiring virtues and if we are to encourage and guide others helpfully in that regard. Telling someone, "It really doesn't matter much what you do this time; you can always just decide to act differently if similar circumstances arise again" could be seriously misleading. In addition, a person cannot come to have certain states of character just by *deciding* to. A decision to make the effort to acquire a certain disposition, if conjoined with resolve and relevant forms of attention and self-awareness, can be a necessary part of an undertaking to shape one's own character, but it is just a part. Acquisition of a virtue is *work*.

It needs to be admitted that whether one is the sort of person to have the relevant types of self-awareness and concern needed for revision of dispositions (let us stipulate, in the direction of virtue) can *itself* be influenced by natural temperament and habituation. The people by whom one is surrounded can influence whether one becomes self-aware and self-critical. Being habituated in an environment in which one is expected to give reasons for acting, explain one's choices, consider whether acting (or reacting) in a certain way is or is not commendable, will generally make it more likely that one will acquire habits of self-awareness, including how one's actions *exhibit* character and can also *affect* character. But the influences of others are not simply stamped onto a person, shaping dispositions without any role for receptivity and the ability to reason, to choose, and to adopt a perspective.

There is a role for voluntariness in the way one's habits shape states of character. As a person matures, so does the ability to inform voluntariness with reasoning and with judgment, and to make one's own decisions. While early habituation is almost entirely a matter of how other persons (in a sense, the practical reasoning of those persons) encourage certain dispositions in us, the habituation influencing us is increasingly a matter of how we habituate *ourselves*. Development of our capacities for reasoning, judgment, and self-awareness, in conjunction with experience provides us with greater ability to decide how and why to act, and supplies a more substantial basis for evaluating, choosing, and acting.

The ability to deliberately shape our own dispositions interacts with the influence of habituation by others and with juvenile, pre-rational habituation. In the one respect we become more self-determining while, in accord with the other, our capacities are exercised in a context shaped by other factors.

However, even youthful habituation can be, in part, a training of self-determination, a matter of encouraging attachment to certain kinds of objects, and shaping modes of attention, perception, and sensibility. This is so even if the person being habituated is not yet fully aware of how her abilities to be self-determining are being shaped. If we are fortunate in how we are habituated, it will be less, rather than more, a matter of just being pushed or forced to act in certain ways without helping us understand why it is better to act thusly rather than some other way. Aristotle, for example, notes: "For children and the other animals share in what is voluntary, but not in decision; and the actions we do on the spur of the moment are said to be voluntary, but not to express decision" (1111b 7–10). In abusive or coercive forms, habituation *imposes* dispositions in ways that can obstruct self-determination (and we will see the relevance of this to criminal justice in section 1.5), but, hopefully, more often, it is a process of encouraging a person's exercise of capacities for voluntariness and self-governance in decision-making and acting.

Unlike a dog or a sheep, a human being can have concerns and commitments regarding what sort of person one wishes to become. Striving to realize them may meet with stiff challenges and frustration. Still, human beings can work at becoming certain sorts of persons, striving to acquire certain states of character. Joel Kupperman, remarking on what is involved in a mature human being having a character, writes:

> character needs to be thought of, not merely as an array of dispositions and abilities, but also as what a person is like. Thus education of character should be regarded not merely as the implanting of something like software for problems of life; it involves shaping the development of what (at the start) are not in the fullest sense persons of certain sorts. (1999, 201)

And in explicating the role of aspiration in the acquisition of virtue Julia Annas remarks,

> Many accounts of virtue give insufficient weight to the drive to aspire. They assume that we learn from our family, school, and friends to be brave, loyal, and

generous, and that this process is something like mindless absorption: we allegedly just come to take on the dispositions which our family and friends call virtuous, without having the distance to criticize them. If this were so, however, each generation would simply replicate the past one... whereas what we find is that each generation alters its predecessor's conception of some virtues, while others fall out of favor altogether. (2011, 22)

This point holds in the context of acquiring states of character generally, and is not limited to the virtues. Example and habituation by others have important roles but a person can mediate and modify those influences by his own interests and investments in how his agential capacities are shaped and oriented. This is not to say that persons typically have explicit, carefully elaborated conceptions of what sorts of character they wish to acquire. Many people may give only intermittent or shallow thought to the matter. However, we can have a role in determining our reasons for acting and the motives prompting us to act and we can judge their place in our enacting what we take to be desirable, worthwhile, required, or appropriate. Even when we disavow reasons or motives the disavowal can reflect awareness of a role for our agency in what we do and what we are like.

Someone who gives thought to how to express their malice or their jealousy (without wondering whether expressing it is a good idea) is still doing something a non-human creature cannot do. It is true that how one habituated by others is part of the explanation of whether one's habits are praiseworthy or objects of ethical criticism but that also depends on her own decisions, actions, and judgments. In any case, despite the influence of habituation, and what may be (in some circumstances) only modest opportunities to resist it, the notion that a feature of character is something rigid, sub-rational, and fixed in its role in a person's actions is just a mistake.

One can, for example, strive to control a volatile temper, learn to be more patient and considerate, attempt to acquire a more disciplined approach to one's work and responsibilities. We might come to certain realizations about our characters at points when it seems late to try to change but the possibility of the realization and the attempt at revision are distinctive capacities of human beings. We do not know whether our efforts will be efficacious because we do not know how fully fixed our dispositions have become. We can still acknowledge reasons for making the effort to change and can be motivated to make the effort. Insisting that, "That's just the way I am; I cannot change that," is almost certainly a poor excuse and an even poorer justification.

Yet, it is true that people tend to become more or less settled in mature dispositions, in acquired 'second natures,' i.e., specific forms in which their capacities and abilities are developed and exercised. Our lives would be very different if that were not so. People typically have guiding concerns, characteristic responses and attitudes, and they tend to engage with other people and the world in ways that reflect lasting valuative concerns and commitments. While rational capacities enable us to critically reflect on ourselves and to consider how we should try to change, those capacities do not remain in a state of unstructured, fully plastic openness. We tend to exhibit what become *characteristic* habits of motivation, reasoning, judgment, and choice, and the plasticity of character diminishes over time.

The barrier to precise knowledge of the respective causal roles of voluntariness and the influence of others is not a basis for denying that the agent is at least partly responsible for the now settled disposition even in the absence of any intention to have become settled in it. Often, when someone admonishes, "You don't want to make a habit of that," the advice reflects the recognition that (i) acting a certain way can shape a disposition to act that way, and that (ii) voluntariness has a role in shaping dispositions whether or not that shaping is in agreement with an intention to acquire just those dispositions.

1.4

The concept *character* has familiar uses in much of our thought about how our own lives are going and what is most important to us. Self-understanding and attaining a coherent, narrative self-conception often involve beliefs (and judgments) concerning states of character. They can be prominent in aspiration, regret, projects of change and reform, how we project ourselves into the future, and how we understand our own past. A particular episode may be the *occasion* for self-evaluative thought but often the *focus of concern* is what sort of person one is, and what the episode indicates about that issue. In thinking about our lives and experience we do not limit ourselves to considering particular episodes and particular experiences. Instead, we tend to place those and their significance in a larger context, often shaped by notions concerning

aspects of character and how experience impacted what we are like or what was at stake concerning what we are like.

A person's self-knowledge, if it is honest and informative, will include notions of what that individual values, her guiding concerns and commitments, and the prevailing contours of her reactive attitudes and sensibility. Also, as Kupperman points out, "[a] quality can be part of someone's normal pattern of thought and action, in the intended sense, without there being any specific occasion on which [the] quality is likely to be expressed. Thus someone's character may include the fact that he or she is capable of great cruelty, even if this refers to occasional (and not entirely predictable) cruel acts." (1999, 202). A feature of character can influence judgments, decisions, and actions in direct, clear ways or in less obvious but still genuine ways.

In regard to how character states can determine limitations on what it is practically possible for us to do, and how such limitations can be strengths or defects, Bernard Williams writes:

> We are subject to the model that what one can do sets the limits to deliberation, and that character is revealed by what one chooses within those limits, among the things that one can do. But character (of a person in the first instance; but related points apply to a group, or to a tradition) is equally revealed in the location of those limits, and in the very fact that one can determine, sometimes through deliberation itself, that one cannot do certain things, and must do others. Incapacities can not only set limits to character and provide conditions of it, but can also partly constitute its substance. (1981, 130)

The actual scope of what a person is free to do is not fully defined by what is, in an abstract sense, causally possible in a set of circumstances. One's character makes a crucial difference to what is practically possible, necessary, and impossible. (And, as Williams notes in the quoted passage, a person's judgments and choices can shape character as well as reflect it.)

Moreover, not all limitations concerning practical possibility are weaknesses. The firmly honest and courageous person may find it impossible to do something self-servingly corrupt. And as Williams says, "[t]he incapacities we are considering here are ones that help constitute character, and if one acknowledges responsibility for anything, one must acknowledge responsibility for decisions and action which are expressions of character—to be an expression of character is perhaps the most substantial way in which an action can be one's own" (1981, 130).

Moreover, the person who admits his ambition and willingness to treat others unfairly for the purpose of his own advantage does not diminish his liability to blame by admitting the truth about some of his defects of character.

Also, someone's insistence that he "had no other choice" or "was left with no alternative" or did "the only thing I could do" can tell us as much about that person's self-conception as about the character-independent possibilities in the circumstances. A person with vices may take a perverse pride in his ruthlessness and be glad to have an opportunity to torment someone. The circumstances do not force the ruthless person's hand, though he enjoys pretending they do. We might not wish to *take* responsibility for a state of character but that is not in its own right evidence that we are not, in fact, responsible for it, our voluntariness having a role in acquiring it.

Failure to take interest in what sort of person one is becoming is what we might call an *aretaic* failure, even if it does not include some notable moral failure. A person's actions, decisions, responses, and attitudes reflect normative valences and we (reasonably) expect persons to be self-aware regarding them. We evaluate those valences and how a person regards them, as well as individual actions. It is difficult to see how one could effectively aspire to virtue or how a person could aim to overcome a fault or a weakness without addressing the matter as a project concerning states of character in more than a merely 'local' or episodic sense.  In thinking about what one wishes to accomplish or what one wishes to change in her life, or in reconsidering priorities, there is almost inevitably a role for considerations concerning lasting states of character, related in various ways to numerous dispositions and matters concerning judgment and decision. The ability to make the desired changes often depends upon matters of character even if the idiom of 'character' does not figure explicitly in the person's reflections.

Our lives and our self-conceptions would be much more fragmented if we did not acquire relatively stable states of character, if states of character were mainly 'local,' domesticated to particular contexts or circumstances. To be sure, we can still be opaque to ourselves, uncertain of how to evaluate ourselves, and not sure about what we are capable of and what are our limits. We can be surprised and disoriented in deep and disruptive ways, even about ourselves. It is evident that there are numerous ways in which self-knowledge is difficult and uncertain. However, without content based upon our grasp of our own characters it is difficult to see what would be the form and matter of our self-conceptions (whether or not they are honest and accurate). They are an important basis for being able to think about the temporal extendedness of our lives and the relations we take there to be between past, present, and future (whether or not we are correct in those judgments).

Though I will argue that, generally, states of character should not be interpreted as local and not enduring, there are ways a characteristic can be reflected in different ways in different contexts. A person might think, "Why am I able to be confident and resolute in some contexts but I am tentative and insecure in others?" One of the challenges in striving to acquire virtues is to acquire them with stability and adaptability, so that their exercise is not limited and narrow. If a virtue is mainly local, that is evidence of it being only partial and defective. Exhibiting courage involves meeting different kinds of challenges in diverse contexts. Not all courage is physical courage and sometimes just telling the truth, or not shrinking from a potentially embarrassing encounter, can take courage. A *principle* concerning honesty may be fairly simple and straightforward but a virtue is not a principle. As Gary Watson notes:

A virtue is not a proposition one can consult or apply or interpret; it does not in the same sense prescribe any course of action. Only something like a principle can do that. On the other hand, one's virtues may enable one to endorse, apprehend, correctly apply, or disregard some principle of action. (1990, 454)

In addition, relations to other virtues (courage, justice, benevolence, compassion, patience, etc.) can be complex. There is much more to honesty than 'just telling the truth.' It is a mistake to think in terms of 'one disposition—one virtue' just as much as (in most cases) it is a mistake to think 'one gene—one trait.' Acquiring a virtue depends upon the interaction of multiple dispositions and attitudes. A state of character, whether a virtue or not, is generally not a stand-alone feature of an agent. It can involve relations between numerous dispositions, aspects of sensibility, and patterns of motivation. While we refer to a particular state of character (e.g., honesty or greed or pride or shamelessness), because of the focus of our interest in the action in question that state is not an isolable building-block of the person's character. It is likely to be related to numerous elements of character as an identifiable but non-separable thread in an overall fabric.

1.5

We can turn now to some of the specific issues concerning character and punishment in a liberal polity. The extent to which states of character are a proper concern of the state is a contested, complicated issue in a liberal democracy. Some theorists have argued that concern with character is in serious tension with liberalism. Jeffrie Murphy suggests one way this might be so.

> In short: our society, supposedly a liberal society, sometimes does in fact administer punishment in part on the basis of beliefs about the defendant's inner wickedness. The focus upon such wickedness is no doubt sometimes simply as a predictor of dangerousness—and is thus consistent with the harm principle—but sometimes it operates with an independent life of its own. The criminal may be punished primarily for breaking the rules, but we often feel free to give him some additional punishment if we think he broke the rules because of traits of character we find loathsome. Is this kind of retributivism consistent with liberalism or does it represent a departure from liberal values? (1998, 98)

Without entering debates concerning sentencing directly we can still see that considerations concerning character are relevant to criminal sanction in a liberal polity in an important way. I want to say something briefly about the importance of retributivist considerations because they are relevant in a significant way. They reflect acknowledgment of persons as agents capable of acting for reasons and meriting respect under a rule of law justified, in part, by the endorsement of the law by those to whom it applies. In that regard, retributivist considerations register the standing of persons in a liberal order and to dispense with them, perhaps appealing exclusively to consequentialist considerations, would mean a loss of something normatively important.

In *Presumed Dangerous* Michael Corrado argues that it is not "open to us to abandon the idea that punishment is limited to the retributive" and that retribution is "the very heart or the meaning of punishment" (2013, 67). He regards non-retributive punishment as contrary to "common sense and ... deeply rooted intuitions about justice" (2013, 67). This strong assertion of retributivism is almost certainly a minority view among contemporary philosophers but Corrado's analysis highlights the connection between retributivist considerations and regarding persons as voluntary, accountable agents who are bearers of important rights. A rationale for punishment limited to minimizing harm or to other consequentialist concerns does not include conceptual resources adequate to register the distinctive status of persons as accountable, rights-bearing agents in relation to a liberal rule of law. A wholly consequentialist conception of punishment is permissive in principle, in morally objectionable ways, inasmuch as it could, for example, steadily expand grounds for preventive detention. (That is an especially significant issue if there is public support for 'putting away the bad guys so that they can't hurt anyone else,' or for 'keeping anyone with a personality disorder off the streets,' even if such persons have completed their sentences, or for preemptive approaches to dealing with concerns about terrorism.)

The chief respect in which character is important in regard to punishment in a liberal polity is that, very often, the terms and conditions of incarceration are antithetical to the principles of a liberal polity even considered apart from debates about what types of conduct are criminalized, and whether character should figure in sentencing. They are in tension with liberal principles because of the kinds of damage prisoners suffer, primarily through the impact on their character states and agential capacities. There is considerable evidence that the conditions of incarceration to which many prisoners are subject undermine capacities needed to re-enter civil society successfully.[2] Prisoners are worsened through demoralization in ways that encourage vice, undermine development of prudential agency, and impede or erode a civil disposition. Demoralization runs deeper than a mood of discouragement; it impacts abilities.

Many prisoners have little or no opportunity for meaningful activity or interactions with other persons, and access to information, instruction, and other constructive undertakings is often severely restricted. The effect extends beyond unhappiness, boredom, and frustration. In many cases, incarceration has become not only removal from civil society but exclusion from participation in contexts and activities involving the exercise (and development) of capacities of the sorts needed to live in civil society. The effect of the combination of the conditions of incarceration and the length of sentences can be enduring. In that sense, punishment goes on after completion of sentence, amounting to a violation of the notion of just desert.

---

[2] Haney (2006: especially chs 5–8) provides an excellent summary and analysis of the ways in which incarceration encourages vice and crime, with extensive reference to much of the relevant empirical literature.

Even without intending to worsen prisoners and damage civil society current practices have that impact and, to some extent, the state is responsible. As Craig Haney writes, "It is not surprising that the overcrowded conditions and anti-rehabilitation ethos that characterized the last several decades in American corrections appear to have greatly increased the criminogenic risks that persons must overcome following incarceration" (2006, 224). Haney quotes Joan Petersilia's summary of research on released prisoners.

> The average inmate coming home will have served a longer prison sentence than in the past, be more disconnected from family and friends, have a higher prevalence of substance abuse and mental illness, and be less educated and less employable than those in prior prison release cohorts. Each of these factors is known to predict recidivism, yet few of these needs are addressed while the inmate is in prison or on parole. (2003, 53)

Some of the attitudes and habits prisoners find helpful to them during their incarceration are not well suited to civil society. The dispositions of trust and trustworthiness, the willingness to cooperate with others, expectations of reciprocity and good faith in all manner of interactions and exchanges—these are not reinforced in prison. Indeed, their opposites are likely to be reinforced to an extent that cannot be easily shed upon release from prison.

These considerations are not introduced to build a case against punishment or for abolition of incarceration as a form of punishment. Moreover, there are prisons in which conditions are not nearly so damaging and prison officials and staff members deserve credit for working to minimize abuses and many of the worst features of incarceration. Nonetheless, these points highlight the fact that current conditions of incarceration are known to worsen many prisoners in ways that exceed whatever deprivation of freedom and its pleasures they might deserve on the basis of their criminal conduct.

It is hardly surprising that prisoners would become despondent and, in many cases, also feel that they are completely at the mercy of a system that treats them in arbitrary and inscrutable ways. Studies of prisoners in the United States and in the United Kingdom show that "[p]risoners became ever more cynical and distrusting, and their behaviour increasingly and narrowly instrumental or strategic. They were experts in manoeuvre—and yet outflanked by an unfathomable system that had all the power" (Liebling ms, 5).

Many prisoners are not only ill-equipped to return to civil society, they regard criminal justice and the rule of law as lacking legitimacy. In many instances, the causes of that perception of doubtful legitimacy actually *are* good reasons for thinking that there is, in fact, a deficit of legitimacy. Also, persons who doubt the legitimacy of the rule of law may be less inhibited about committing additional crimes. Thus, even if criminal sanction does not aim at damaging and worsening prisoners it can do considerable damage in forms that are coercive, and illiberal, and also counterproductive. The misery experienced by a great many prisoners does not generally motivate efforts at ethical self-correction; bitterness, distrust, and alienation are at least as—if not much more—likely.

It might be argued that the impact of the prison experience is more situational than enduring, that the habits and outlooks acquired by prisoners are not indicative of a change in enduring character states. Whether they are deliberate strategies of coping or non-voluntary, is there reason to believe that prisoners sometimes actually undergo changes in states of character and agential capacity? Consider the analysis by Doris and Murphy (2007) of soldiers in combat and their argument that, often, soldiers should be regarded as having diminished responsibility for morally unjustifiable acts—such as the intentional killing of civilians who do not appear to pose a threat, or the murder of prisoners who are in no position to defend themselves or escape. Their view is that the conditions to which soldiers are subject in combat can cause them to become cognitively impaired to an extent such that they are less than fully responsible for wrongful acts. They argue that this is a situational phenomenon, not an example of enduring states of character being formed. Once back in a peacetime environment many such soldiers realize the enormity of their acts and may be wracked by painful regret, disturbed at what they were capable of doing.

There is not space for a thorough discussion of the view, as presented in 'From My Lai to Abu Ghraib: The Moral Psychology of Atrocity,' though I will remark on some of their illustrations, to indicate why I regard them as problematic, tendentious, and implausible. For example, they remark that "SS officer Jochen Peiper claimed not to have slept for nine straight days during the fight (during which Peiper's troops massacred several dozen American POWs on December 17, 1944)" (2007, 37).

Peiper had, by that time, very considerable experience as an SS officer in charge of murdering very large numbers of civilians and POWs on the Eastern Front. He had joined the SS in 1933 as an enthusiastic Nazi. The notion that a partial exculpation of the Malmedy massacre is that he and his troops were exhausted is not convincing. The authors also say that, "U.S. personnel report being instructed to circumvent this inconvenience (that 'firing white phosphorous at people is a war crime') by calling for white phosphorous strikes not against enemy soldiers, but against their equipment" (2007, 42). They do not mention that (i) the prohibition is against firing it at people known to be civilians, or that (ii) white phosphorous is widely—and legally—used as an anti-armor weapon, or that (iii) in many cases US forces were aware that Iraqi forces had abandoned their tanks, armored vehicles, and trucks, and the weapon was used to render such equipment useless to the Iraqis. Numerous examples in the article invite questions, with important qualifications being left unmade or significant contextual factors not being included. Having mentioned them, we should put aside concerns about some of their illustrations, and focus on their explanatory claims.

One of their main points—one that comports with the situationist and 'local' conception of character states Doris has defended—is that "combat and related phenomena frequently induce, in quite normal subjects, transient cognitive impairments that enable morally reprehensible behavior" and situational influences "can result in aberrant behavior coming to seem appropriate" (2007, 31, 36), such that on account of impairments in "normative competence," "soldiers are typically not responsible for much of their combat behavior" (2007, 39, 38). The situation of prison inmates might appear to be analogous; i.e., is it the case that the ways that they respond to their conditions do not involve changes in states of character or enduring erosion of agential capacities but, instead, situationally induced, temporary changes?

In making the case for enduring states of character I have not argued that mature states are so fixed that, aside from the sorts of changes that come with aging, there is no plasticity whatsoever in one's character. What appears to happen to some incarcerated persons is that the conditions are so restrictive in regard to freedom, so demoralizing (literally, in not permitting judgments and activities of the kind constitutive of moral life) that their attitudes, willingness to trust, their patterns of motivation, and so forth are changed in significant, enduring ways. Often, they appear to be more than situationally induced local changes that do not extend into other contexts or persist after leaving prison.

Given the diversity of sensibility we should expect a broad range of responses to the conditions of incarceration, some prisoners affected in deeper, more lasting ways than others. Differences in prisoners' sensibilities, life histories, prior experiences, self-confidence, and resolve can make a difference to the impact of incarceration. Still, part of what makes the miserable conditions of incarceration so objectionable is that their effects often do extend beyond causing suffering while in prison. They impact prisoners by diminishing their capacities for prudential practical rationality and for the kinds of regard of others crucial to many forms of interaction in civil society.

One of civil society's most significant features is that it not only involves but also requires persons recognizing each other as agents, and, accordingly, as owed certain forms of regard. Awareness of being seen by others as an accountable, independent, respect-meriting agent can influence one's exercise of agency and thereby support the acquisition of prudence. Through being regarded as an agent in diverse contexts one can come to a fuller understanding of oneself as acting for reasons and of how to respond to others' exercise of agency. The mutual recognition can be an important basis for trust and trustworthiness, the expression of reactive attitudes and emotions, and interaction on the basis of an honest expression of them. If a person is (i) denied any but the most regimented, limited interaction with others, (ii) is denied any but regimented, limited occasions for deliberation, weighing of considerations, and fitting one's decision into a more than merely episodic context of action, and if (iii) one has severely limited opportunities for cultivating different kinds of relationships with the diversity of forms of emotionality they involve, (iv) while being denied recognition by others except in rule-governed (in the sense of order-preserving) and regimented ways, perhaps we should not expect that person's agency to remain intact. An effect on the person's states of character and emotionality is hardly surprising. The demoralization is more than a temporary coping strategy to be discarded upon release from prison. It is also more substantial than a mood.

The deficit of civil disposition is not confined within prison walls or to the persons punished. It is aggravated by uncivil attitudes *toward* prisoners and ex-prisoners on the part of many people in free society. As a result of those attitudes many ex-prisoners find it extremely difficult to find work, establish residence, build a credit record, and so forth. Granted, many ex-prisoners have multiple convictions and many are bad risks in various respects. Still, many ex-prisoners are stigmatized out of proportion with their records and continue to face undeserved obstacles to reintegration. Their punishment is continued by official and unofficial means, and the opportunity to reintegrate in society is stunted in several ways. Disenfranchisement is an example of an official impediment, denying ex-prisoners a key participatory role in the society's political life. Felony convictions disqualify former prisoners from voting in many jurisdictions and in fourteen US states convicted persons are permanently prohibited from voting. In approximately thirty states parolees are prohibited from voting (Haney 2006, 111). In addition, "the Personal Responsibility and Work Opportunity Reconciliation Act...imposed a lifetime ban on assistance to needy families (including food stamps) to anyone with a felony drug conviction; drug users and their families and friends are likely to lose publicly assisted housing as well as their welfare benefits" (Haney 2006, 113).

Even apart from an overall strategy of reorienting imprisonment toward rehabilitation (something not defended here) there are good reasons for minimizing the needless, significant harm done to prisoners. As Haney notes, "Prisoners are now exposed to harsh prison conditions overseen by prison officials attempting to manage far too many people, with far too little to do, who are incarcerated for far too long a period of time" (Haney 2006, 222). That encapsulates much that is at the root of the damage being done. Many sentences—even for what are minor crimes—are very long, and given the surge in criminalization in recent decades, there are very large numbers of prisoners spending very long periods in badly overcrowded conditions. In many prisons the emphasis on order and security has led to severe limitations on what sorts of activities and interactions are permitted to prisoners. Large numbers of prisoners experience a combination of severe overcrowding, near-total prohibition of meaningful activity, intimidation and blackmail by other prisoners, lack of physical and mental health resources, very limited visits by family and loved ones, and outbreaks of violence as the main interruption of what otherwise is mind-numbing tedium. This tends to worsen people rather than stir their consciences into recognition of their wrongdoing and a resolution to ethically self-correct. Gresham Sykes writes:

> Whatever may be the personal traits possessed by these men which helped bring them to the institution, it is certain that the conditions of prison life itself create strong pressures pointed toward behavior defined as criminal in the free community. Subjected to prolonged material deprivation, lacking heterosexual relationships, and rubbed raw by the irritants of life under compression, the inmate population is pushed in the direction of deviation from, rather than adherence to, the legal norms. (2007, 22)

The prison experience can lead to a worsening of prisoners' characters and erosion of their willingness to regard criminal justice as legitimate. Both results diminish the civility of civil society.

Whether by design or not, incarceration often reinforces just those dispositions and attitudes unsuited to civil society, with many ex-prisoners lacking both the resources and the relevant abilities to try to 'make it' in free society. Prisoners' strategies for dealing with disagreement and conflict, for protecting themselves and asserting their independence, for making judgments about who deserves respect and who is to be treated with contempt, and so forth during many years of incarceration are likely to encourage and reinforce vices. Vices can become more firmly entrenched and more difficult to overcome on account of the kinds of rationalization, self-deception, and misrepresentation to which they give rise (Liebling ms, 6).

The prison experience is often abundantly supplied with the sorts of conditions making trust, trustworthiness, and restraint—all crucial to a civil disposition—seem like forms of weakness. Even if, at sentencing, a convicted person recognizes the moral intelligibility meant to be communicated by conviction, with the passage of time the message may be undone by the miserable realities of prison life. As one British prisoner said in an interview: "We're human beings at the end of the day; we're people. OK, some of us have done some very bad things, some of us have done some not quite so bad things, but that doesn't make us... we're still, you know, we still love and feel and have the same emotions as everybody else." This was part of the overall picture of prisoners feeling that, as one put it, "You hit a wall where nothing matters. Suddenly, you are capable of anything. You'd betray anyone... You lose your moral compass" (Liebling ms, 6).[3]

Sykes points out that "The prisoner is never allowed to forget that, by committing a crime, he has foregone his claim to the status of a full-fledged, *trusted* member of society" (2007, 66). The confinement of imprisonment "is a constant threat to the prisoner's self-conception and the threat is continually repeated in the many daily reminders that he must be kept apart from 'decent' men" (2007, 67). Coping with that is a key part of the psychological survival of incarceration. Badly inadequate preparation for life in free society after release, and the need to adjust oneself to hierarchies of prisoner power structures, are among the conditions and policies that worsen and damage inmates. Civil society is then diminished by large numbers of ex-prisoners returning to it unable to function as prudent, self-determining agents. They lack a civil disposition and constructively developed capacities for practical reasoning and judgment.

The ways in which prison habituates many prisoners in vice constitute a form of *coercive corruption* sufficiently powerful to impact character. That is a respect in which current carceral practice is both illiberal and a cause of self-wounding on the part of society. In a liberal polity it is important that criminal sanction should communicate a morally intelligible message of censure. The intelligibility depends upon there being adequate reasons for criminalizing the conduct in question, adequate reasons for the type and severity of the punishment imposed, and the carrying out of sentence in a manner that does not obscure or invalidate those first two considerations via abuses or arbitrariness. Even if punishment is deserved, the moral intelligibility of censure and the legitimacy of punishment are called into doubt by the kinds of conditions prevalent in contemporary practice. The receptivity that could be helpful to ex-prisoners—which can be summarized as the willingness to extend toward them a civil disposition—is often denied. Its absence can deepen demoralization and harden the barriers between ex-prisoners and others, further diminishing the civility of society.

---

[3] Gabriele Taylor (2006) explores the ways in which certain centrally important vices frustrate the individual's desires and damage rational agency and also how some vices are 'capital' vices in the respect that they tend to give rise to additional vices.

1.6

It is widely and plausibly held that in a liberal polity a person's character is not properly a direct concern of the state and the state's responsibility does not extend to being a moral teacher or a guardian of souls. Yet, one of the considerations strongly in favor of the liberal order is that it preserves the political/legal conditions in which individuals are able to enact moral and other values in ways that are crucial to human beings' experience of their own lives as being gratifying and worthwhile. Moreover, the concept *character* is explanatorily relevant to some of the main issues concerning criminal sanction in a liberal state. Considerations of character figure in our self-conceptions, our aspirations and regrets, in the narratives of self-understanding so important to how we appreciate the coherence (or the lack of it) of our lives, and in what we take to be our most important successes, failures, undertakings, and concerns. If character is impacted powerfully by prevailing carceral practice the results can be, and are, socially significant.

There are difficult questions concerning the voluntariness of states of character, the interactions between them, their durability and plasticity, and so forth. Nonetheless, the dispositions, attitudes, and concerns constitutive of character provide a significant conceptual idiom for self-knowledge, for our knowledge of others, and for the explanation of human agency. I have argued that if the state organizes and directs institutions and practices that damage human beings by encouraging vice and eroding agential capacity, that activity of the state is politically illiberal and morally problematic. The conditions in which many persons are imprisoned *do* encourage vice and erode agential capacity. Moreover, many prisoners enter prison with little education or nearly illiterate, with little history of continuous employment and few marketable skills, coming from criminogenic environments, and feeling unjustly treated by society on account of poor life prospects and absence of opportunity. Many already suffer a deficit of civil disposition. They then experience punishment in conditions that worsen them. That reinforces the uncivil disposition many members of society already harbor *toward* them.

This is not part of an argument for trying to turn criminal sanction into rehabilitation or reform. The poor record of such attempts from earlier in the twentieth century gives rise to considerable skepticism. Just training enough prison and other staff to have the relevant expertise would be a daunting task, not to mention several other grounds for doubt. Nevertheless, it is clear that much current carceral practice needlessly undermines and impedes the civil disposition ex-prisoners need if they are to participate in free society. Looking more closely at the relevance of states of character to the prospects for a sustainable liberal democracy could prove to be a vitally important step in the direction of at least containing some of the damage being done to individuals and society.[4]

Works Cited

Annas, Julia. 2011. *Intelligent Virtue*. New York: Oxford University Press.

Aristotle. 1999. *Nicomachean Ethics*. Translated by Terence Irwin. Second edition. Indianapolis: Hackett Publishing Company, Inc..

Corrado, Michael. 2013. *Presumed Dangerous: Punishment, Responsibility, and Preventive Detention in American Jurisprudence*. Durham, NC: Carolina Academic Press.

Doris, John M. and Dominic Murphy. 2007. From My Lai to Abu Ghraib: The Moral Psychology of Atrocity. *Midwest Studies in Philosophy* 31: 25-55.

Galston, William. 2002. *Liberal Pluralism*. New York: Cambridge University Press.

Haney, Craig. 2006. *Reforming Punishment: Psychological Limits to the Pains of Imprisonment*. Washington, D.C.: American Psychological Association.

Kupperman, Joel. 1999. Virtues, Character, and Moral Dispositions. In *Virtue Ethics and Moral Education*, ed. David Carr and Jan Steutel. London: Routledge, 199-209.

Liebling, Alison. ms. Moral and Philosophical Problems of Long-Term Imprisonment.

Murphy, Jeffrie. 1998. Legal Moralism and Liberalism. In *Character, Liberty, and Law: Kantian Essays in Theory and Practice*. Boston: Kluwer, 89-117.

---

[4] I would like to thank the editors of this volume for their close attention and numerous helpful suggestions throughout the process of developing my paper. In addition, Routledge granted permission for me to include some ideas and arguments I presented in recent work, especially, 'Punishing Society: Sanctioning Others and Harming Ourselves,' in *Criminal Justice Ethics*, December 2014. Finally, some of the ideas articulated in this paper were developed in the course of work supported by a grant I received from the National Endowment for the Humanities 'Enduring Questions' program. That grant supported the development of a course, Is Virtue Its Own Reward, in which the relationships between agency, virtue, vice, and happiness were central concerns.

Petersilia, Joan. 2003. *When Prisoners Come Home: Parole and Prisoner Reentry*. New York: Oxford University Press.

Shils, Edward. 1997. *The Virtue of Civility*, ed. Steven Grosby. Indianapolis: Liberty Fund.

Sykes, Gresham. 2007. *The Society of Captives*. Princeton: Princeton University Press.

Taylor, Gabriele. 2006. *Deadly Vices*. New York: Oxford University Press.

Watson, Gary. 1990. On the Primacy of Character. In *Identity, Character, and Morality: Essays in Moral Psychology*, ed. Owen Flanagan and Amelie Rorty. Cambridge, MA: MIT Press, 449–69.

Williams, Bernard. 1981. Practical Necessity. In *Moral Luck: Philosophical Papers 1973–1980*. New York: Cambridge University Press, 124–31.

2

Virtue Ethics and Criminal Punishment

Katrina L. Sifferd

2.1 Introduction

Criminal punishment is designed to serve particular societal-level functions. These are often called the principles of punishment, and there are four that are referred to most often: retribution, deterrence, incapacitation, and rehabilitation. The principle of retribution states that violators of the law should get their 'just deserts,' and thus punishment should serve to provide harmful consequences in response to a harmful act. The principle of deterrence attempts to influence an offender's decision-making with the threat of punishment. The principle of incapacitation also aims to stop defendants from offending, but there is no attempt to influence decision-making; instead the offender's environment is manipulated to make reoffending impossible (usually via incarceration). Finally, rehabilitation is the idea that offenders can be reformed such that they won't reoffend.

These *functions* of punishment fall into broad categories of *justification* for punishment. A justification for punishment provides good reasons why society is warranted in denying offenders' liberties based upon their performance of certain acts. Deterrence, incapacitation, and rehabilitation are often seen as utilitarian aims, and thus are primarily justified based on their consequences, while retribution is usually justified based upon deontological notions of moral judgment and desert. A third sort of justification for punishment is offered by virtue theorists, who view punishment as a means to encourage virtuous character development, and punish vicious characters. Rehabilitation is the function of punishment most easily justified from the perspective of virtue theory, although some have argued the theory can justify all four of the principles of punishment.

All of the major justificatory theories of punishment—deontological, utilitarian, and virtue theory, as well as the more recent theories that emphasize the communicative aspect of punishment (e.g., Duff 1996)—rest upon the cornerstone notion that citizens and offenders are rational agents. Citizens are culpable for their criminal acts precisely because, as rational agents, they can understand legal rules and punishment as reasons to act or refrain from acting: such abilities ground what H. L. A. Hart termed 'capacity responsibility' (Hart 1968). If persons, or classes of persons, do not have the capacity to understand the rule of law and/or make decisions regarding whether to follow legal rules, then the institution of law as structured fails as applied to that person or class (Hart 1968, 227).

Punishment aims in part to communicate with offenders (namely, to convince offenders that their act was wrong), and influence their future decision-making (Duff 1996). Thus the aims of retribution, deterrence, and rehabilitation each depend upon offenders' rational capacities: retribution requires that an offender understand why he is being punished; deterrence attempts to convince an offender not to reoffend, and rehabilitation attempts to reform an offender so he will be less inclined to chose to commit crimes in the future. Conviction of a criminal offense does not rescind one's standing as a rational agent (Hart 1968, Duff 2002). As preeminent US federal appellate judge Richard Posner has noted, if the status of rational agency was revoked due to criminal behavior, we might come to view offenders as "members of a different species, indeed, as a type of vermin, devoid of human dignity and entitled to no respect"[1] instead of as agents who retain the capacity to undergo moral change.

In this chapter I use virtue theory to critique certain contemporary punishment practices. From the perspective of virtue theory, respect for rational agency indicates a respect for choice-making as the process by which we form dispositions, which in turn give rise to further choices and action (Pincoffs 1980). To be a moral agent requires one must be

---

[1] *Johnson v. Phelan*, 69 F3d 144 (1995), Posner dissenting.

able to act such that his or her actions deserve praise or blame; virtue theory thus demands that moral agents engage in rational choice-making as a means to develop and exercise the character traits from which culpable action issues. With respect to criminal offenders, virtue theory indicates the state is obligated to recognize offenders' right to form their own moral character via rational choice-making, even while under state supervision. I will argue below that punishment practices should limit choice-making only to the extent necessary to achieve the functions of punishment: whenever possible, punishment should preserve opportunities for the rational exercise of character and development of virtue. This means that even within a prison setting incarcerated offenders should be able to make some choices about their daily lives (e.g., regarding whether to follow the rules of prison, how to manage their relationships with other prisoners and prison staff, etc.). Offenders should also be offered opportunities to develop virtuous traits through rehabilitative programming such as drug addiction treatment, educational programming, and job training.

I will also argue that two contemporary punishment practices unjustly undermine an offender's moral agency. The first is the overuse of isolation sanctions, which very severely limits offender choice-making. The second is chemical castration, which results in limiting an offender's capacity to develop his character within a specific realm of choice-making. I conclude that these two punishments violate offenders' moral agency, and that this violation cannot be justified by appeal to the aims of incapacitation, deterrence, retribution, and rehabilitation.

2.2 Contemporary Formulations of Character Traits

Virtue theorists argue that character traits, which are in a constant process of development or decline, ground morally relevant human action. Aristotelian virtue theory claims that character traits like honesty, kindness, and courage become stable as a result of the process of habituation (Aristotle 1985). Habituation involves practicing the trait via the use of practical reason, which allows a person to determine which actions are appropriate in any given situation. A stable disposition to act in accordance with a trait, such as honesty, is built as a result of making appropriately honest choices over time.

Contemporary versions of virtue theory emphasize that both reason and character traits are vital to moral action, providing detailed accounts of the operations of practical reason and the structure of character traits, often taking into account psychological data (see, for example, Webber 2006, Webber 2013). Much recent work in virtue theory has defended virtue ethics against the threat of 'situationism' lodged by John Doris (Doris 2005) and others. Evidence of the large effects relatively small features of the environment (such as ambient noise or whether one is late) can have on behavior led situationists to argue that robust or 'global' character traits simply do not exist. Virtue theorists have responded by arguing that much of the situationist data has been overblown, and that despite small situational effects, character traits can be considered stable dispositions to action when one has an appropriately sophisticated notion of the way in which multiple environmental factors interact with numerous dispositions to act in real time to produce action (Annas 2003, Webber 2006). Thus Webber (2006) argues that situationism is only a threat if behavior is seen as produced by straightforward stimulus and response pairs. This view of human action is obviously untenable: human action results from the complex interaction of multiple motivating predispositions and environmental factors (Webber 2006). Character traits should thus not be seen as simple responses to environmental stimuli, but instead one disposition among many that might lead to certain behavior in certain situation; as "dispositions toward certain behavioral inclinations in response to particular kinds of stimulus" (Webber 2006, 206). Even Doris admits to what he calls 'local' character traits, where a trait can be considered stable given a particular context.

As an example of the complex ways character guides action, consider a case where the traits of kindness and honesty may demand different actions: your friend asks you how she looks in an expensive new dress. Kindness demands a 'white lie,' but honesty demands that you tell her she looks pear-shaped. What is the right action? This is likely to depend on the circumstances. Can she still return the dress or is she already wearing it out at a restaurant? Is your friend very sensitive or does she have a thick skin? Here, as is the case for most human action, identification of the right act requires weighing the relative importance of the two virtues and various situational factors. Even one who possessed the character traits of kindness and honesty would need to employ her practical reason to determine the correct course of action.

According to Julia Annas, the capacity for practical reasoning has both an affective and intellectual component (Annas 2003, Annas 2004, Annas 2011). Emotions indicate whether one feels good or bad about performing a certain act, creating an internal system of reward and punishment. This component of Annas's theory is necessary to explain why character traits motivate a person to act: a good moral education will teach a person to feel good about the right actions and bad about the wrong ones. The intellectual aspect of the self is capable of understanding whether the reasons one has for acting are good or bad (and thus, whether the act should be considered good or bad). Our emotional and intellectual reasoning capacities are developed by the process of education begun by our parents, teachers, role models, and eventually peers, and then continued in our adulthood by our own ability to critically assess our moral opinions.

This process of moral education takes time, and it is a process that is never finished. Take as an example the trait of stewardship to the planet. At first, two-year-old Gabby may learn from her parents that it isn't okay to litter. As an eight-year-old, Gabby then gains an understanding (from lessons at home and at school) that taking care of the planet means recycling whatever we can so less gets thrown in a landfill. As a high school student, Gabby takes an environmental science course and sees films on environmentalism, thus developing a more sophisticated understanding of how consumption of disposable coffee cups and other packaging may be irresponsible even if they get recycled, and about the way in which American methods of consumption disproportionately hurt the poor and marginalized. As Gabby's reasoning capacity grows, she becomes more deft, versatile, and thoughtful in the application of her value of stewardship to action.

Thus developing a virtuous character trait requires developing expertise just like being good at any craft. This is a point that Aristotle makes very explicitly in the *Nicomachean Ethics* (Aristotle 1985, 1103a30) and that Julia Annas examines (Annas 2011). An expert electrician will know how to solve novel problems, and will be able to articulate to a novice why a particular solution is the right one (Annas 2011, 19). Similarly, expertise in a character trait will mean that a person can apply the trait in new or difficult situations, and later provide reasons as to why they acted in such-and-such a way. Rote-memorization and rule-following is often the beginning stage of acquiring a skill, but expertise exhibits intelligent flexibility. Thus, practical reason is critical to the process of "becoming just by doing just actions, temperate by doing temperate actions, brave by doing brave actions" (Aristotle 1985, 1103b).

To summarize, contemporary virtue theory examines the role environment, practical reason, and predispositions to act play in moral action. Reason plays two roles with regard to character. First, it is vital to development of character, via habituation of traits; and second, allows for the expression of those traits as action. To claim that a character trait is a 'stable' means the trait predisposes one to act in such-and-such a way in such-and-such a situation. Human action is the result of many motivations and depositions to act which are relevant in any given situation.

2.3 Criminal Character

Virtue theory was the dominant approach in Western moral philosophy until roughly the Enlightenment, when utilitarian or deontological theories arose as the prevailing methods for justification of moral judgments (and by extension, criminal law and punishment). However, the past fifty or so years has seen renewed interest in virtue theory, partly due to Anscombe's famous article "Modern Moral Philosophy" (Anscombe 1958). There has been specific interest in the intersect of virtue theory and criminal punishment in the last fifteen years (see, for example, Brown 2002, Huigens 2004, and Tadros 2011).

Virtue theory has been used to justify punishment by emphasizing the criminal law's obligation to "promote human flourishing by instilling and cultivating the moral virtue, promoting sound practical reasoning and punishing those who display vice" (Yankah 2009: 1169). The theory is best suited to justify punishment's function of rehabilitation, which aims to reform offenders' characters such that they won't recidivate. However, many aspects of the common law system of punishment reference an offender's character. For example, increased sentences in accordance with three-strikes and felony murder laws and capital sentencing procedures indicate concern for an offender's underlying character traits or dispositions (Huigens 2002). Even the recent focus on retribution as the primary justification of punishment—evident in the US especially—seems to reflect moral judgments based not upon harmful acts, but upon vicious traits of character (Huigens 2002).

One of the central problems in the criminal law is that the imposition of punishment cannot be justified by a single ethical theory (Brown 2002). Different theories of justification best explain different functions of punishment: deontological theory most easily justifies punishment based on moral wrongs; and utilitarianism best justifies punishment based upon social order concerns via incapacitation or deterrence of dangerous persons. Because of this, attempts to make utilitarianism or deontological theory the sole justification for criminal law have been unsuccessful (Brown 2002). Indeed, many contemporary scholars, including Robert Nozik and Antony Duff, argue for a 'hybrid' theory of justification, which utilizes multiple justifying theories (Nozick 1981; Duff 2002).

It is thus not surprising that very few believe virtue theory can act as the sole justification for criminal punishment. One issue is that criminal guilt does not seem primarily to depend upon assessment of character, but instead on whether a person performed an intentional harmful act. An intentional killing of another human being is usually determined to be murder regardless of whether the act was in keeping with, or contrary to, an offender's character (Duff 2002; Yankah 2009). Even so, all of the functions of punishment can be made sense of from the lens of virtue theory: deterrence and incapacitation can be viewed as attempts to influence choices and character; and retribution as moral judgment which refers to, and should be respectful of, character. As noted above, rehabilitation is the function of punishment most easily justified from the perspective of virtue theory, because of its focus on altering in a more permanent way an offender's choice-making. One of the reasons virtue theory has been less utilized by contemporary legal theorists than other justifying theories, at least until recently, may be due to the relative diminishment of the principle of rehabilitation in the past fifty years. For the first six decades of the twentieth century, rehabilitation was often thought to be the dominant principle of punishment, especially among correctional elites and criminologists (Cullen and Gendreau 2000). Rehabilitation has since fallen out of favor, especially in the US, due to the monetary cost of rehabilitative programming and the political cost of supporting such programs. Drug addiction treatment, job training, educational programs, and therapy are all still used in many US prisons, although cuts in funding and a lack of commitment to the programs have made their effectiveness questionable.

Although it has been underemphasized in the past, I feel virtue theory is an important tool for analyzing the operations of the criminal law because of its focus on moral development, and because it provides a fuller description of the way human rational agency creates culpable action than the other two theories. While it is helpful to see an actor as interested in maximizing his utility, or as motivated to act in accordance with moral duty, virtue theory provides a detailed account of how a moral agent develops a predisposition to act in such-and-such a way over time, and how law and punishment might influence this process. Whether a violator of law acted out of character or from viciousness can be important considerations with regard to punishment, even if they aren't directly relevant to guilt. A murder performed in keeping with a disposition to act violently and to devalue life should be determined to be deserving of harsher punishment than an out of character act (e.g. a murder committed by a normally peaceful parent who discovers his child has been raped).

Considerations of character are also important when evaluating the overall effectiveness and justice of a particular system of criminal punishment. The threat of punishment should make the acquisition of virtue easier, not harder, for citizens, by providing external pressure to cultivate virtuous traits. As Huigens notes, general deterrence of the population from crime can be seen as an effect of virtue (Huigens 2002). It never even occurs to most people to rob a bank or a store, even though they see one every day. This internalization of moral and legal norms—as H. L. A. Hart terms the phenomenon (Hart 1968)—reflects the acquisition of dispositions toward honesty, or lawfulness, of which the threat of punishment plays a role.

More specifically, virtue theory highlights a particular ethical side-constraint on punishment: methods of punishment should still allow for the development and exercise of character, at least in so far as this is possible within a system that serves the functions of incapacitation, deterrence, retribution, and rehabilitation. As legal scholar Yankah notes, "All would agree that a morally justified legal system cannot make impossible (or overly difficult) a life of value or virtue" (Yankah 2009, 1181). Ideally, punishment should not result in worse characters, especially as the vast majority of offenders are eventually released. Punishment ought not to preclude the possibility of the development of virtue, unless this preclusion is absolutely necessary to achieve one of punishment's central aims (retribution, deterrence, incapacitation, rehabilitation). Any punishment that infringes upon moral choice-making and thus agency, where the infringement is not clearly designed to accomplish one of the four functions of punishment, is unjust.

2.4 Virtue and Punishment: an Example

The ethical constraint virtue theory places upon criminal punishment can be explored further by use of an example. Webber (2006) discusses a study regarding the regional differences in the disposition to be violent. According to the study, in the US white males in large southern cities are no more likely to commit homicide than their counterparts in large northern cities, but those who do commit homicide are significantly more likely to do so as the result of an argument; and outside cities, southern white males are twice as likely as their northern counterparts to commit homicide as a result of an argument (Webber 2006). Experimenters guessed that these differences were due to a southern culture of honor, and designed a study to test this hypothesis. In the study, northern and southern male college students were asked to finish a story about a situation where one man saw another trying to kiss his fiancé (Webber 2006). Half of the men were insulted in the hallway just before being told the story. 75 percent of insulted southerners ended the story with one of the men suffering injuries or threats, whereas only 20 percent of control southerners did so (Webber 2006). Having recently been insulted made no statistically relevant difference to how northerners ended the story (Webber 2006).

This tells us, according to Webber, that the trait of being strongly inclined to respond violently when insulted is more prominent in southerners than northerners (Webber 2006). In my mind, the difference in strength of inclination to respond violently in certain situations can manifest in two different ways. First, it may be a difference in the strength of the disposition to act aggressively itself. For example, as a general rule, males have a stronger disposition to act aggressively than women. So the reason southern males react more strongly may be that the emotional component of aggression after being insulted is stronger in southern males than in northern ones. Or, it may be difference in the rational processes of the actor that give effect to the feelings of aggression. One might feel very angry and aggressive in response to some environmental stimulus, but still not act aggressively or violently because one determines via the reasoning process that such action is wrong or unwise.[2]

To take the example a bit further, imagine Jack, a white southerner. He was at a party one night when another man, Tom, starting flirting with his girlfriend. When Jack approached Tom and accused him of being inappropriate, Tom insulted him. Jack then beat Tom severely, and Tom ended up paralyzed.

Jack has been found guilty of attempted murder. At sentencing, a jury is asked to consider the following three options: (1) life in prison without the possibility of parole; (2) a twenty-five-year sentence with involuntary anger management therapy, and the possibility that Jack can earn early release; or (3) a short sentence of three to five years with the involuntary administration of aggression-reducing drugs for the rest of Jack's life.

Both anger management therapy and the aggression-reducing drugs might be considered rehabilitative treatment. Before discussing in detail Jack's punishment, let me say a few words about these rehabilitative programs from the virtue theory perspective more generally. Traditional rehabilitative programs such as anger management and behavioral therapy often aim both at enhancing reasoning processes and diminishing the strength of certain dispositions to act via the process of habituation. For example, anger management therapy may train an offender to stop and count slowly to ten before acting upon a feeling of anger. This encourages the use of practical reason before acting. Another tool commonly used by cognitive behavioral therapists is called 'systematic desensitization' (McGlynn, Smitherman, et al. 2004). The technique exposes a person to stimuli to which he tends to have a very strong emotional reaction, with instructions on how to better manage and reduce that reaction over repeated exposures to the stimuli.

Other rehabilitative programs focus on changing situational factors that encourage destructive dispositions, such as educational programming or job training (Bouffard, Mackenzie, et al. 2000). By providing an offender with an education or job prospects, the programs attempt to

---

[2] My colleague Bill Hirstein and I have argued elsewhere these rational processes are necessary to criminal responsibility, and that they can be understood in terms of executive functions in the brain (Hirstein and Sifferd 2011). We have also argued that many criminal defenses can be understood as deficits in this rationality (Sifferd and Hirstein 2013).

remove an environmental factor that is linked to criminal behavior (joblessness) and place the offender in an environment where following the law is an easier choice.

Treatment of addiction or other psychological disorders also attempt to either diminish the strength of certain dispositions (in the case of addiction), improve reasoning (in the case of many psychological disorders), or both (Wexler, Falkin, et al. 1990). Addiction rehabilitation can work to try to decrease the strength of the disposition to administer the drug via pharmaceutical and situational means. In the former case, medicine may be given that lessen cravings or even make the addict sick when they administer the drug they are addicted to. Addiction rehabilitative programs also attempt to increase the addict's ability to make a reasoned choice not to take the drug via cognitive behavioral therapy (Bahr, Masters, et al. 2013). Often these two sorts of treatment are given in tandem, where drugs may be prescribed to decrease cravings, while therapy works to increase rational control (Bahr, Masters, et al. 2013). Similarly, an offender with obsessive compulsive disorder (OCD) may receive medicine that lessens his anxiety levels, in coordination with cognitive behavioral therapy, which increases his ability to use his reason to keep his dispositions to certain behavior (locking doors, washing hands, etc.) in check.

Note that all of the rehabilitative interventions discussed so far work within the normal structure of habituation and practical reasoning except the use of certain medicines to treat addiction or psychological disorders such as OCD. As such, the majority of programs are 'indirect' in that they work via the rational processes of the offender and not directly on the offender's dispositions themselves. In the latter case of addiction or psychological treatment, however, these programs seem to work to lessen certain dispositions directly via brain interventions.

Let's return to Jack's punishment. Option one was to sentence Jack to life in prison without the possibility of parole (or an LWOP sentence). LWOP sentences ought to be reserved for very serious crimes and our most deserving criminal offenders, although they are relatively common in the US.[3] One of the problems with locking offenders up

---

[3] In contrast, the European Court of Human Rights recently ruled that all offenders sentenced to life imprisonment have a right to a prospect of release (van Zyl Smit et al. 2014).

and 'throwing away the key'—besides the obvious cost to taxpayers—is the psychological impact this will have on offenders. Offenders with no possibility of release would seem to have little opportunity or motivation to improve their characters. First, LWOP offenders are less likely to be offered rehabilitative programming, and second, they are less likely to participate in any programming they may be offered. There is no reason for the state to assist in Jack's rehabilitation such that he will be less likely to recidivate, because he will never be released. And there is no need for Jack to learn new skills that might assist him in the community (such as job skills). Finally, many of the character traits that might benefit Jack once released may be of dubious value in a maximum security prison where LWOP offenders are often held, such as the traits of moderated aggression, a good work ethic, and honesty.

Of course, it is still at least *possible* an LWOP offender might wish to develop virtuous character traits, and be able to do so, even given the very limited opportunities for virtuous choice-making in prison. However, it is clear that an LWOP conviction makes this much less likely than sentences of incarceration with a chance of release. This infringement upon moral development may be warranted where an offender commits a particularly heinous crime (or series of crimes): for example, one might imagine a serial killer or pedophile for which an LWOP would be warranted. In Jack's case, however, especially if this is his first offense, an LWOP sentence seems much too extreme. Life in prison seems a disproportionate punishment for Jack from a retributive perspective. Let's assume Jack is twenty-five: fifty years seems much too long a sentence, even given the hardship he caused his victim. Further, if the therapy mentioned in option two works to help Jack manage his anger, life in prison won't be necessary for incapacitation; and even without therapy Jack, like many violent offenders, is likely to 'age out' of his violent tendencies by middle age.[4] Finally, there is no evidence that an

---

[4] The justification for granting life without parole (LWOP) sentences is usually retribution, although some argue the sentence serves the function of incapacitation, the idea being that very dangerous offenders should never be trusted to leave prison. However, lifelong incapacitation of offenders is rarely necessary to keep them from recidivating. Inmates serving long sentences who are then released have a very low rate of recidivism, partly due to their advanced age when released. Sentences in the US are five to seven times longer than sentences for comparable offenses in Europe, but despite this, recidivism rates in Europe are lower than in the US (Dow 2012). One study found that four of every five (79.4%) lifers released in 1994 had no arrests for a new crime in the three years after their release. This

LWOP sentence is more likely to deter potential violent batteries than a substantial sentence of twenty-five years (Tonry 2008). In short, none of the aims of punishment seem to be served by Jack serving an LWOP sentence.

Option three (a short sentence with lifelong involuntary administration of aggression-reducing drugs) alters Jack's disposition to act aggressively directly via brain interventions. Initially, one might not think this is such a bad thing. It is very likely to result in Jack being less dangerous. One problem, however, is that administration of these drugs will not just alter Jack's disposition to respond aggressively to insults, but also alter his disposition to respond aggressively in every situation. And one can easily imagine a scenario where responding aggressively would constitute a virtuous act: If Jack sees a little girl being beaten by a gang of boys, responding with the appropriate amount of aggression would constitute the virtues of courage and good Samaritanism. A more likely scenario might be Jack needing to exhibit aggression to keep from being victimized if he were released back into violent neighborhood. The capacity to get angry, and even the willingness to threaten aggression, might be absolutely necessary for Jack to take public transport or walk safely down his street.[5] Such actions may not be considered wrong or vicious—and may even be considered virtuous—if they constitute the right amount of aggression exhibited under the right conditions (assuming Jack only threatens violence and does not commit a violent act).

In general, we ought to worry about the way in which such aggression-reducing drugs might work. Would they remove Jack's ability to get angry completely and make him permanently docile? Would Jack's ability to play competitive sports or compete for clients with other workers be compromised due to the drugs?

Upon close examination the aggression-reducing drugs do not seem to act as a rehabilitative treatment, but instead as an attempt by the state to incapacitate Jack without the cost of incarcerating him. As already discussed, according to traditional virtue ethics the development of

---

compares to an arrest-free rate of just one third (32.5%) for all offenders released from prison. This means that released lifers are less likely than the general prison population to recidivate.

[5] It may be that these situational conditions are the reason why Jack cultivated a trait of aggression to begin with.

virtue is like development of expertise in a craft. This expertise allows one to make very specific, detailed decisions regarding virtuous action given a particular situation. If the aggression-reducing drugs completely remove Jack's aggression, and are given to him for the rest of his life, Jack will never be given the opportunity to develop many virtues associated with the considered practice of aggression, including courage. That is, he will never have the chance to learn to express just the right level of aggression under the right circumstances. In this way the drug would severely undermine Jack's moral development and agency.

Contrast this result with the administration of medication to diminish an offender's cravings for illegal drugs. This direct intervention does not interfere with dispositions that might be virtuous: such medicines tend to suppress withdrawal symptoms, relieve cravings, or block the effects of certain drugs so the motivation to take them is removed (Mitchell, Wilson, et al. 2012). When such a drug is given in concert with therapy, it may assist moral development by decreasing the salience of very strong desires such that an agent can better use his practical reason. Administration of such drugs is rarely permanent, but continues only as long as is needed to assist in an addict's rational decision-making. Similarly, a drug that decreased a person with OCD's anxiety to normal levels would not on its face inhibit moral development. As long as the patient could still experience anxiety in adequate levels in truly anxiety-deserving situations, the medicine would not seem to impact his moral agency.

Several conditions would have to be met for Jack's aggression-reducing drug to play a similar rehabilitative role to the medication given to drug addicts or an offender with OCD. First, the drug would have to 'tone down' and not fully remove his aggression, so as to target mental causes likely to cause criminal harm (e.g., very strong desires to harm others) and be less likely to impact legal behavior (e.g., scaring someone off with a show of aggression). Second, the drug would have to be given in tandem with therapy, so that a therapist might help Jack learn to make better choices with regard to his expressions of aggression while his aggression levels are low. This also may require that Jack be released while on the medication and in therapy, so that he is subject to situations where he is asked to moderate his aggression. (Given the conditions of prison, it would be quite difficult, and possibly unsafe, to ask Jack to take these drugs while incarcerated.) Third, the administration of the drug should not be permanent but temporary, until his therapist or other medical professional determines that they are no longer needed because Jack is no longer likely to cause harm due to his aggression. And fourth, such drugs should be given only voluntarily, where Jack has consented that he wishes to change his trait of aggression. (More on this requirement immediately below.) Only if all of these conditions were met could a sentence of aggression-reducing drugs be a justified rehabilitative punishment. If aggression-reducing drugs are given as stipulated—as a permanent sanction, and provided without therapy or the oversight of a medical professional—then option three violates Jack's rational agency.

Option two (a long prison sentence in conjunction with anger management therapy) is most respectful of Jack's rational capacity to form his own character, despite the fact that the therapy is involuntary, and seems appropriate, given the severity of Jack's crime and the various functions of punishment. Therapy could help Jack develop expertise regarding which sorts of situation require aggression and which don't. Or, if Jack practices psychological resistance, his character won't change in response to the therapy. If he does resist, he will continue to be incapacitated but his character will remain his own. The reason why aggression-reducing drugs should only be given voluntarily is precisely to preserve this opportunity for an offender to resist a state-imposed character change. The state ought not to require an offender to make changes in his character via direct brain interventions, because this would entail use of state power to force conformity with a state notion of virtue.[6] Certainly, a criminal conviction does not justify state-mandated changes in an offender's character. However, if a character change is desired and the therapy works, Jack may undergo character development and be a good candidate for early release.

Above I claimed that any punishment that infringes upon moral choice-making and thus agency is unacceptable unless that infringement aims to fulfill a function of punishment. The above example provides further evidence for this claim by examining a hypothetical case where certain punishments—involuntary administration of aggression-reducing drugs

---

[6] The idea of state-enforced character changes via direct brain interventions is especially worrying when one considers the changing notions of what constitutes a bad character: e.g., the fairly recent shift from seeing homosexuality as a criminal wrong to a constitutionally protected right in the US.

and LWOP—were unjust because they eliminated or severely compromised the possibility of moral development and virtue without justification.

2.5 Isolation Sanctions and Current Chemical Castration Programs

In this section I will explore in more detail certain contemporary punishment practices through the lens of virtue theory. Specifically, I will argue that many cases of isolation sanctions, and every instance of chemical castration, unduly infringe on moral development agency without sufficiently promoting a principle of punishment.

2.5.1 Isolation sanctions

Philosopher Lisa Guenther provided this description of solitary confinement in a 2012 opinion piece for the New York Times:

> There are many ways to destroy a person, but the simplest and most devastating might be solitary confinement. Deprived of meaningful human contact, otherwise healthy prisoners often come unhinged. They experience intense anxiety, paranoia, depression, memory loss, hallucinations and other perceptual distortions. Psychiatrists call this cluster of symptoms SHU syndrome, named after the Security Housing Units of many supermax prisons. Prisoners have more direct ways of naming their experience. They call it "living death," the "gray box," or "living in a black hole." (Guenther 2012)

In a census of state and federal prisons taken in June 2000, approximately 80,000 prisoners were reported to be in solitary confinement (Gibbons 2006, 461). Rikers Island alone has over eighty solitary confinement cells, according to the New York City Bureau of Prisons. Across the US, use of solitary confinement is on the rise: in supermax prisons, tens of thousands of prisoners are isolated, and many traditional prisons also isolate some portion of their population (Weir 2012). Although isolation sanctions were originally designed to be a sanction of the last resort, prisoners are now often forced into isolation upon a first offense of failing a drug test, arguing with a guard, or fighting with another prisoner (Guenther 2012).

Isolation sanctions can almost completely remove an offender's capacity for choice-making. All versions of solitary confinement mean living twenty-three to twenty-four hours a day in a cell. Sometimes inmates are granted one hour for exercise, which usually takes place alone in an exercise room or a 'dog run' (Haney 2003). Solitary confinement cells generally measure from 6 × 9 to 8 × 10 feet. They can have solid metal doors so inmates cannot see outside, and inmates inside are often banned from using a TV, radio, or reading supplies (Haney 2003). Supermax prisons are specially designed facilities for isolation, and can be either stand-alone or connected to larger prisons. Supermax prisoners are confined to single cells around the clock, released only three to five hours a week for showers or exercise, and subject to continual surveillance (Lovell, Johnson, et al. 2007). On the very rare occasions when they are in the same room with another person, supermax prisoners are often caged or bolted down (Lovell, Johnson, et al. 2007).

In response to successful lawsuits filed by prisoners, some states have moved away from the most severe forms of solitary confinement to 'administrative segregation' where inmates are allowed to communicate with other prisoners during their one hour of recreation; receive visitors, mail, and phone calls; and take part in religious and educational services (Berger, Chaplin, et al. 2013). One recent study, which attempted to examine the impacts of administrative segregation in a Colorado prison, found elevated levels of mental illness amongst those prisoners in segregation, but failed to find that these illnesses worsened as a result of the segregation (O'Keefe et al. 2013). However, some have questioned the validity of the study, partly because the prisoners studied had already been subject to an extreme version of solitary confinement for up to a week before they meet with researchers, and then were sent to less restrictive segregation (Weir 2012). In addition, there is some evidence that prisoners in solitary confinement at supermax prisons fare worse than prisoners in the general population once released. A 2007 study found that prisoners released directly from a supermax prison committed new crimes sooner than prisoners who were transferred from segregation to the general population for several months before being released (Lovell, Johnson et al. 2007).

There is no doubt that all prisoners experience a diminishment of their capacity for habituation of traits. There will be less opportunity in prison to practice vicious traits (although many bad actions are performed by incarcerated offenders), but also virtuous traits such as honesty, kindness, or courage, than there would be outside of prison. However, prisoners usually retain choices regarding who to talk to, what to read or watch, and whether to exercise, follow the rules, or work a prison job. Some take advantage of these little freedoms to develop virtuous character traits, although many don't. In isolation sanctions, even these small opportunities are often removed. The forced idleness of isolation can deny offenders any choices short of the position they sit, stand, or lay in, and whether to eat the food delivered to them. This complete lack of choice doesn't just halt character development, but can lead to psychological hardship in the very least and complete breaks with reality for some. It isn't surprising that denial of the most basic human capacity for choice-making, the capacity that grounds the formation of character and self, comes at a price.

Supporters of isolation sanctions often claim that they are necessary to incapacitate unruly prisoners. In very rare, extreme cases it is possible that isolation is necessary to stop an offender from seriously injuring other prisoners or prison staff. However, due to the extent of the infringement on development and character, proof of an imminent and serious threat to self or others should be necessary to justify isolation on the basis of incapacitation. And this level of proof is certainly not met in most cases where prisoners earn isolation sanctions now (Guenther 2012).

Retribution, deterrence, and rehabilitation do not support the practice. Even our worst offenders, those sitting on death row, do not automatically earn isolation as retribution for their crime. And the impact of isolation is too unpredictable to justify a deterrent effect: a prisoner would often not know if he was likely to be subjected to isolation if he were sentenced again to prison. Finally, there are obviously no rehabilitative gains from the practice.

Rarely the psychological impacts of isolation are so extreme that repeated exposure to isolation could make an offender permanently incapable of moral development, even once released from prison. As one offender subjected to the practice noted: "I went to a standstill psychologically once—lapse of memory. I didn't talk for 15 days. I couldn't hear clearly. You can't see—you're blind—block everything out—disoriented, awareness is very bad...I think I was drooling—a complete standstill. I never recovered" (Guenther 2012).

2.5.2 *Chemical castration*

Chemical castration is used in different ways by different criminal jurisdictions. In the US, it may be used as punishment to be applied in addition to incarceration; or, it can be a restriction placed on offenders when they are released on parole (Scott and Holmberg 2003). In some cases an offender may be eligible for a shorter sentence if they agree to castration, and in others, offenders will have served a full sentence before being released on parole with the condition that they agree to castration. At least six US states and quite a few European nations (including the UK, Denmark, Sweden, Poland, and the Czech Republic) have chemical castration programs as a part of their criminal justice system. In the US, the drug medroxyprogesterone acetate (MPA) is most often used for chemical castration (Scott and Holmberg 2003). MPA is an analogue of the female hormone progesterone, used to reduce the normal level of testosterone in a male by 50 percent—a level equal to the level found in prepubescent boys (Smith 1998). The drug reduces sex drive in men, often diminishing ejaculation fluid to zero, and may eliminate the capacity for an erection (Smith 1998). Chemical castration is not only used as punishment for sexual assaults against children. In the state of Louisiana, for example, chemical castration is a possible sentence for all persons convicted of rape (Millholon 2008).

The aims of retribution and incapacitation are both used by policy-makers to justify the imposition of chemical castration. Sexual offenders are thought by some to deserve the removal of a sexual life in accordance with the old-fashioned interpretation of retribution as lex talionis, where an eye for an eye is legitimate punishment. Chemical castration also holds the allure of incapacitating a sexual offender for the rest of his life without taxpayers bearing the cost of lifelong incarceration. However, neither of these offered aims justifies state-enforced chemical castration of sex offenders. With regard to the aim of retribution, state-sanctioned mutilations or physical harms caused for retributive purposes can undermine the state's moral authority and rule of law, and assessing what sort of harm constitutes proper eye-for-an-eye punishment is dubious, at best. Modern liberal democracies do not usually punish offenders who are found guilty of battery via physical beatings, or sexually assault offenders who are found guilty of rape.[7] It is fairly easy to understand why once one attempts to figure out what aspect of a criminal's person

---

[7] In the US, certain states with capital punishment statutes do kill offenders who murder. However, there is much debate regarding whether capital punishment is indeed a just punishment. Capital punishment is rarely used in first world countries outside the US.

should bear the brunt of lex talionis-style retributive sentiment. For example, is rape a crime of physical violence, or sex, such that a rapist be punished by a beating, or by forced sex? What if the offender enjoys forced sex, or physical harm? In the case of chemical castration, why is the removal of sexual capacities a proper lex talionis response to sexual assaults, many of which are best seen as crimes of violence? What if the offender is a pedophile, who desperately wants to rid himself of his sexual desire for children? In this case, chemical castration wouldn't seem retributive enough. Hopefully these disturbing questions make clear why most nations reject punishments based upon old-fashioned notions of lex talionis.

Chemical castration can also not be justified by the aim of incapacitation. When compared to a traditional sentence of incarceration, it seems clear that chemical castration is likely to have a weaker incapacitative effect than a long prison sentence. Chemical castration may stop an offender from committing a sex crime—although this is debatable; see Ryan (forthcoming) regarding the lack of evidence that chemical castration has any effect on recidivism—but incarceration incapacitates offenders from almost all crime. Even if chemical castration severely limits sexual desire, if a sex offender committed his sex offense due to a desire for violent control of women or children castration may fail to incapacitate.

Neither can chemical castration be justified by appeal to its deterrent effect. There is little evidence that changes in punishment regimes—even fairly extreme changes such as the imposition of the death penalty—have any effect on rates of crime (Tonry 2008). And certainly, possible offenders are just as likely to be deterred by a threat of a long incarceration as chemical castration, especially where chemical castration is offered as a condition for early release.

Even so, from the virtue theory perspective it might seem that chemical castration is an appealing option. If chemical castration worked as some of the US castration statutes seem to assume (Scott and Holmberg 2003), the state would be able to remove one area of choice-making from sex offenders—choices that have to do with sex—and not others. This means that an offender could continue to develop his character in most realms, while at the same time be incapacitated with regard to the type of crime for which he was convicted. In this way castration would seem to infringe less on an offender's moral development than traditional sentencing options.

However, on closer examination, there are several problems with chemical castration when viewed through the lens of virtue theory. First, as indicated above, it isn't at all clear that chemical castration is capable of actually fully incapacitating sex offenders with regard to sexual capacity (Ryan, forthcoming). But more importantly from the virtue theory perspective, chemical castration is often legislated as a permanent sanction, which in the US is often administered to offenders without adequate medical oversight and accompanying therapy (Scott and Holmberg 2003). The statutes that allow chemical castration position the sanction not as a means to rehabilitate sex offenders, such that they can make more virtuous decisions with regard to their sexual expression, but as retributive or incapacitative punishment. This means that an offender who is sentenced to castration may be expected to continue to take the castrating drugs for the rest of his life, and as a result will experience permanent diminishment of his sexual life. Such permanent castration will make moral development with regard to an offender's sexual life very difficult, if not impossible.

Remember Jack, the southerner discussed above who was found guilty of attempted murder. I argued that the involuntary administration of aggression-reducing drugs would not only impact his disposition to respond violently to threats, but would also impact his capacity to develop virtuous traits related to aggression such as courage. So too does chemical castration impact not only an offender's disposition to desire illegal sexual partners, but any sexual partner. The removal or diminishment of sexual capacities will have a suffocating effect on an offender's ability to develop virtue with regard to being a kind and thoughtful partner, one of the most central and important components of a human life. That is, if a chemically castrated sex offender experiences severe and permanent diminishment of his sexual desire, he will never have the opportunity to redirect his sexual desire to legal, consenting targets, or learn to express his sexuality in the right way, at the right time.

My analysis might be different, however, if MPA was given to sex offenders in accordance with the criteria I discussed above with regard to administration of aggression-reducing drugs. If those criteria are met, MPA might actually be considered rehabilitative treatment for certain sex offenders that could encourage rational moral development. First, MPA would have to be administered only to sex offenders who experienced overwhelming and intrusive sexual desires, where these desires are the cause of the crime for which the offender is being punished. This means the court, like drug courts, would have to be in the business of determining whether an offender was a good candidate for medical treatment. Second, MPA would have to tone down and not fully remove sexual desire, so it targeted mental states more likely to cause criminal harm (e.g., overwhelming and persistent desires for illegal partners) and would be less likely to impact legal behavior (e.g., desires for legal partners). Third, the drug would have to be given in tandem with therapy, so that a therapist might help the chemically castrated offender re-target his sexual desire while such desires were less salient. Fourth, MPA would have to be given to offenders only once they were released from prison, so that they can be subject to situations where sexual desire might be legally expressed. Fifth, the administration of the drug should not be permanent but temporary, until his therapist or other medical professional determines that they are no longer needed because the sex offender is no longer likely to recidivate. And sixth, MPA should be given only voluntarily, where a sex offender who is a good candidate for treatment has expressed a wish to get treated with MPA, and thereby wishes to change his character.

In sum, the virtue theory perspective allows us to see that permanent removal of any particular realm of decision-making denies an offender the possibility of moral development within that realm. While prison denies an offender the ability to make most harmful choices based upon their desires, it still preserves some possibility that the offender may practice a virtue such that he can align his desires with the moral good and develop a virtuous character. Similarly, prison may allow an offender to maintain a vice if he wishes. Direct brain interventions, such as MPA, are ethical only where they assist an offender to change his character as he desires. Permanent or involuntary direct brain interventions deny an offender his moral agency and thus his humanity.

2.6 Objections to the Use of Virtue Theory as a Constraint on Criminal Law

Although Yankah recognizes that virtue theory places an important ethical constraint on criminal law and punishment, he worries that use of 'virtue jurisprudence' could lead the law to label criminal offenders as possessing a permanent character flaw, and further encourage the use of sanctions that already serve to create a criminal 'caste' of persons who are viewed as unfit citizens (Yankah 2009, 1200).[8] Some of these sanctions include revocation of rights to vote and work in many fields, and permanent monitoring of offenders. Others are 'informal' sanctions: society's treatment of prior offenders as outcasts who no longer deserve our respect, which can manifest as rampant discrimination.

I disagree that this is a likely or even logical outcome of the application of virtue theory to punishment practices. One problem with Yankah's analysis is that he seems to confuse stability with permanency when speaking of character traits. As indicated above, contemporary virtue theory envisions character traits as dispositions to act that are constantly evolving, depending on choices a person makes and one's environment. It is true that both vicious and virtuous traits can become so stable that they are habitual, such that acting in accordance with these dispositions is almost second nature. But while it may be difficult to dislodge a well-established trait, it often is still possible, especially with help. Just as many people with severe phobias of flying can, with assistance, manage their fear well enough to begin to fly, so too can many violent persons, with help, learn to control their anger and aggression.

Yankah's simplistic portrayal of character traits reflects a shallow understanding of the role that practical reason and environment play in choice-making, especially for those who commit crimes. I have met many offenders who claim that prison, where they are assured of their 'three squares' and a bed to sleep in, allows them to make better choices than the neighborhoods they come from. Within this environment, they can begin to abide by simple moral rules, even if they feel deeply ambivalent about following them. Eventually, they might begin to feel good about following certain rules and staying out of trouble, or even about being helpful. In 2012, a *New York Times* article documented the rise in prisoners with dementia, and a program that allowed other prisoners to work as caregivers for the demented. As a result of the

---

[8] Yankah also claims that virtue jurisprudence necessarily conflicts with "the autonomy of the legal subject" (Yankah 2009, 1197), but this concern only applies when one is using virtue theory to justify the structure of criminal offenses and the application of force in punishment. As I do not use virtue theory in this way, I need not address this concern.

program, Shawn Henderson, who got twenty-five years to life for a 1985 double murder and was twice denied parole, earned his release. Mr Henderson claimed that doing a job where "you get spit on, feces thrown on you, urine on you, you get cursed out" helped teach him to cope outside prison. "Now when I come into an encounter like that on the street, I can be a lot more compassionate," he said.

It may be that Mr Henderson joined the program solely due to a selfish desire to get out of prison. He may have cared for his patients solely from duty at first. But it is possible that via the program, he actually was able to cultivate the trait of compassion. Another inmate caregiver is quoted in the article as saying, "I didn't have any feelings about other people. I mean, in that way, I was a predator." As a result of the program, he says, "I'm a protector."

I'm not going to claim that this sort of moral development in prisoners is common. However, the program discussed above seemed to provide the environmental push some inmates needed to start down the road to developing virtue. Instead of envisioning offenders as members of a permanent criminal caste, virtue theory can recognize the potential of offenders, and endorse offering offenders opportunities for development. This is precisely because it claims persons, including offenders, are constantly evolving moral agents. Only in the rarest of cases should a person be seen as permanently vicious; instead, offenders need personal and environmental support to encourage the strengthening of virtuous traits.

2.7 Conclusion

From the perspective of virtue theory moral agency requires choice-making as a means to develop and exercise character traits. I have argued that any punishment that infringes upon moral choice-making and thus agency, where the infringement is not clearly designed to accomplish one of the four functions of punishment, is unjust. I then examined current chemical castration punishments, and certain uses of isolation sanctions, and concluded that they are unethical punishments, because they deny choice-making and undermine the offender's ability to maintain or develop his own character.

Acknowledgements

The author gratefully acknowledges Nicole Vincent's helpful comments and criticisms of an earlier draft of this chapter.

Works Cited

Annas, J. 2003. Virtue Ethics and Social Psychology. *A Priori: The Erskine Lectures in Philosophy.* Retrieved 24 July 2015, from <http://apriorijournal.net/volume02/Annas1.pdf>.

Annas, J. 2004. Being Virtuous and Doing the Right Thing. *Proceedings and Addresses of the American Philosophical Association* 78 (2): 61-75.

Annas, J. 2011. *Intelligent Virtue.* Oxford: Oxford University Press.

Anscombe, G. E. M. 1958. Modern Moral Philosophy. *Philosophy* 33 (124): 1-19.

Aristotle. 1985. *The Nicomachean Ethics.* Indianapolis: Hackett Publishing Co.

Bahr, S., Masters, A., and Taylor, B. 2013. What Works in Substance Abuse Treatment Programs for Offenders? *The Prison Journal* 93: 251-71.

Berger, R., Chaplin, P., and Trestman, R. 2013. Commentary: Toward an Improved Understanding of Administrative Segregation. *Journal of the American Academy of Psychiatry and Law* 41 (6): 1-4.

Bouffard, J. A., Mackenzie, D. L., and Hickman, L. J. 2000. Effectiveness of Vocational Education and Employment Programs for Adult Offenders. *Journal of Offender Rehabilitation* 31 (1/2): 1-41.

Brown, D. K. 2002. What Virtue Ethics Can Do for Criminal Justice: A Reply to Huigens. *Wake Forest Law Review* 37: 29-50.

Cullen, F. T. and Gendreau, P. 2000. Assessing Correctional Rehabilitation: Policy, Practice, and Prospects. Washington, D.C.: US Dept of Justice, National Institute of Justice.

Doris, J. 2005. *Lack of Character.* Cambridge: Cambridge University Press.

Dow, D. R. 2012. Life Without Parole: A Different Death Penalty. *The Nation.*

Duff, A. 1996. *Criminal Attempts.* Oxford: Clarendon Press.

Duff, R. A. 2002. Virtue, Vice, and Criminal Liability: Do We Want an Aristotelian Criminal Law? *Buffalo Criminal Law Review* 6 (1): 147-84.

Gibbons, J. J. 2006. Confronting Confinement: A Report of the Commission on Safety and Abuse in America's Prisons. *Washington University Journal of Law & Policy* 22: 385-562.

Guenther, L. 2012. The Living Death of Solitary Confinement. *New York Times Opinionator.*

Haney, C. 2003. Mental Health Issues in Long-Term Solitary and Supermax Confinement. *Crime & Delinquency* 49 (1): 124-56.

Hart, H. 1968. *Punishment and Responsibility: Essays in the Philosophy of Law.* Oxford: Clarendon Press.

Hart, H. L. A. 1968. *Punishment and Responsibility: Essays in the Philosophy of Law.* Oxford: Clarendon Press.

Hirstein, W. and Sifferd, K. 2011. The Legal Self: Executive Processes and Legal Theory. *Consciousness and Cognition* 20 (1): 156–71.

Huigens, K. 2002. Homicide in Aretaic Terms. *Buffalo Criminal Law Review* 6 (1): 97–146.

Huigens, K. 2004. On Aristotelian Criminal Law: A Reply to Duff. *Notre Dame Journal of Law, Ethics & Public Policy* 18: 465–99.

Lovell, D., Johnson, L. C., and Cain, K. C. 2007. Recidivism of Supermax Prisoners in Washington State. *Crime & Delinquency* 53 (4): 633–56.

McGlynn, F. D., Smitherman, T. A., and Gothard, K. D. 2004. Comment on the Status of Systematic Desensitization. *Behavior Modification* 28 (2): 194–205.

Millholon, M. 2008. Jindal Signs Chemical Castration Bill. *Louisiana Advocate*, 26 June: 6.

Mitchell, O., Wilson, D., Eggers, A., and MacKensie, D. 2012. Assessing the Effectiveness of Drug Courts on Recidivism: A Meta-analytic View. *Journal of Criminal Justice* 40: 60–71.

Nozick, R. 1981. *Philosophical Explanations.* Cambridge: MA: Harvard University Press.

O'Keefe, M. L., Klebe, K. J., Metzner, J., Dvoskin, J., Fellner, J., and Stucker, A. 2013. A Longitudinal Study of Administrative Segregation. *Journal of the American Academy of Psychiatry and the Law* 41 (1): 49–60.

Pincoffs, E. L. 1980. Virtue, the Quality of Life, and Punishment. *The Monist* 63 (2): 172–84.

Ryan, C. Forthcoming. Is it *Really* Ethical to Prescribe Antiandrogens to Sex Offenders to Decrease their Risk of Recidivism? Under review.

Scott, C. and Holmberg, T. 2003. "Castration of Sex Offenders: Prisoners Rights versus Public Safety. *Journal of the American Academy of Psychiatry and the Law* 31: 502–9.

Sifferd, K. L. and Hirstein, W. 2013. On the Criminal Culpability of Successful and Unsuccessful Psychopaths. *Neuroethics*: 1–12.

Smith, K. L. 1998. Making Pedophiles Take Their Medicine: California's Chemical Castration Law. *The Buffalo Public Interest Law Journal*: 1–42.

Tadros, V. 2011. Obligations and Outcomes. In *Crime, Punishment, and Responsibility: The Jurisprudence of Antony Duff*, ed. R. Croft et al. Oxford: Oxford University Press, 173–92.

Tonry, M. 2008. Learning from the Limitation of Deterrence Research. *Crime and Justice* 37: 279–311.

van Zyl Smit, D., Weatherby, P., and Creighton, S. 2014. Whole Life Sentences and the Tide of European Human Rights Jurisprudence: What Is to Be Done? *Human Rights Law Review* 14.1: 59–84.

Webber, J. 2006. Virtue, Character and Situation. *Journal of Moral Philosophy* 3 (2): 193–213.

Webber, J. 2013. Character, Attitude and Disposition. *European Journal of Philosophy*. Published online.

Weir, K. 2012. Alone, in 'the Hole': Psychologists Probe the Mental Health Effects of Solitary Confinement. *Monitor on Psychology* 43 (5): 54–6.

Wexler, H. K., Falkin, G. P., and Lipton, D. S. 1990. Outcome Evaluation of a Prison Therapeutic Community for Substance Abuse Treatment. *Criminal Justice and Behavior* 17 (1): 71–92.

Yankah, E. N. 2009. Virtue's Domain. *University of Illinois Law Review*: 1167–212.

3

Character, Will, and Agency

Roman Altshuler

Character is commonly understood as a set of dispositions to respond in certain ways to one's surroundings, and as such is a broad category. It can include, for example, dispositions to feel or to react to events, or even more broadly, dispositions to see particular features of one's surroundings as salient and calling for action, thus playing a role in motivating action as well as moral perception. But aside from character, it seems, we also have a will, a capacity for making decisions, and the relation between these two features of agency is frequently overlooked. I will be concerned first to suggest that there are good reasons to think there is a tension between holding that both character and the will have a role to play in human agency, and that this tension inclines supporters of one toward eliminativism about the other. But I will also argue that eliminativism is inadvisable: neither character nor the will can be eliminated from our understanding of agency without a cost, because each serves functions for which the other is unsuited. However, I will aim to cast doubt on the idea that this consideration genuinely implies that will and character must be distinct phenomena; instead, acting volitionally and acting from character (for lack of better terminology) may provide different descriptions of the same events. This will require modifications to the standard views of both will and, to some extent, character. Finally, however, I will argue that this should not be taken to mean that we can speak of will and character interchangeably or, conversely, that we should be free to do away with one of them. Character talk and will talk—and the self-conceptions that go along with such talk—serve important and irreducible purposes.

3.1 Toward a Single Theory of Agency

Authors focusing on character tend to avoid talk of the will;[1] similarly, those concerned with the will frequently avoid character, unless they are attempting to eliminate the former by reducing it to the latter. This eliminativism makes perfect sense, on both sides. Character, after all, is supposed to determine our agency. While the dispositions involved in character may be dispositions to feel, reason, or desire in particular ways, they are first and foremost dispositions to act. In his discussion of the virtues of character, Aristotle, for example, notes that virtue involves having the right knowledge, the right motive, and the right disposition toward one's passions, but no one can accomplish the human function without virtuous *action*. Production of such action is, in other words, the *point* of virtue. And, as many writing on character have pointed out, character is intimately tied to prediction of behavior: to know someone's character is to know, or at least be in a position to make strong predictions about, the person's future behavior.

With the will, however, we find ourselves in a similar position. If an action is to be attributable to me as an agent, it must be because I somehow chose or decided to carry it out. Were my arm to simply jerk as a result of an electrical current applied to my nerves, the resulting movement would not be an action at all but simply a spasm. So our acts of will, our volitions, however we choose to interpret them, must explain why some movement of my body took place if that movement is to be an action. And now it seems that we have a problem, since both character and will seem to play the same theoretical role: they explain why an action took place. But if actions are explicable in terms of both character and will, it begins to look as if actions are overdetermined. Why, after all, would we *need* two distinct ways of explaining why an action took place?

It does not help here to point out that on most currently dominant accounts actions are explicable in terms of some combination of beliefs and desires, since those alone cannot explain why an action took place.

---

[1] There are, of course, apparent exceptions. But many are not genuine exceptions to the rule. For example, Hudson (1980) argues that understanding character traits requires attention to the role of strength and weakness of will: being virtuous, on his view, involves not simply acting rightly or having the right motives, but acting rightly because one wills to act on those motives. But strength of will is itself a character trait, so that the notion of will referenced here is fully subservient to that of character.

Even if we grant, and this is far from a given, that any time we act there must be (at a minimum) some belief–desire pair behind the action, the belief–desire pair by itself is not sufficient to explain why we performed that action rather than some other, given that there are often a number of distinct ways to satisfy a given desire and belief (Goldie 2004a), nor, for that matter, why we performed that action at all, since we have many desires we never act on. Even if we grant, as Michael Smith (2012) holds, that citing beliefs and desires places actions within a familiar context of explanation, questions about why the agent had those beliefs and desires, or about why she acted on them, remain. The belief–desire explanation is incomplete unless it is filled out with either character or will.

On one hand, we might explain how the agent saw the situation and why seeing it in this way gave rise to certain desires—this is a type of explanation in terms of character (Butler 1988). As Annette Baier notes in her incisive paper on Hume and character, we can often cite beliefs or desires of the agent as explanation because so long as these are themselves ordinary enough, reference to them will suffice to make the action intelligible. But "when either the motivation or the beliefs of the agent themselves cry out for explanation... citing them does not satisfy our wish to understand, nor end our puzzlement. Then a description of the agent can help," because "[t]he kind of person one is helps determine both the sort of desires one has and acts on, and the way one selects advisors and forms one's beliefs" (Baier 2009, 246). So belief–desire pairs are, on this account, merely steps in the transition from character to action. While Baier herself rejects the implication that all action explanations must cite character, this is ultimately due to her view of explanation: she takes an explanation to be sufficient so long as it makes the explanandum intelligible, something explanations in terms of belief–desire pairs can usually accomplish when the beliefs and desires themselves are intelligible enough. That we often *can* make an action intelligible without reference to character, however, does nothing to show that a certain understanding of character is not already presupposed in that intelligibility; many commonplace actions are, after all, perfectly intelligible even without reference to any beliefs or desires of the agent, but presumably no defender of the belief–desire theory would be willing to dispose of mental states in such cases.

Alternatively, we might note that the agent *chose* to act on this particular desire rather than some other in these circumstances, and this will provide us with an explanation in terms of the will. For, a defender of the will might argue, desires do not simply push us into particular actions, but must first be in some way endorsed by the agent. An agent might take acting on the desire to be more intelligible than the alternative, for example (Velleman 1992), or as providing an answer to the question of what to do (Hieronymi 2009); here the will as a capacity for practical reason steps in to fill out the belief–desire conception. On other views, the idea of the will as a separate executive capacity may be brought in to make sense of the choice among desires. Perhaps the will manufactures desires of its own; on one view, motivational states can lead to intentional action only if they are themselves produced by and under the direct control of the will, so that those states are better characterized as choices or decisions than simple desires, to which we are passively subject (Wallace 2006). In any case, however, if *either* a volitionist or characterological account can be brought in to explain action, agency will appear overdetermined. Attempts to avoid this problem of overdetermination lead to a tendency in the direction of taking either character or the will as providing the *ultimate* explanation, to which the other is subservient. But of course if we can explain an event in terms of one factor, which is itself explicable in terms of another, the instability quite naturally leads toward an attempt to eliminate the subservient explanation.

There is a further way to skirt the issue: one might simply insist that character does not determine action at all. One version of this view, for example, might hold that our formative experiences, those that have shaped our character, are not sufficient to determine our actions in every possible situation. When we find that our character conflicts with our values, we can set out to revise that character and engage in self-correction. The patterns of acting and desiring that constitute our way of life do not force us to follow them. On the basis of such considerations, Michele Moody-Adams (1990), for example, concludes that we have an ability to act out of character, and this ability is the reason that character is not destiny. Alternatively, we can note that traits of character do not fully determine actions—traits may be only probabilistic predictors of behavior.

Such arguments, however, do little to provide a rationale for appealing to the will. Granting that we can sometimes act 'out of character,' or resist our habitual ways of acting, raises the question of just what sorts of things can incline us away from those habitual ways. Say that a typically courageous person fails to act courageously on a given occasion. Is this evidence that courage does not in fact determine her actions? It is reasonable to think that, if the agent really had a robust disposition to act courageously, some abnormal features were operating here. Perhaps she encountered a situation all the courageous habituation of her past hadn't prepared her for; maybe she was simply fatigued or overly emotional (Goldie 2004a); or maybe another disposition provided a weighty enough consideration. Baier illustrates that "[w]hen we act out of character in some respect, it will be still in character in another respect" through a series of examples drawn from Hume's *History*; "[e]ven Becket, when he donned the character of sanctity and started mortifying his hitherto well-indulged flesh, still showed his old concern for how he looked—sackcloth peeping out from his archbishop's robes" (Baier 2009, 254). While people do act in unpredictable ways, this shows at best that we did not know enough about them or their circumstances to make confident predictions; that features of their character combined with features of their situation to produce an unexpected result.

Nor does the claim that traits of character do not fully determine actions help much. The word 'determine' is often used in a strong sense that does not allow for exceptions, and Moody-Adams's argument may be drawing on this sort of usage. It may well be false that character determines agency in the sense that if we know everything about a person's character and everything about the environmental factors she is exposed to, we may still be unable to predict her behavior with absolute certainty. However, as just noted, whatever determined the action had to come from somewhere—from the agent's motivational structure or from the environment. If something about the action was not so determined, this can at best show us that determinism is not complete. In this case, we can rephrase from the claim that character determines agency, to the more nuanced one that insofar as agency is determined, it is determined by character.

But there is no obvious opening for the will here; if there is any role for it to play, it is either as a feature of character or as an overdeterminant of features of action already determined by character. Rather, the argument seems to be based on the mistaken view that character consists simply of neatly defined traits of character. If we recognize that character involves far more complexity, however, it will quickly start to look as if 'acting out of character' just involves acting on less dominant—or heretofore less noticed—aspects of one's character. Alternatively, if we want to hold on to the idea that character is constituted entirely or primarily by character traits, we can adopt a context-relative view of such traits to allow that, for example, being honest when threatened with physical force and being honest when one can profit by lying are distinct traits (Upton 2005). Features of one's character can easily be at odds. We can see this by asking why the agent decided to act out of character. It will be hard to answer that question without appealing to other dispositions to act. Arguments of this sort play a common and familiar role in undermining free will and moral responsibility.

3.2 Forms of Eliminativism

I have been arguing that it is difficult to avoid eliminativism, and this is borne out in the literature. In the nineteenth century, for example, the thought that character, together with environmental cues, determines action seems to have been commonplace, and frequently came bundled with a wider kind of determinism. Schopenhauer, for example, built a complex metaphysical system on which each individual's behavior over the course of a life is fully fixed by their phenomenal character, itself a manifestation of an underlying noumenal character, and to illustrate his point he compared what seems to us self-determined, chosen behavior with the development of an ice crystal—the crystal may appear unique, but it develops according to the necessary rules of its crystalline nature (Schopenhauer 2010, 205). At the (otherwise) opposite end of the philosophical spectrum, Mill insisted that "given the motives which are present to an individual's mind, and given likewise the character and disposition of the individual, the manner in which he will act might be unerringly inferred" (Mill 1988, 23). But unlike Schopenhauer, he largely dispensed with metaphysics, noting only that "this proposition I take to be a mere interpretation of universal experience, a statement in words of what every one is internally convinced of" (*ibid.*).

In the twentieth century the strategy is not significantly different. Powerful compatibilist approaches to the free will debate have built upon Harry Frankfurt's work on the idea of identification: I act of my own free will, on this view, when my second-order volition happens to conform to the desire I actually act on (Frankfurt 1971); or, alternatively, in later work, when I am satisfied with the desires I act on (Frankfurt 1992). But on this view what I do is either not up to me at all—if, for example, I am in the grip of forces I do not identify with but cannot defeat—or it is a result of the sort of character I happen to have. A similar theme runs through the work of Bernard Williams, who views character as constituted by our projects and desires, so that we can make no decisions unless they are supported by those desires (Williams 1993; Williams 1981a). This tendency is developed further by authors like John Fischer, who see intentional actions as actions stemming from moderately reasons-responsive mechanisms, which we form and take responsibility for in the course of normal development (Fischer and Ravizza 1998).

It might seem that I am being unfair. After all, the authors just mentioned are specifically attempting to explain such notions as the will, free will, and decision, among others. But in their attempts to do so, we find a clear leaning toward explaining these concepts in terms of, and as dependant on, a prior and more robust notion of character. Sometimes the attempt is implicit; other times it is explicit, as in Williams's famous argument that all reasons are internal reasons—that nothing can count as a reason for me to act unless there is a clear path to that reason from my subjective motivational set which, of course, Williams tends to identify with my character (Williams 1981b; Williams 1973). Even when the move is implicit, however, my point is that such accounts seem to make a separate volitional capacity redundant; character can do all the explanatory work.[2]

There are similar strategies on the other side. The logic is, again, simple. Whenever we encounter a choice, we are capable of exercising our capacity for willing by making a decision about how to act. True, our character might incline us in one direction or another, but character is not deterministic; we can choose which inclination to follow, and we can do so because we have a will. If we go down this path, however, the role of character retreats. Character does not determine action at all; rather, it suggests courses of action, which we validate or invalidate by our will. This threatens, however, to reduce character to little more than the Summary view, on which character traits simply are patterns of behavior.

---

[2] For a detailed account of Williams on character and its relation to an agent's subjective motivational set, as well as a critique of his attempt to reduce the will to character, see Altshuler (2013).

This view has been roundly criticized, among other reasons, for being unable to make sense of the explanatory role appeals to character can serve on such a conception (Brandt 1970; Gilbert 2006). The explanatory work is being done entirely by our acts of willing in particular situations; if any patterns emerge in our willing, those patterns have no existence independent of the instances of willing themselves. Volitional explanation simply displaces character explanation. The Summary view also allows that character traits serve a predictive function, but cannot explain why. If the traits just *are* patterns of past behavior, there is no reason to think that they can have any bearing on future behavior unless there is a further mechanism at work motivating the past actions and (thereby) making future actions along similar lines more likely. The view thus fails to make sense of the function of character, reducing all agency to willing.

Now, such an approach may appear too extreme, if for no other reason than because eliminating character altogether seems to do too much violence to our ordinary ways of understanding and evaluating agents. The alternative is to find a more palatable view, one on which our actions are indeed determined by character, but that character is the result of willing. Robert Kane is perhaps the most notable proponent of such an account. Arguing that we could not be responsible for our actions unless we chose them, Kane maintains that while our actions are determined by character in most cases, in rare instances we are capable of 'self-forming willings,' that is, volitions that bring character traits into existence (Kane 1996). By freely choosing to lie in one situation, for example, I do not merely choose that one action, but open myself to a future of being open to dishonesty. This view seems to preserve a role for character—in fact, it stresses that the majority of our actions are entirely fixed by character—but the appearance is deceptive. Character now becomes a mere diachronic effect of willing. More significantly, character is always fully open to revision: if I can will new character traits into existence, there is in theory, if not in practice, no limit to what I can will.

Again, my point is not that proponents of character are necessarily eliminativists about the will or vice versa. And there are, in fact, some ingenious attempts to reconcile the two sides. Developing Sartre's account, for example, Jonathan Webber argues that character may be fixed by projects, which may or may not be compatible with a fairly high degree of freedom of choice (Webber 2006). This is reasonable; it can hold that character inclines us in certain directions, but the will is needed to take the extra push to action. But any such view, which attempts to separate character and will into distinct phenomena, is likely to be unstable, for reasons that I have been pressing. In fact, I suspect that the best strategy is to recognize the common nature of character and will. The question is whether such a strategy must take an eliminativist form.

3.3 Distinct Roles

Before moving on to that question, we should examine whether eliminativism can be carried out, in either direction, without serious loss. There are good reasons for thinking that character and will are distinct phenomena: they seem to serve distinct functional roles. Character, among other purposes, serves the function of providing third-personal explanations of behavior; will, again among other functions, aims at providing justification. That I have a jealous disposition, for example, may go a long way toward explaining why I have planted a GPS tracker on my partner's person; it does nothing to justify it. The fact that I *think* I have reason to plant the tracker is itself explicable in terms of my character traits, moreover, and thus it may seem as if there is little for my will to do—between my character and my action, will can serve at best an intermediate position; in acting as I do, I am merely playing out my character, much the way Schopenhauer's ice crystal merely follows the directives of its crystalline structure. Suppose, for example, that I were capable of refusing to plant the tracker—of returning it to the store and never thinking of it again. If I could do that, perhaps some other feature of my character can explain it; say, the tension between trust and jealousy, and the importance to me of trust, has gotten to me. But if this is *not* the explanation, if I simply *chose* to return the tracker and that is all there is to the story, it is not clear what it would mean to describe me as a jealous person, to attribute a character trait to me.

Let's say that we settle for the first option: that I return the tracker because some disposition of my character, rather than my will, outweighed my jealousy. On a popular strain of thought about the will, it is in fact my character that sets my goals; all that's left is to act them out. This is why Aristotle stresses that deliberation is about means, not ends; it is virtue that fixes the appropriate ends. Why, on such a view, would justification be missing? Why isn't "doing this would be incompatible with trust" a good enough justification? The problem is that the justification wouldn't, in this case, provide an explanation of my action. I did not in fact return the tracker because trust gave me reason to do so, but because trust happened to be a trait of my character. So while this picture is perfectly compatible with my acting well or badly, in ways that can and those that cannot be justified, it is not compatible with my having a justification of my action that can explain why I so acted.

The role played by the will in allowing for justification of my action is a normative one. The role of the will on this picture is not merely to allow me to act well, but to allow me to *choose* to act well. What is necessary is that the will be able to serve an executive function. We can see this more clearly when we think about acting badly, especially when we do so in the knowledge that we are doing so—that is, in cases of akrasia. Say that I recognize that my planting the tracker is incompatible with trust, and that I ought to do what is compatible with trust. If I set it anyway, it seems I have acted wrongly. But unless I chose to do so, it is unclear that I have really *acted*, and by extension that my 'action' can have any moral status. That is, if my action stemmed from a defect in my character's ability to pursue the good, it is unclear that it was an action at all, rather than something more akin to a spasm. This is what seems to follow on the view that akrasia involves an overriding of the will by passion. Of course here I am assuming that choice—and thus will—is necessary to a bit of behavior's being an action. On the character side, we can reject this assumption. We might stipulate that anything brought about by any aspect of my character, broadly construed, counts as an action. Or we might hold that actions, to count as *actions*, i.e., doings attributable to the agent, must stem from fixed dispositions, or perhaps from dispositions that are representative of the agent in some sense that can be further specified. In these cases, counter-normative agency will qualify as genuine agency, but it will be unclear how we might hold someone responsible for it or speak of being obligated to avoid it, and attribution to an agent along such lines threatens to sever the connection with authorship. The exercise of counter-normative agency is thus frequently cited as requiring an account of the will, since without it akrasia becomes mysterious as an exercise of agency, or conversely threatens to sever agency from normativity and authorship altogether (Watson 2003; Wallace 2006).

This latter point ties in with some standard arguments about responsibility, since it seems as if to be *responsible* for our actions, we must be capable of actively choosing them on the basis of reasons. Actions that merely stem from character, it seems, can be responsible ones only on the assumption that we choose our characters. This view is common to positions as diverse as those of Robert Kane and Galen Strawson; Kane (1996) argues that we can be responsible in acting from character only insofar as our character stems from prior self-forming actions, while Strawson (1994) holds that responsibility is impossible, since all such actions must themselves be determined by character. Yet both take character without will to be a bare given, something for which no one can be responsible.[3] At the executive level, it seems we are able to act out of character—that is precisely how people can turn their lives around, by choosing to act counter to their dispositions. But once again, we are faced with a problem: if we *can* act counter to our dispositions, this seems to suggest that they are only dispositions to act insofar as we endorse them or choose to act on them. And if that is the case, it is not clear that they really are dispositions to start with. Moreover, leaving the will out once again seems to cut us off from authorship of our character; that character may change, but with no will driving the change, it is a blind process without an author.

It looks like we cannot simply eliminate the will in favor of character, because we will then lose the executive power that comes with it, and which is needed for justification, responsibility, and control. But we cannot simply settle for the opposite view, that of eliminating character in favor of the will. For if we do that, we will leave it utterly mysterious how it is possible to predict the future actions of ourselves and others, or just why it is that we seem to make similar decisions over time—that is, why our actions come in patterns. As I've noted above, attempting to eliminate character in this way will leave us with nothing more than the Summary view—the view that character, if there is such a thing, is just the sum total of our intentional actions. But if each exercise of agency in this scenario is caused by an individual act of willing, dispositions of character serve no *explanatory* role. What, then, would license me to infer anything about your future behavior from your past behavior?

---

[3] For a position similar to Strawson's, see Nagel (1986, ch. 7).

There is a further problem in the wings. Let's say that we accept an account on which the will has primacy and character is threatened by a corresponding reduction to the Summary view. We will lose more than just intuitiveness. For what will motivate us to make choices or commit to following through on them if not character? The executive power by which we commit ourselves to our resolutions seems to presuppose our having the dispositions to care about and bind ourselves to those resolutions. This seems to me to be one of the major weaknesses of many will-centered accounts, such as that presented by Korsgaard (1996; 2009). What unifies the agent's actions with cross-temporal principles, on this view, is just something like the agent's practical identity. But so long as that identity is itself constituted by nothing other than practical commitments, it is far too thin to make sense of agents' actually sticking to their identity in the face of conflict rather than abandoning it at the first sign of trouble. Thus, responding to Michael Bratman's view of planning for the future as structured by higher-order policies (Bratman 2000), Goldie notes that "people can, and often do, lead unreflective lives, being playful, patient, temperate, forgiving, modest, and so on, without giving any reflective thought to their policies" (Goldie 2012, 96). My point here is stronger: it is not simply that we typically do not need to think about our policies insofar as they are encoded into our dispositions and do not require explicit thought to adjust to, but that policies or commitments cannot maintain their intrapersonal diachronic authority without support from dispositions. Aside from having principles and seeing that they have practical reason to abide by those principles, agents also need to *care* about the principles, at least implicitly.

This point is the main appeal behind a rival account such as that developed by Frankfurt (2006), on which what binds us to a particular identity is that we *care* about it, and caring involves wanting to go on caring. As I've already suggested, Frankfurt's account takes things to the opposite extreme of eliminating the will or at least reducing it to character. We can attempt to split the difference with a beefed up account of the will, on which it is not simply a capacity for choosing, but also for creating new motivations, and something like this view seems to me to be right (Davenport 2007). But such motivations must still link up with a preexisting motivational framework. And separating this power to create new motivations from any dispositional background leaves any exercise of the power itself unmotivated.

3.4 The Single Phenomenon View

If character and will serve distinct functions in this way, it seems that neither can be eliminated in favor of the other. But the functional distinctions I've just discussed are more fluid than I've made them appear. If we can establish what counts as a reason, or a good reason, independently of willing,[4] then responding to reasons (or to good reasons) in certain circumstances may itself be a character trait.[5] This would at the very least give agents the power to act in accordance with—or contrary to—right reason without requiring recourse to a specialized faculty of willing, though admittedly we would be left with no control over our exercise of this power of responding to reasons itself. Reasons-responsive views pay the price of losing the sense that it is the *agent*, not merely her dispositions or mechanisms, that responds to reasons. It is in part for this reason that Fischer and Ravizza, for example, complement their view with the agent's *ownership* of her reasons-responsive mechanisms, though it is unclear that this addendum can succeed. If those mechanisms can fail to belong to the agent, it seems, so can the mechanisms by which agents come to own them (Shabo 2005); unless, perhaps, the agent's distinctive activity as will comes into play. Yet such views do blur the boundaries between will and character by bestowing some of the former's normative function on the latter. If, on top of this, we recognize that our decisions are constitutive of character (and vice versa), the case for thinking a distinct capacity is necessary for executive functions is weakened: character will itself be an executive faculty, by virtue of responding to reasons and giving rise to (and itself embodying) decisions.

---

[4] Some versions of Kantian constructivism, for example, follow just the line I am leaving out here. Korsgaard (2008), for one, develops the view that for something to count as a reason, it must be willed, or at least must be capable of being willed by an ideal agent (her view is a bit sketchy on the details). But even on this view, it is not the case that just *anything* could count as a reason, since there are things ideal agents must will, and things they cannot will. If so, we can treat constructivism—for the purposes of this paper—as a type of moral realism, on which reasons are established independently of any subjective exercise of willing.

[5] Something like this view is suggested by McDowell (1998). Goldie argues that "all character traits are *reason-responsive*" (2004b, 13), though he is working with a much narrower version of character than one I have been discussing, since on his view character refers to deep ethical dispositions and is distinguished from the sorts of non-moral mannerisms and ways of behaving he places under the heading of personality.

So instead of separating character from will as two distinct phenomena, we may do better to think of our agency as having a dual nature, neither fully passive nor fully active, a view that has the added benefit of being able to explain just *why* we can both explain (in non-rational terms) and justify the very same actions without requiring that giving two such explanations necessarily overdetermines the action. The space of reasons need not be ontologically sui generis. But this dual nature should not give us reason for eliminativism. Without recourse to character, we would lose our strongest explanations of why certain agents are likely to *consistently* respond to relevantly similar reasons in similar ways; and we would lose also the ability to explain what motivates even justified action. But without will, while we could establish more and less desirable ways of acting, we would lose the connection between action on one hand, and normativity and responsibility on the other.

I have been assuming throughout that reduction of character to will, and vice versa, is roughly equivalent to eliminativism. This suggestion can be fleshed out through an analogy: suppose that one argues that (1) all mental phenomena just are, in reality, physical phenomena. This seems like a straightforward eliminativism: all that is left, on such a view, is to figure out the exact physical specifications of each mental phenomenon and dispense with the folk terminology. But one could also maintain that (2) although mental phenomena just are physical phenomena, we may retain the folk terminology because we do not yet know how to match it fully to the physical vocabulary, although with the caveat that even if the folk terminology is too slippery to simply replace by physical terminology, ultimately it refers—though in a vague way—only to fully physical phenomena. This, too, seems to be a kind of eliminativism, since the distinction between the mental and the physical is a merely semantic one. Finally, one can hold that (3) although mental entities exist, they are entirely constituted by physical ones. This, I suppose, is what is normally thought of as reductionism, though sometimes the term is used for (1) or (2). But I am not convinced that it avoids being substantially different from eliminativism: unless we are willing to grant that mental phenomena have functions that physical phenomena themselves do not (for example, to repeat an old argument, mental phenomena are intentional, and it is not clear how physical phenomena could be), we continue talking about mental phenomena only provisionally—perhaps we do not know *how* to say what we need to say in purely physical vocabulary, but the conviction is that it must be possible to do so, if perhaps not at our present stage of scientific development.

I do not here wish to maintain that reductionism is *necessarily* a form of eliminativism. To say that smoke is a collection of airborne particles, or a toupee a contraption of artificial hairs held together by cloth and glue, surely reduces the smoke and toupee without eliminating them; the smoke is real, as is the toupee, in that they really are their constituents arranged in a certain way. Nor do I want here to endorse the claim suggested in the above example, that reductionism about the mental just is eliminativism about it. But it seems to me that in reducing character to will or vice versa, one is generally committed to an eliminativism. Of course, following strategy (2) or (3), someone like Williams can continue to use volitional terms, despite holding that there is nothing behind them but character. But in that case either the usage is ultimately obfuscating an underlying disconnect, or it simply helps itself to volitional features it cannot in fact grasp.[6] So if I am right and character and will really do have distinct functions, then one cannot be reduced to the other without eliminating it. As I suggested above, *some* functions of the will may be performed by character, and the reverse is likely true as well. But complete reduction of one to the other will leave a functional remainder (this is one reason that the point does not apply to the toupee or smoke examples above: neither a toupee nor smoke has any function that cannot be equally well filled by its constituents). This gives us reason to think that character and will must be kept discursively separate in order to accommodate their functional distinctions, but not to claim that they must be ontologically separate as well.

Isn't that last concession a kind of eliminativism? It might seem so, if we think the suggestion is that there is a specific kind of phenomenon to which I propose ascribing the functions of both will and character. So, for

---

[6] For a justification of this claim in Williams's case, and an argument for the claim that it is insufficient to explain the volitional features it relies on, I again refer readers to my longer discussion in Altshuler (2013). A quick example: Williams argues that "if one acknowledges responsibility for anything, one must acknowledge responsibility for decisions and action which are expressions of character" on the grounds that expressing an agent's character is paradigmatic of being an agent's own (Williams 1981a, 130). But it is not clear how one can explain *why* being one's own brings responsibility with it if ownership rests on being a feature of the agent's subjective motivational set rather than choice.

example, if the claim were that our agency can be completely described using only physiological terms, and that this capacity then expresses itself in diverse functions that can be roughly described in character terms or volitional terms, the proposal would indeed be eliminativist. But I am not claiming that agency is any completely describable thing. No doubt there is a physical vocabulary in terms of which our agency can be partially described, and no doubt such a vocabulary serves important functional purposes. But it does not follow that any one description is *complete* and thus capable of serving as a ground to which all other descriptions can be reduced. As agents, we do things that are frequently predictable, that are legitimate targets of praise and blame, that express patterns of activity over time, that respond to reason and deliberation, and, yes, that involve neural firings and muscle fibers. We need diverse vocabularies to grasp these different functions; no one of them is sufficient.

Of course this is not to deny that a vocabulary *could* be devised that can capture all of the functions of agency. My claim here is simply that the vocabulary of character cannot replace that of will, nor vice versa, and that we have no reason to think the two are fully reducible to any existing third vocabulary, even if we have reason to think that they are not ontologically distinct determinants of agency. Davidson famously argued that mental and physical events are the same events under different descriptions. Here I am making a similar claim: acting from character and willing an action can give us two different descriptions of the same exercise of agency. Some descriptions will allow us to draw conclusions about how the agent is likely to act in the future; other descriptions will allow us to hold the agent responsible. But my view also differs in important ways from Davidson's model. First, while Davidson of course did not hold that every physical event can also be described as a mental event, he did hold the reverse. But I make no such claim. Some of our actions from character are ones we could not, without significant distortion, describe as volitional exercises. But it is also true that some choices are ones we would be hard pressed to attribute to character, except in the vaguest terms—by noting that an agent has a disposition toward arbitrary behavior, for example. This is one reason the use of distinct vocabularies is often called for.

But many exercises of agency admit equally well of both kinds of descriptions, and here is the second difference from the Davidsonian model: while it is often appropriate to describe the same exercise of agency in both kinds of terms, the descriptions can easily blend together. Thus, we may say of the inveterate procrastinator that he has chosen to put off yet another task, and we may likewise, as noted above, speak of normative features of character. The reasons such cross-talk is possible is that character and will do not belong to sharply delineated spaces, the way that physical and mental descriptions supposedly belong, respectively, to the space of law and the space of reasons. The latter distinction is established, in my view, less because there is a sharp divide in nature to which it corresponds and more as a bulwark against the creeping fingers of reductionism. In the case of character and will, their cross-bleeding and nature as determinants of action give rise to the same reductionist tendencies. But such reductionism, I have been urging, should be resisted without a corresponding insistence on a division in nature. If the aim of reductionism is simplicity, we can satisfy that aim by drawing sharper lines between various normative and explanatory functions of agency and grouping those functions into families of descriptions with less distortion than obtains when we attempt to eliminate the boundaries altogether and either reduce all acting on reasons to features of agents or reduce all constancy to a mysterious repetition of free acts.

The distinct functions of will and character, in other words, need not require us to take will and character as two distinct phenomena, or two ontologically distinct capacities, and we can thereby address the problem of overdetermination. But the distinct functions should, at the very least, require us to adopt a dualism in our talk about agency. Understanding agency should not demand that we attempt to explain character in terms of the will or the will in terms of character. But it should lead us to see agency as having two distinct functional roles, with the implication that a proper understanding of the relation of character to the will must lead to a careful delineation of the functions of both so as to allow for our practices of both explanatory and normative discourse, although there may well be a great deal of terminological and functional ambiguity at the edges. An explanation of how we can choose on the basis of motives without thereby undercutting the normative authority of choice demands ontological parsimony along with discursive multiplicity.

Works Cited

Altshuler, Roman. 2013. Practical Necessity and the Constitution of Character. In *The Moral Philosophy of Bernard Williams*, ed. C. D. Herrera and Alexandra Perry. Newcastle: Cambridge Scholars Publishing, 40–53.

Baier, Annette. 2009. Acting in Character. In *New Essays on the Explanation of Action*, ed. Constantine Sandis. Basingstoke: Palgrave Macmillan, 241–56.

Brandt, R. B. 1970. Traits of Character: A Conceptual Analysis. *American Philosophical Quarterly* 7 (1): 23–37.

Bratman, Michael E. 2000. Reflection, Planning, and Temporally Extended Agency. *The Philosophical Review* 109 (1) (January): 35–61.

Butler, D. 1988. Character Traits in Explanation. *Philosophy and Phenomenological Research* 49 (2): 215–38.

Davenport, John J. 2007. *Will As Commitment and Resolve: An Existential Account of Creativity, Love, Virtue, and Happiness*. New York: Fordham University Press.

Fischer, John Martin, and Ravizza, Mark. 1998. *Responsibility and Control*. New York: Cambridge University Press.

Frankfurt, Harry. 1971. Freedom of the Will and the Concept of a Person. *Journal of Philosophy* 68: 5–20.

Frankfurt, Harry. 1992. The Faintest Passion. *Proceedings and Addresses of the American Philosophical Association* 66: 5–16.

Frankfurt, Harry. 2006. *Taking Ourselves Seriously and Getting It Right*. Stanford: Stanford University Press.

Gilbert, Margaret. 2006. Character, Essence, Action: Considerations on Character Traits after Sartre. *The Pluralist* 1: 40–52.

Goldie, Peter. 2004a. What People Will Do: Personality and Prediction. *The Richmond Journal of Philosophy* (7): 11–18.

Goldie, Peter. 2004b. *On Personality*. London: Routledge.

Goldie, Peter. 2012. *The Mess Inside: Narrative, Emotion, and the Mind*. Oxford: Oxford University Press.

Hieronymi, Pamela. 2009. The Will as Reason. *Philosophical Perspectives* 23 (1): 201–20.

Hudson, S. D. 1980. Character Traits and Desires. *Ethics* 90 (4): 539–49.

Kane, Robert. 1996. *The Significance of Free Will*. New York: Oxford University Press.

Korsgaard, Christine. 1996. *The Sources of Normativity*. Cambridge: Cambridge University Press.

Korsgaard, Christine. 2008. *The Constitution of Agency*. New York: Oxford University Press.

Korsgaard, Christine. 2009. *Self-Constitution: Agency, Identity, and Integrity*. New York: Oxford University Press.

McDowell, John. 1998. Virtue and Reason. In *Mind, Value, and Reality*. Cambridge, MA: Harvard University Press, 50–73.

Mill, John Stuart. 1988. *The Logic of the Moral Sciences*. Chicago: Open Court.

Moody-Adams, Michele. 1990. On the Old Saw That Character Is Destiny. In *Identity, Character, and Morality: Essays in Moral Psychology*. Cambridge, MA: MIT Press, 111–31.

Nagel, Thomas. 1986. *The View from Nowhere*. New York: Oxford University Press.

Schopenhauer, Arthur. 2010. *Schopenhauer: The World as Will and Representation*. Trans. Christopher Janaway. Cambridge: Cambridge University Press.

Shabo, Seth. 2005. Fischer and Ravizza on History and Ownership. *Philosophical Explorations* 8 (2): 103–14.

Smith, Michael. 2012. Four Objections to the Standard Story of Action (and Four Replies). *Philosophical Issues* 22 (1): 387–401.

Strawson, Galen. 1994. The Impossibility of Moral Responsibility. *Philosophical Studies* 75: 5–24.

Upton, Candace L. 2005. A Contextual Account of Character Traits. *Philosophical Studies* 122 (2): 133–51. doi:10.1007/s11098-004-6218-6.

Velleman, J. David. 1992. What Happens When Someone Acts? *Mind* 101: 461–81.

Wallace, R. Jay. 2006. *Normativity and the Will*. New York: Oxford University Press.

Watson, Gary. 2003. The Work of the Will. In *Weakness of Will and Practical Irrationality*, ed. Sarah Stroud and Christine Tappolet. New York: Oxford University Press, 172–200.

Webber, Jonathan. 2006. Sartre's Theory of Character. *European Journal of Philosophy* 14: 94–116.

Williams, Bernard. 1973. The Makropulos Case: Reflections on the Tedium of Immortality. In *Problems of the Self*. New York: Cambridge University Press, 82–100.

Williams, Bernard. 1981a. Practical Necessity. In *Moral Luck: Philosophical Papers, 1973–1980*. New York: Cambridge University Press, 124–31.

Williams, Bernard. 1981b. Internal and External Reasons. In *Moral Luck: Philosophical Papers, 1973–1980*. New York: Cambridge University Press, 101–13.

Williams, Bernard. 1993. Moral Incapacity. *Proceedings of the Aristotelian Society* 93: 59–70.

4

Practical Necessity and Personality

Katharina Bauer

When we try to explain important decisions, we sometimes tend to imply their *necessity*: We say things like *I have to do this, I do not have a choice* or we quote one of the most famous historic examples (even though it is probably not historically true)—Martin Luther's: 'Hier stehe ich, ich kann nicht anders' ('Here I stand, I can do no other'). Such phrases refer to fundamental convictions or beliefs and they can also be interpreted as existential expressions of a person's character and identity. As such, they seem to have a special value and authority. However, they could also be regarded as unjustified exculpations. It would be a typical reaction to ask: 'Did you really *have* to do this? Didn't you just wish to do it? Did you consider all alternatives?' Situations and utterances of practical necessity are used to discuss different positions of ethics and morality. Kantian-inspired moral philosophy underlines the absolute and objective necessity to follow the categorical imperative, which is distinguished from the subjective necessity of hypothetical imperatives. Contrary positions defend the specific authority of a less rational inner necessity of the character or the will. The different positions are related to the ideals of autonomy and authenticity.

I will argue for three theses about practical necessity and personality. First, that there are expressions of practical necessities which allow an insight into deep structures of personality and self-understanding. Experiences of *personal necessities* or incapacities can reveal limits of one's character and help to distinguish one's ground projects and essential convictions from less important aspects of one's self-conception. Second, that personal necessities cannot be reduced to the necessitation of moral law. They point at a limit where someone would have to *become another person* (in his own view), if he was forced to an alternative decision. I will suggest that this limit is marked by a loss of autonomy *and* authenticity. Third, that expressions of personal necessities call forth the respect of the other towards an individual personality. Whether those expressions are understandable and acceptable as exculpations depends on cultural patterns and is restricted by basic ethical demands. The response of the other can be a call for *self-reform*, which does not have to conflict with the authenticity or with the autonomy of the self. Still, as far as someone argues that alternative action might affect the 'limits of his personality' in a particular situation, this argument should always be considered with special diligence and respect, even if acting according to the personal necessity means to break a rule. I will draw from these theses the conclusion that personal necessities reveal the tension between an understanding of individual persons as *examples* of humanity and virtuousness and as *exceptions* from abstract, calculable terms and wrongheaded conformity.

4.1 Experiences of Personal Necessity as Focal Points of Character

It is quite sure that Martin Luther did not really say the famous words 'Here I stand, I can do no other' when he was defending himself against the accusation of heresy in Worms. Nevertheless they have become proverbial and Luther's composure in this situation has become exemplary for a person who is standing for something, defending her attitudes and convictions in the face of a high personal risk and neglecting easier alternatives. The expression 'Here I stand, I can do no other' refers to both the particular character of the situation and the particular character of the person who is involved.

Usually Luther's attitude is interpreted as an example for the strength of an individual personality or for a firmness of character. He is regarded as a virtuous or moral person. Anyhow, there are also aspects of his personality that are fascinating beyond moral judgements and there are aspects that might contest his moral integrity like many of his statements about the Jews or about women or his ambivalent comportment during the Peasant's Wars. In Worms, Luther is true to himself and holding fast to his ideals to advance innovation and reform, therefore he risks his life. To appreciate his steadfastness does not automatically mean to share the convictions he is standing for. Furthermore, he is steadfast but not inflexible. To become the famous reformer he had to undergo a substantial change and conversion. His writings are testimonials of vital deliberation and self-reflection during his conduct of life. Daniel Dennett underlines that 'Luther claimed... that his conscience made it *impossible* for him to recant' and that 'he was not trying to duck responsibility'.[1] His reference to practical necessity is not meant to be an exculpation. And the necessity of his decision does not follow from desires or volitions, but 'reason dictates it'.[2] In fact, Luther finishes his apology in Worms with reference to his conscience. And he admits that he would be ready to recant as soon as the evidence and accordance of his writings to the contents of the scripture were disproved. Still, it does not seem sufficient to explain his behaviour as the outcome of cool and rational calculation. He has to give his whole personality in pledge for his convictions. Of course, Luther could have done otherwise and it is quite sure that he was well aware of the opportunity to take the line of least resistance. Perhaps this would have even been more reasonable in some respects. But in the act of resistance he shows that this alternative is no alternative for him. In this situation he turns out to be the one who cannot recant. His steadfastness can be regarded as a personal necessity and it can be explained by the fact that any other alternative would mean a radical betrayal of himself as it would mean to sell out the values he is standing for and the ground project of his life.

But what about less heroic versions of personal necessity, in particular if there is no reference to conscience or evidence? Subjective expressions of personal necessities often seem to imply that someone cannot really give rational reasons for actions or legitimate a decision—at least in the very moment of the decision. Pointing at the inescapable necessity does not explain *why* something has to be done. But whenever someone seriously asserts that something is necessary *for himself* he gives an insight into the structures of his individual personality and in particular

---

[1] Dennett 1984, 133. [2] *Ibid.*

of his self-understanding: when *I just have to do this, because I am who I am* this personal necessity can be regarded as an integral part of my story and as an unfolding of my implicit idea of who I am or who I would like to be. I can try to make this idea understandable to others—and this can help me to understand myself. Asserting the necessity can be a kind of self-assertion.

The term *personal necessity* shall express the experience that an action seems inevitable and without alternative for a particular agent even though he knows that other persons could act otherwise in the same situation and under the condition that this inevitability and incapacity of alternative action is closely related to the individual personality of the agent. *Expressions* of personal necessity call forth a hermeneutical approach to personality and an intersubjective process of mutual understanding. Addressed to others, they also reveal the human want to express one's personality. *Experiences* of personal necessities can be interpreted as *hermeneutic phenomena*, which help to understand how we understand ourselves in different situations, decisions, and actions, what we care about and regard as important for our life and our identity. This does not mean that experiences of personal necessity are necessary conditions of self-knowledge or self-development. It does not mean that those who express personal necessities are immune against self-deception or that the self-conception could be equated with the definite truth about the self. And one should not expect that *one* universal model of self-understanding and personality might be revealed by the examination of personal necessities. But if we can never get rid of our personal, individual, 'phenomenal' (and not purely 'noumenal') perspective, a sober description and investigation of such phenomena may help to point out different aspects of human self-understanding—not only individually but also with regard to socio-cultural identities—and it affords different situational judgements about the right to justify decisions by means of personal necessity.

Whenever someone says that an action or a project seems to be necessary for him according to his individual personality, this can be regarded as important evidence of how strongly he or she identifies with a certain role or aspect of his or her personality. *I have to do this* then means *I have to do this, because doing this is essential for being myself*. Thus, if we want to find out how a person understands her personality and what she regards as essential elements of her identity and ground projects of her life, we should ask her what she considers not only as important or worthy but as *necessary* for (being) her. Internalized convictions, goals, and habits can become obvious in actions that follow from personal necessity. A person who is confronted with the experience that she has to do something and can do no other can discover in that very moment what she is standing for and who she wants to be. Exceptional circumstances in which someone's self-understanding is challenged and in which he or she experiences a personal necessity or incapacity can reveal limits of one's character and help to distinguish one's ground projects and essential convictions from less important aspects of one's self-conception. Personal necessities mark the limit where someone would have to become another person to act differently—according to his own perspective. And those limits call for attentiveness when we are judging another person from an external perspective, even though they cannot justify every action and decision.

4.2 Practical Necessity: Practical Reason or Personality?

Nomy Arpaly points out that 'Luther's purported ability not to do otherwise does not make his stand any less meaningful, but if anything that it actually lends it some added weight'.[3] It is the weight of morality as such, provided that expressions of practical necessity are regarded as avowals of moral commitment. Then *I have to do this* only underlines the necessitating force of moral law and it really means *I ought to do this*. Still, many such expressions have to be interpreted as declarations of a different kind of a less reasonable and more subjective necessity. Sentences like *I have to do this* or *I cannot do this* are often related to a self-expression of character or individual personality which is not reducible to an expression of moral ideals. Human personality cannot be reduced to the ideal of a mere 'moral subject'. On the other hand, the ideal of an unfolding of individual personality does not necessarily imply a full release from moral ideals. A 'complete personality' should also be a 'good person'. Based on a review of different theories of moral and personal necessity, I will argue against a one-sided emphasis either on

---

[3] Arpaly 2006, 42.

a moral necessity that rules out personal reasons or on a defence of individual personality against the necessitation and restrictions of morality.

4.2.1 Kant's moral necessity and the necessities of self-government

Practical necessity can be understood as a rational necessity to follow moral obligations and categorical imperatives. Then it is (as Leibniz already points out) nearly congruent to the concept of duty. Indeed, Kant uses the term necessity to define duty as the 'Notwendigkeit einer Handlung aus Achtung vor dem Gesetz' ('the necessity of an action from respect for the law').[4] According to Kant, moral necessity is furthermore related to a *necessitation* (*Nötigung*), which is authoritative and forces us to override our appetites. This semantic level of practical necessity is essential for theories of personal autonomy and moral responsibility. It implies that it is only legitimate to plead that *one just had to do this* without any alternative, if the principle of the action was formed by practical reason. Thus the necessity is congruent to the necessitating force of moral law—a self-imposed law, which expresses our autonomy. The accordance to the law is guaranteed by the test procedure of the categorical imperative, so that the maxim of the individual action can be universalized. Kant stresses that hypothetical imperatives (I have to do X to achieve Y) also imply a kind of necessity. But after all this necessity is subjective and depends on an alterable intention (if I do not intend X any longer, I do not have to do Y).

We are unconditionally necessitated to act morally, i.e. to act not only according to duties, but also *from duty*, thus fundamentally motivated by the duties that we have as rational beings. The binding force of morality cannot be totally comprehensible for us, because of our finiteness and 'phenomenality'. Kant is well aware of the fact that empirical persons are never purely rational, reasonable, and unselfish. Human beings have to synthesize the phenomenal and noumenal dimensions of their identity. And they have to be necessitated to act morally. The only chance to realize their own rationality is to govern their desires by the authoritative force of duty, which means to let oneself be guided by the necessity to act

[4] Kant 2011, 29.

out of reverence to the law. Kant's reverence to the law is associated with self-respect: we regard with awe the moral law within ourselves just like the starry sky above us. The respect for the moral law within ourselves also implies respect towards all rational beings, which should thus never be treated as mere means but always as ends in themselves. But does this really explain the individual motivation to act *against* personal interests?

Christine Korsgaard localizes the motivation to act morally and to be a good person in the Platonic ideal of the need (or necessity) to exist as a unity or at least to understand oneself as a *whole* person. In her theory of 'self-constitution' Korsgaard combines Immanuel Kant's term of necessitation with another aspect of practical necessity: the basic fact and necessity that persons *have to act*—action is the function of personhood. We have to follow hypothetical and categorical imperatives necessarily, because our actions aim at efficacy and autonomy and because acting is essential for our self-constitution. Surprisingly, Korsgaard sounds like an existentialist philosopher when she points out that acting 'is our *plight*: the simple inexorable fact of the human condition' and a 'necessity you are *faced* with'.[5] Nevertheless, she shares the Kantian view that our practical rationality and moral autonomy allow us to rule and control all contingencies of our existence.

According to Korsgaard the expression *I have to do this* is based on the principle *I have to act* and specified to the imperative *I have to act this way* by the necessities of practical reason and by the necessitation to act according to moral law, which is motivated by our human condition to act and to exist as unified agents. Moral necessity comes down to the fact of our existence, but the normative direction is already implied in the constitutive structures of our rationality. For Korsgaard normativity is defined by the criterion of a successful, continuous process of self-constitution. Here she refers to an Aristotelian model of human nature and the teleology of our function (*ergon*): in deciding about our actions we give ourselves a *form*—and the boundaries of this form are decisive for our future decisions.

From a Kantian view the sentence *I have to do this* does only express a necessity if it can be translated into the sentence: *I have to do this, because it has to be done—everybody should do this in my place.* But what is *my*

---

[5] Korsgaard 2009, 1f.

place if everybody (or anybody) could do what I have to do? Korsgaard suggests that we can have *private or agent-relevant reasons*, but they have to be interwoven into the textures and networks of public interest—into Kant's famous Kingdom of Ends. She premises that our personal ambitions and reasons are automatically subordinated to the universality of practical reason. We identify ourselves as we identify with a particular role in the harmonious interaction of human beings who treat each other as persons—as ends and not as mere means. Our individual identity can only be fulfilled as an *example* of humanity. After all the self-knowledge of our phenomenal practical identity, which is formed by our social role and our individual biography, only seems to be important for Korsgaard because it helps to govern ourselves more efficiently.

But do we really always have to 'pull ourselves together' to be ourselves? Luther might have to do it for being able to resist his fears when he is faced with the challenge of the accusation. But in other situations letting oneself go can be regarded as a very important factor of authentically being oneself.[6] This holds true when persons express themselves in situations of love or charity and subsequent supererogatory actions, in producing a piece of art or in finding creative solutions. By letting themselves go and by letting themselves be guided by emotions, intuitions, and desires they do not only unfold their individual identity but also contribute to society and to the public project of humanity in each of those cases. Self-expression, which can go along with the experience of a strong personal necessity, is thus an important factor in making our individual and social lives meaningful and precious. Still, Korsgaard does not really deny this (and this also holds true for Kant): the reasonable government of moral law with its procedural and formal character coordinates spaces of individual freedom that may allow for different ways of individual self-fulfilment of one's own practical identity. However, not only rigid forms of Kantianism tend to deny the positive aspects of letting oneself go instead of pulling oneself together. Thus (as Korsgaard explicitly concedes) they have difficulty dealing with the uniqueness of the unfolding of individual personalities and the necessitation that follows from their individual form and not from the formality of universal law.

[6] Cf. Schechtman 2004.

4.2.2 Personal necessities and the limit of 'becoming another person'

An alternative model, which pleads to strengthen the role of individual reasons and necessities, can be found in the thinking of Bernard Williams. He has established the idea of a particular kind of *personal necessity* that can override moral reasons. Williams criticizes the formality of rigid forms of Kantian and utilitarian ethics and the ambition to establish a discourse of moral philosophy that claims the status of a science.

In the experience of having no alternative, we have the chance to experience our own character and the lines of demarcation that mark the figures of our personality. Practical necessity is a personal incapacity of alternative action. The form of the self is something that can be explored and fulfilled from the inner perspective of the individual person. But it cannot be formed and controlled completely by an intelligent self-designer. However, the inner necessity and internal reasons we have to follow do not prevent us from being responsible or blameworthy for our actions. On the contrary: for Williams the limitations of a determined character that become perceptible in practical necessity (as well as in the feeling of shame) are essential to form a responsible personality. A character is formed by constitutive luck and social circumstances as well as in the history of personal decisions and actions (the past) and the ground projects (the future) which make somebody's life worth living for himself. And this character can be the addressee of the imputation of actions and of responsibility.[7] The form of my character determines what I can do and where other alternatives are no alternatives *for me*. The expression *I have to do this* really means *I have to do this, because I am who I am*.

Similarly, Harry G. Frankfurt develops the idea of a *volitional necessity of love* that shapes our personality: A wholehearted identification with something or someone I love is the way to identify myself and organize the multitude of my volitions. Frankfurt's argument oscillates between the logic of the argument *I have to do this, because I am who I am* and *I have to do this, to become who I am or rather who I want to be*. Frankfurt distinguishes different levels of the will: on the first level, we

---

[7] Cf. chapter 1 in this volume, section 1.3.

want something, on the second level we decide whether we wish to want what we want. The motivation for a person to identify herself with her first-order wishes and to agree with the limitation of choices by an inner necessity arises from the need for unity, identity, and orientation. Frankfurt emphasizes practical necessity in contrast to an overestimation of freedom in modern societies: 'For it is true, both of freedom and of individuality, that they *require* necessity.'[8]

Thus, a part of the interest in the question of practical necessities, determinations, and orientations can be interpreted as a reaction to the pluralism and the range of possibilities in modern societies. Personal necessities are regarded as necessary to generate a unity of a personal identity that is *making sense*. They imply a strong ideal of authorship and authenticity of the self—in opposition and as a reaction to postmodernist theories of a fragmentation of the subject or the person, which are, according to John Doris, proved by the findings of psychology. The basic personal necessity seems to be *the necessity to be oneself* 'completely' and in an identifiable way. But is it really necessary for every person to constitute an identity that is as individual and constant as possible? This presupposition is questioned at the least by Derek Parfit's constructionist view, which is based on John Locke's theory of personal identity. Parfit describes it as an experience of release that he does not feel bound to a constant and continuous identity, whereas Williams emphasizes the need to find one's life bound up with ground projects as a 'condition of having any interest in being around in that world at all'.[9] Therefore he seems to disregard the possibility of a 'flexible self' that can free itself from the actuality and condition of its character by means of self-reform.

From a Kantian perspective it is an important aspect of our autonomy that we can 'free ourselves from our (empirical) selves'—which means to free ourselves from our desires and govern them by moral law. Williams only considers the most radical way of 'self-release', which is suicide. While the necessitating force of our will to survive and to continue our own lives seems unquestionable for Frankfurt, Williams is more radical here. His favourite example of practical necessity is a character of an antique tragedy—Sophocles' Aias. He wants to take revenge, but instead

[8] Frankfurt 1999, 109. [9] Williams 1981a, 14.

of his enemies he kills a herd of cattle, because a goddess (Athena) has punished him for his hubris. Aias feels so ashamed of his deed, that he sees no alternative but suicide. 'Now I am going where my way must go,' he says. Williams points out why there is no alternative for Aias: it is because of his individual identity and more exactly because of his *ethos*. His role as a warrior and the social constraints are so strong that the only other way he could go would be *to become another person*. For Williams this way out is impossible—it is *an impossible demand* to change your personality or character completely. This holds true even more as this personality is not the result of a purely autonomous decision, but it also has been formed by others, by the orientation towards social role models or the ideal of an *ethos* and is thus not an object of total self-control, but to some extent necessitated by the circumstances. Is there really no other way out for Aias? It is important to reflect on the context of the ancient tragedy in this case—and Williams provides for the presupposition of fate and supernatural necessities in this context. Williams does not intend to make a person's action more calculable. But in reaction to the fragmentation of the modern world he seems to search for another kind of *form*, a consistency and stability of character and personality. This attempt is quite parallel to Korsgaard's search for unity and self-control (and to her reference to the Aristotelian concept of form).

Modern theories of practical necessity are trying to deal with a tight-rope walk between an active, creative, and self-governing personality—formed by self-determination—and the consideration of passivity towards its determinations. I hold the view that a good relationship to oneself and to others can only be realized in an ongoing procedure of an intermediation between our demands of rational (and moral) self-control, self-restrictions and clear rules, orientations, and boundaries and our striving for self-fulfilment, self-expression, and individual difference. Or as Marya Schechtman puts it, the 'task of being oneself' involves 'seeking the appropriate balance between constraint and liberty—between self-expression and self-control'.[10] Schechtman recommends a democratic self-conception according to the model of a 'liberal democracy'.[11] In the 'democratic self' there are 'guidelines within which we can safely be more passive'[12] and there must be room for inner conflicts

---

[10] Schechtman, 2004, 426. [11] *Ibid.* [12] *Ibid.*

as far as they are carried out in constructive ways and do not lead to self-destruction or self-alienation. Of course, this liberal democratic constitution of the self has a lot of parallels with Korsgaard's concept of self-constitution, except that for Korsgaard the constitution shall particularly fix the procedural guidelines of self-government and self control. The person is defined by acting, and by an active and rational control over contingency and passiveness—or by their oppression.

The individual balance point of each personality between constraint and liberty, action and passivity is not determined once and for all. It has to be redetermined again and again in particular situational decisions. In the individual process of this intermediation in her self-concepts, plans, and decisions, referring to the experiences and the continuing story of one's individual self-synthesizing between different ideals, desires, and expectations a person tries to find out what *she* has to do, because it has to be done *and* because it *is her* who has to do it. It is not convincing that persons only want to play their part in the history of humanity and therefore to constitute themselves as stable and well-organized entities and agents. This might be a motivation for many achievements of morality and culture, but in some cases it might be much more important to be motivated by the idea to unfold, shape, and re-form one's individual story and personality continuously and creatively. Based on this presupposition a special weight and value cannot only be attributed to moral necessities or to the idea that someone just has to advocate for high ideals like Luther. It can also be attributed to personal necessities that follow from the demand to 'just be yourself' and express your personality.

4.2.3 The criteria of autonomy and authenticity

How can the question be answered if someone is forced to become another person because of neglecting his personal necessities or whether he could just turn into another version of himself? From a modern perspective, it seems very easy to say that Aias could have acted otherwise: he could have decided to leave his home and family, to give up his role as a warrior, to settle down as a farmer, and develop a completely new self-conception. And it is not clear that this change would have meant to 'become another person'. Compared to the context of the antique tragedy, the extreme demand to 'become another person' might have been attenuated by the achievements of modern liberal societies that open spaces to reinvent one's practical identity. There are still much clearer cases of a serious change or loss of personality. To update the example one could think of the case of the German writer Wolfgang Herrndorf, who committed suicide in August 2013. His 'Athena' was an incurable brain tumour that had already started to threaten his self-control, self-knowledge, and personality. Shortly before his death he wrote: 'I am not the man that I was. My friends are talking to a zombie.'[13] Of course, there is an important difference between a disease that changes personality and social constraints or necessitation of others. Still, it was not immediately the disease and its influence on his character that forced Herrndorf into suicide. It probably was his fear to lose himself or to 'become another person' successively. He explicitly dealt with this threat in his blog 'Arbeit und Struktur' and more indirectly in his novel *Sand*.[14] Herrndorf was afraid to lose his autonomy as well as his authenticity. In such cases being necessitated to 'become another person' thus seems to mean to be driven into situations of hopelessness: the alternative to 'just be yourself' is blocked.

I do not think that it is possible to establish universal criteria to identify the limits of individual personalities. But I think it is decisive here to point out *who* should answer the question of 'becoming another person': the question of personal identity necessarily has to consider the perspective of the first person singular. When Michael Quante tries to distinguish between *Persönlichkeitswechsel* and *Persönlichkeitsentwicklung*, thus between a radical change and a continuous development of personality, he hints at a problem of the first-person perspective: We tend to integrate most of the changes into a coherent biographical story. But there are also stories of conversions or reversions that imply the idea of *becoming another personality* sometimes underlined by a change of name. And it seems obvious for us that there are diseases (such as Herrndorf's brain tumour or Alzheimer's) which seem to force persons into becoming another personality or at least into a fundamental loss of their personality. Quante states that one might not find concrete criteria or an absolute limit for a change of personality, as the phenomenon of personality is much too complex and flexible. It is a gradual concept. Thus, a continuous development of personality is distinguished from a

---

[13] Cf. Herrndorf 2013, 418.
[14] Cf. <http://www.wolfgang-herrndorf.de>; Herrndorf 2013; Herrndorf 2011.

radical change, as the personality is understandable as the same personality from the first-person perspective and from the perspective of interpreting others. This sameness is guaranteed by an active integration into one's biography and by identification with certain wishes and experiences.[15]

Experiences of personal necessity can be regarded as experiences of a limit of one's own self-conception, which cannot be surpassed without completely abandoning one's identity and the motivation to continue one's life. With Williams the particular value of a decision that follows from a personal necessity derives from the value that we ascribe to our lives and to the possibility to lead our own lives according to our ground projects. In this way personal necessity is again a 'dictate of reason' as defined by Thomas Hobbes: it is necessary for survival and self-preservation and beyond that for the possibility of *eudaimonia*. I prefer a less radical and tragic idea of personal necessity, which still refers to the limit of 'becoming another person' or, more precisely, 'another personality': there are boundaries of our self-conception that determine *how far a person can continue and value her life as her own life authentically and autonomously—according to her self-understanding and how well she is integrated into interpersonal and social relationships with others*. Those boundaries call for the respect of the other. But they also call for critical self-investigations. A person can legitimately state that she is necessitated by a personal necessity, if she is convinced that carrying out or forgoing to carry out a particular action in a particular situation would mean to exceed this limit.

Understood as a capacity of self-control (and not in the pure Kantian sense) autonomy plays an important role in understanding experiences of personal necessity. Even Williams, who is so concerned with luck and contingency, alludes to the ideal of a self-conscious subject whose character is formed by his decisions and who has his own life in his hands. Although there is no other way to go for Aias, it remains decisive that *he* is the one who goes this way and annihilates his personality. This is necessary for *him* and *he* cannot turn into another person without a fundamental loss of authenticity. The authenticity which is at stake here should be understood as a kind of 'self-authentification' by a constant

[15] Cf. Quante 2007, 174.

process of understanding and of identification with a self-conception without implementing the idea of a singular and timeless 'true self' to which a person has to be truthful. Thereby I would like to grasp the idea that being forced to give up one's ground projects or to neglect one's necessities of love can mean being driven into a deep alienation from an *elaborated and ingrained self-understanding*. It might remain possible to continue your life as another version of yourself, but the price would be a serious loss of (what I call) authenticity. A mere loss of authenticity might be compensated by autonomous acts of reidentification and self-reform. And the necessitation to 'become another person' does not automatically follow from a severe loss of autonomy. But a real threat of losing one's autonomy *and* authenticity is a real threat of one's personality without fail.

4.3 Personal Necessity and the Demands of Interpersonal Relationships

Expressions of personal necessities call for the respect of the other towards an individual personality. But justifications that refer to personal necessities will not and should not always be understood and accepted. The understandability of individual personality depends on cultural patterns and is restricted by ethical demands. Whether someone would be forced to become another person or not, if he could not do what 'he has to do', can only be answered from his own perspective. But this perspective is inseparable from interpersonal relationships. Other people can call for further justifications and for a critical self-investigation and even for a 'self-reform', if they are affected by actions which follow from personal necessities. This does not violate the individual personality of the particular self, as far as the ideal self-conception is understood as an intermediation between the ideal to be consistent and identifiable by means of 'necessary structures' of one's personality and the ideal of a procedural and creative relationship to one's own 'reformable' personality.

The call for respect towards personal necessities can be a call for exceptions to the rule in favour of the rich diversity of human personalities. But the expression 'Here I stand, I can do no other' can also reveal a steadfastness of being exceptionally virtuous. Thus, personal necessities point to another process of intermediation, which is important for self-constitution and ethical interaction. An intermediation between an understanding of individual persons as *examples* of humanity and virtuousness and as *exceptions* from abstract, calculable terms and wrongheaded conformity.

4.3.1 No alternative?—Limits of understanding

To illustrate how far a justification by a personal necessity seems understandable, I will deal with one of Bernard Williams's most famous examples. The painter Gauguin decides to move to Tahiti, hoping for new inspiration for his work of art but, for sure, also hoping for a pleasant life. He leaves behind his wife and family in Paris. Williams considers how luck or bad luck (a shipwreck on the journey, for example) could have prevented Gauguin's success as a painter. In the very moment of his decision he cannot even be sure that his talent—depending on the constitutive luck of his personality—is strong enough to profit from the inspiration of the South Seas. Luckily he does, and for Williams this success rules out moral objections against his decision, even though it does not prevent Gauguin from having remorse against his family. Gauguin's story can also be interpreted as an example for a personal necessity: one might argue that Gauguin has to follow his vocation as an artist—for the benefit of art but also to express his personality authentically in realizing his ground project and unfolding his talents. Indeed, this kind of vocation might be the most popular and traditional pattern of personal necessity in the modern world—a cultural pattern that idealizes the individuality, authenticity, and originality of the artist.

If Gauguin would have justified his emigration to Tahiti by an inner necessity one could say that his statement implies a self-projection. He has to do what he does, because he understands himself—according to his ground project or life plan as well as according to constitutive features of his characteristic personal capabilities—as an artist, as a painter who needs inspiration, who dedicates his life and sacrifices his personal relationships to his work. Retrospectively this self-conception seems to be justified by his success as a painter and the wonderful paintings, which we can still enjoy and which had influence on other artists. From that consequentialist perspective the necessity to go to Tahiti would probably seem less necessary for a mediocre hobby painter. And *his* statement *I have to do this* would sound like a self-fashioning to justify that he prefers the South Sea beauties of Tahiti to his spouse and that he wants to shuffle out of the responsibility for his family. But his desires for sunshine, beautiful landscapes, and beautiful women, and the fact that he enjoys painting and feels the desire to be an artist, could also be regarded as inner necessities that just correspond to the determinations of *his* character. Then the statement *I have to do this* seems to express a correct self-understanding, too. Nevertheless many observers would tend to doubt the necessity of his decision. A comparison of the examples shows that we judge the explanatory force of such statements by different measures. The pattern of the necessity to develop one's talents as an artist, for example, seems to be more valuable than the idea to follow other inner incentives and desires.

As the vocation of the artist shows, the accordance with socio-cultural patterns and role models is an important factor in our evaluation of personal necessities. Those socio-cultural and traditional patterns of identification do not automatically have to be cut and dried. They can offer differentiated opportunities and 'forms' for a successful self-constitution, which are still subject to change. Such patterns can be reinterpreted and revised critically in the historical process of cultural developments. The ideal of an individual self-fulfilment that has become quite popular since the 1960s, for example, affords some sympathy for the hobby painter who moves to Tahiti. In Gauguin's case the estimation of the value of arts, and probably correspondingly also the idea of a certain value of the artist's individual talent or even genius, can be regarded as a measure for the integrity and unity of his biography—which is not a measure for morality. Even though Gauguin's personal necessity can be acknowledged with regard to his role as an artist, that does not mean that it justifies his behaviour as an irresponsible husband.

What about the moral value of Gauguin's decision? Of course there would have been alternatives for a man like Gauguin. He could perhaps have taken his family with him as a more responsible husband. He could have continued to paint in Paris or to discover other French or European landscapes. His paintings of Brittany are well known and beautiful and they already foreshadow the particular style of his Tahiti paintings. So he could perhaps also have leveraged his talent elsewhere. Still, it cannot be denied that to a certain degree any alternative to his decision would have forced him to become 'another person'—or at least 'another artist'. The 'Gauguin' we all know and the most famous works of art that are associated with this name would not exist. The biographical narrative that can be told retrospectively to answer the question 'Who was Gauguin?' would have been changed radically. Under certain circumstances a severe threat to his personality would be obvious. Gauguin would be alienated from his self-conception in a society that prohibited creativity or painting. Or he would be forced to give up his ground projects and he would lose his authenticity and autonomy, if his wife suppressed him and did not allow him to paint any longer. In such cases most people would understand that he really *has to* go.

For Bernard Williams it is first and foremost Gauguin who has to judge his own decision and deal with the possibility of remorse. But in *Shame and Necessity* Williams underlines that the perspective and potential recognition of the other is an integral part of Aias' *ethos*. In the process of self-identification every person (even—or in particular—the artist) depends on the recognition of others, which is an integral part of her self-constitution. Thus, each singular person has to learn to understand the core and the borders of her identity in a continuous process of self-understanding, which cannot be fulfilled in a solipsistic structure but only if it is embedded into a plurality of social relationships.

Furthermore, there are basic ethical demands that limit the acceptability of a personal necessity. Our sympathy for Gauguin's decision depends on the influence on the life of his wife and children and on their opportunities of self-fulfilment. If Gauguin had stated that he would not only have to leave them behind but to kill them, because he wanted to get rid of them or perhaps even to find a kind of subversive aesthetic inspiration in that 'experiment', his vocation as an artist would not help him very much to gain the respect of others for his decision. And the measure for the validity of a personal necessity is not only the inner coherency of a character. The world view as well as the self-concept of Anders Behring Breivik, the assassin of Utøya, for example, seem to be quite coherent—a closed system, as far as we are willing to regard him as a terrorist and not only as a psychopathic personality. Luckily most people would not respect his assertion that *he just had to* kill seventy-seven people, even though he might regard and justify his deed as a personal necessity as well as a political or even 'moral' one. Probably he would have had to 'become another person' to avoid his deed. And again, most of us would answer that a radical change of his personality seems to be a legitimate demand, but there would be surely much more disagreement about whether he would have to kill himself (as Aias) to avoid the deed.

With Kant persons have an essential duty to sustain their life and personhood, because they can only understand themselves adequately as ends in themselves. But they also have the duty and the possibility to change. Persons who already have achieved a moral standpoint may still have to reform their conduct and their habits. But in *Religion within the Boundaries of Mere Reason*, where he deals with the possibility of radical evil, Kant points out that becoming moral really asks for a radical revolution and not only for a reform of one's own character, even for a complete rebirth. However, as in politics, it seems difficult to impose a revolution on people. We commonly accept limits of the right to *force* persons to change or abandon their personality in moral judgements and legal practice. But we also regard it as an ideal to assist autonomous attempts of self-improvement and to eliminate social conditions or practices, such as forms of punishment, that constrain the opportunity to become a better version of oneself.[16]

4.3.2 A call for respect, a call for justification, and a call for the 'reformability' of the self

The reference to a personal necessity—if it is not regarded as the universal necessity of practical reason—might not serve as a moral exculpation. Nonetheless *expressions* of a personal necessity *call* for reverence and recognition. It is an ethical requirement that such a call should be answered. But the ethical demand of responsiveness does not imply that the recognition has to be granted and every personal necessity can be accepted as a justification of any action. Nevertheless, it is important to understand expressions like *I have to do this* in the context of communication: they are addressed to others. Those others are asked to respect the deep structures and the boundaries and limits of an individual personality and self-conception. As far as someone argues that alternative action might affect the 'limits of his personality' in a particular situation, this argument should always be considered with special diligence and respect, even if acting according to the personal necessity means breaking a rule. If alternative action is no alternative *for*

---

[16] See the chapters by Jacobs and Sifferd in this volume.

me without profound changes to my personality I should not be forced to become another person even though I may be prevented from realizing my plans, as far as they constrain or violate other persons.

Nobody has to justify each and every personal decision that seems necessary to himself to everybody in public. But any other person can ask someone to justify a decision as far as it affects her personality or the dignity and existence of others. If there is no alternative *for me*, but there is an alternative for others (for another painter with a similar talent, for another, more responsible husband or just for anybody else), those others can ask all the more for a justification of the decision and thus for an explanation of the personal necessity which is not automatically self-explanatory because of the different perspectives and self-conceptions of other persons. That is why utterances and experiences of a personal necessity ask by all means for a critical self-investigation and thorough self-explanation to others. And at the same time they ask those others for respect and for a recognition of those limits which I cannot cross without completely abandoning myself, or more precisely, without abandoning *my idea of my personal identity*. Such an idea of one's personality does not necessarily correspond to a globalist model of character. On the contrary, the statement *I have to do this* usually refers to particular situations: 'I have to do *this here and now*' or 'I always have to do something like this under certain circumstances.'[17]

Persons long for being understood and respected by others as meaningful and unique personalities. Expressions of personal necessity seem to tell us something both about the fragmentation and diversity of personality and about our *need* to understand our individual personality as consistent, which calls for fixed structures and inner necessities. Doris describes a 'considerable social pressure towards consistency'.[18] But I think there is more than this external social pressure, which might be due to the interest in the calculability and predictability of others' behaviour. Persons also long for an inner consistency and necessary structure of their own identity—for a completeness of a closed order that makes sense, which is accurately described by the German word *Sinnzusammenhang* (a coherency of sense) and which can also be convenient to integrate breaks and ambivalences. This need becomes obvious in our self-narrations—and again, those narrations are

[17] Cf. Williams 1995, 52. [18] Doris 2002, 89.

addressed to others. They are *calling* for an acceptance of a personality as a unity and do not only react to social pressure. At the same time, there is a need to be understood as a person with a certain degree of control over her own identity—as someone who is free to change. I share Doris's objections to strong concepts of character education or character (re) building. Especially when they are institutionalized, such concepts bear the risk of an enforcement of ideologically or economically useful ideals of character. Therefore I would say that the invitation to a critical self-investigation and successful self-constitution or self-reform must stay an individual one that is expressed directly or indirectly in interpersonal or culturally mediated encounters.

As Owen Flanagan puts it, we should recognize a picture of personality that involves the possibility of 'individually and collectively making ourselves into many of the different kinds of beings we can be, and of bringing philosophical criticism to bear in these projects of self-creation' because this way of thinking allows 'appreciating the rich diversity of persons that everywhere abounds'.[19] A creative relationship to oneself and the diversity of possible selves does not lead to arbitrariness, especially not if it is combined with philosophical and critical self-investigations. To some degree our personal necessities are always normative necessities, because they express the shape of our ideals and convictions. And our responsibility towards others implies a responsibility for ourselves, which can be implemented by a critical self-elucidation about our personal necessities and possibilities.

There is a double call for the 'reformability' of the self: on the one hand, others have the right to ask a person to change in favour of contributing to a well-organized interaction in public life. On the other hand, persons call to be understood as 'reformable', developing and adaptive human beings who can plan their future and shape and unfold their personality. In expressions of personal necessity they also call for respect towards the limits of their reformability.

4.3.3 A call for exceptions from the rule (that prove the rule)

The call for respect towards personal necessities can imply a call for an exception towards established and generally accepted rules. But the

---

[19] Flanagan 1991, 335.

exception can prove the rule as far as it is an exception in favour of a creative unfolding of the uniqueness of human individuals in a well-organized sphere of interaction—which should be the essence and final end of ethics.

Despite the reformability and flexibility of the self, it is important that practical necessities can also be exceptional as expressions of steadfastness, as in Martin Luther's 'Here I stand, I can do no other.' What about those people who did not (and perhaps could not) go to the limit by giving electric shocks to another person in the Milgram experiment of obedience? Didn't they follow their inner necessities? It would be interesting then to ask for the structures of personalities, convictions, and self-conceptions that suspended the alternative of going on with the electric shocks *for them*. Persons who autonomously follow internalized moral principles that form an essential part of their personalities can be considered as role models. They are regarded as virtuous. Thus they can offer an orientation to others as to how to try their best to 'form' themselves by their decisions, actions, and life plans in different and individual ways and circumstances, even if a complete autonomous and rational self-forming might be impossible.

For Kant, being moral is the only way to get into a condition which is analogous to felicitousness (*Glückseligkeit*) and to gain a feeling of self-fulfilment and self-respect as a rational and free human being. It is important for him that this is only an analogy, as he wants to eliminate any motivation to act according to duty but the motivation of duty itself. But when he considers the question how to develop good character in the *Doctrine of the Method of Pure Practical Reason*, the motivation by a felicitous self-concept is regarded as a very important first step.[20] And on the other hand even Williams admits that an important form of the personal incapacity that follows from practical necessity is the incapacity to violate the rights of others—probably most of all their right to form and unfold their individual character.[21] Focusing on the legitimate demand of the structures of individual personalities, their striving for self-fulfilment and the necessities that follow from them should not mean that they rule out moral law as such. That would be a self-contradiction as far as this law conduces to a coordination of individual

---

[20] Cf. Kant 1997, 123–33.   [21] Cf. Williams 1981b, 127.

interest and its essence is the respect for the dignity of any other person. But it means to keep an eye on the rigidity of moral norms, particularly with regard to the differentiated moral rules, conventions, and ideologies of societies, which can tend to coerce people to change or suppress their personality.

The individual claims, needs, and desires of non-exchangeable personalities exist and they have to be discussed again and again in interpersonal encounters as well as in interdisciplinary discourses. Sometimes they just have to be answered by love. This does not mean that the claim for a universality that neutralizes individual perspectives in favour of humanity was not justified or should be neglected. Far from it; it is necessary to try to coordinate the individual necessities and spaces of freedom as well as possible, but without prescribing how each individual person has to be and how she should train or develop her character in every detail. A certain formality and neutrality can also allow spaces of individual freedom to open and give way to different opportunities for filling the formal structure with the individual forms of our personalities and our lives. Many expressions of personal necessities call for an exceptional judgement. But the exception can prove the rule. And, with Korsgaard, it can also ask for a revision of the rule. The idea that '*I* have to do this' here and now, but that there might be other alternatives for other persons in the same situation, could also be regarded as an element of what Jacobs regards as a condition of liberal polity: 'recognizing, in an enduring, effective way, that at least some of one's own values cannot be presumed to be correct for everyone'.[22] It means that the agent does not want to turn his personal necessity into a practical necessitation of others.

Aiming at the opportunity of a good life for every person, each person has the obligation to investigate her own character and to 'elucidate' and critically reflect the structures of her own personality towards herself and towards others in a sphere of public reason. But perhaps one should also respect a region of opacity of personality. It can be due to unconscious structures and deep-seated goals. Such internalized virtue-relevant goals can become present in habitual actions, which go along with the thought 'I just have to do this.' Even though this thought does not really present a

---

[22] Jacobs, this volume, p. 11.

reason for the action or even the automatic *re*action, this does not make the action less reasonable or virtuous.[23]

Finally, to respect an opacity of personality can also mean to respect an unexplainable uniqueness of individuality that 'makes the difference' between this particular person and 'anybody in her place', between *my* life, my story, and the history of mankind, between *my* individual perspective and the standpoint of an objective viewer, between *this* human being and humanity as such. Just as 'the self' can be understood only as a procedure of synthesizing different ideals, demands, and facts of our existence, so too humanity can only be understood in the procedure of a continuous interpersonal intermediation between different perspectives. The individual self-constitution of personality as well as interpersonal communication and interaction are in particular intermediating between the following aspects. Each person is as *exemplary* of humanity as she is *exceptional* in being herself. Being an exception—from statistical average, from doing what everybody would do—and being an example—of doing what everybody should do—correlates in virtuous action, which is often (even though not necessarily) accompanied by the experience *I have to do this. Here I stand, I can do no other.*

Works Cited

Arpaly, Nomy. 2006. *Merit, Meaning and Human Bondage: An Essay on Free Will.* Princeton: Princeton University Press.

Dennett, Daniel. 1984. *Elbow Room: The Varieties of Free Will Worth Wanting.* Cambridge, MA: MIT Press.

Doris, John. 2002. *Lack of Character: Personality and Moral Behavior.* New York: Cambridge University Press.

Flanagan, Owen. 1991. *Varieties of Moral Personality: Ethics and Psychological Realism.* Cambridge, MA: Harvard University Press.

Frankfurt, Harry G. 1999. *Necessity, Volition and Love.* Cambridge: Cambridge University Press.

Herrndorf, Wolfgang. 2011. *Sand.* Berlin: Rowohlt.

Herrndorf, Wolfgang. 2013. *Arbeit und Struktur.* Berlin: Rowohlt.

Kant, Immanuel. 1997. *Critique of Practical Reason.* Trans. Mary J. Gregor. In Immanuel Kant, *Practical Philosophy.* Cambridge and New York: Cambridge University Press, 133–271.

---

[23] Cf. Snow 2006.

Kant, Immanuel. 2011. *Groundwork of the Metaphysics of Morals: A German–English Edition*. Ed. and trans. M. Gregor and J. Timmermann. Cambridge: Cambridge University Press.

Korsgaard, Christine. 2009. *Self-Constitution: Agency, Identity, and Integrity*. Oxford: Oxford University Press.

Quante, Michael. 2007. *Person*. Berlin and New York: De Gruyter.

Schechtman, Marya. 2006. Self-Expression and Self-Control. *Ratio* 17 (4): 409–27.

Snow, Nancy E. 2006. Habitual Virtuous Action and Automaticity. *Ethical Theory and Moral Practice* (9): 545–61.

Williams, Bernard. 1981a. Persons, Character and Morality. In *Moral Luck: Philosophical Papers 1973–1980*. Cambridge: Cambridge University Press, 1–19.

Williams, Bernard. 1981b. Practical Necessity. In *Moral Luck: Philosophical Papers 1973–1980*. Cambridge: Cambridge University Press, 124–31.

Williams, Bernard. 1995. Moral Luck: A Postscript. In *Making Sense of Humanity and Other Philosophical Papers*. Cambridge: Cambridge University Press, 241–7.

5

Implicit Bias, Character, and Control

Jules Holroyd and Daniel Kelly

Implicit biases are automatic associations, often operational without the reflective awareness of the agent, which influence action.[1] This influence can be malign—affecting negatively individuals' evaluations and judgements of, and interactions with, individuals in stereotyped or stigmatized groups (social identities such as race, gender, religious identity, age, and mental illness have all been studied). The effects may be relatively minor: implicit biases can increase the number of times one blinks one's eyes when interacting with a member of another race, which in turn can degrade the quality of those interracial interactions. Or the effects may be of grave consequence, such as increasing the likelihood of shooting a black man reaching for an ambiguous object (could be a gun, could be a wallet or mobile phone). Both kinds of effects systemically contribute to and re-entrench patterns of discrimination and marginalization.[2] In the studies that have proliferated on implicit bias, one outcome is indisputable: almost all of us harbour, and are influenced by, some kinds of implicit bias, to some degree.[3]

---

[1] We would like to thank the following people for useful feedback on earlier presentations and drafts of this material: Michael Brownstein, Natalia Washington, Alex Madva, the attendees of the Implicit Bias and Philosophy workshops held at the University of Sheffield, audiences at the University of Edinburgh, and the editors of this volume, Jonathan Webber and Alberto Masala, and anonymous reviewers for this volume.

[2] Amodio, Harmon-Jones, and Devine 2003; Payne 2005.

[3] For an excellent overview of the range of biases and their pervasive effects, see Jost et al. 2009.

Our focus here is on whether, when influenced by implicit biases, those behavioural dispositions should be understood as being a part of that person's character: whether they are part of the agent that can be morally evaluated.[4] We frame this issue in terms of control. If a state, process, or behaviour is not something that the agent can, in the relevant sense, control, then it is not something that counts as part of her character. A number of theorists have argued that individuals do not have control, in the relevant sense, over the operation of implicit bias. We will argue that this claim is mistaken. We articulate and develop a notion of control that individuals have with respect to implicit bias, and argue that this kind of control can ground character-based evaluation of such behavioural dispositions.

First we introduce two perspectives on implicit bias and character (section 5.1). In section 5.2 we evaluate the arguments for the conclusion that individuals lack the relevant sense of control with respect to implicit bias. In sections 5.3 and 5.4 we elaborate on one sense of control—Clark's 'ecological control'—which we argue is a sense of control that enables us to consider implicit biases as 'part of who the agent is', and hence something that is a legitimate candidate for normative evaluation. We go on (in section 5.5) to show that this requires some emendation to recent ways of thinking about the development of moral character and self-regulation.

5.1 Character, Evaluation, and Implicit Bias

Some philosophers who have written on implicit bias have homed in on the idea that such implicit associations are 'rogue' processes, which are not properly seen as part of the agent's character—not indicative of 'who she is'. For example, Jennifer Saul has suggested that we should reject the thought that 'acknowledging that one is biased means declaring oneself to be one of those bad racist or sexist people' (2013, 55). Whilst this is recommended for pragmatic reasons (namely, getting people to acknowledge that they may harbour implicit biases), we take it that the underlying assumption here is that having negative race or gender biases

---

[4] For other questions that have been raised in relation to implicit bias, see Gendler 2011, Holroyd 2012, Kelly and Roedder 2008, Saul 2013. Many other fruitful papers can be found here: <http://www.biasproject.org/recommended-reading>.

does not reflect badly on one's character. Merely being influenced by implicit bias does not mean that one has the character of a racist or sexist person; it takes something other than the operation of implicit racial biases to be properly ascribed the character *trait* racist. Likewise, Joshua Glasgow has emphasized that many of us are *alienated* from such attitudes, and tend to regard implicit bias and the behaviours influenced by them as 'actions and attitudes that do not represent us in any real sense at all' (forthcoming). Glasgow's remarks here resonate with the idea that implicit biases do not constitute 'who we are', or form part of our characters. Finally, Neil Levy (2012) has indicated that the associative structure of implicit biases, and the fact that they are not subject to 'rule-based-processing' in the way that our explicit attitudes are, means that such states cannot play a role in unifying us as agents and can actually undermine our ability to express 'who we are' in our actions over time.

This treatment contrasts with that of Lorraine Besser-Jones, who implies that implicit biases can legitimately be taken into consideration when evaluating a person's character. Insofar as behavioural dispositions are a part of character, and implicit biases produce certain behavioural dispositions, then those implicit biases qualify as part of an individual's moral character, for which they can be evaluated (and perhaps blamed). This emerges in her treatment of the following example (we quote at length):

Take the case of Jane and Mark. Jane believes that everyone deserves equal treatment, and condemns racism. Yet, whenever she sees a black man walking down the street, she averts her eyes and, if possible, crosses the street. She feels guilty when she does so, but nonetheless cannot help herself from acting in these ways. Mark, on the other hand, holds racist beliefs about the inferiority of African Americans. He, too, averts his eyes and crosses the street when encountering a black man. He, too, feels guilty when he does so, after all, it is not as if he holds anything 'personal' against the man, but is simply acting on the basis of what he thinks is right.

Jane and Mark share very similar dispositions—both behavioral dispositions, and dispositions to feel certain ways in response to their behavioral dispositions—nonetheless, all would agree that they have different moral characters: Jane is what psychologists label an 'aversive racist'—one who is 'consciously non-prejudiced yet unconsciously prejudiced'; her character is significantly different than Mark's, whose character is prejudiced on all levels. (2008, 317, see also discussion in her 2014, 82)

Besser-Jones uses this example to make the point that an individual's beliefs, and not simply her behavioural dispositions, are the basis of character: the right account incorporates both, she argues. What is striking from our point of view is that Besser-Jones nonetheless sees the behavioural dispositions involved in Jane's 'aversive racism'—a form of racism underpinned by negative implicit biases—as a legitimate (partial) basis for evaluating her moral character. A full evaluation of her moral character should take into account those dispositions, and the behaviour that manifests them, contra the starting assumptions of Saul, Glasgow, and Levy.

Which view should we endorse? Both perspectives have some appeal: insofar as implicit biases are not under an individual's control and are attitudes from which she is alienated, it does seem somewhat unfair to treat them as evaluable in the same way as her considered and endorsed beliefs and attitudes. Moreover, one might think that implicit biases reflect mere epistemic mistakes rather than character flaws, and that being influenced by them can be evaluated only by tracing back to these original errors, which are not flaws of character.

But there is intuitive appeal in Besser-Jones's position also. Her emphasis is on the extent to which individuals' moral commitments and beliefs interact with and shape their behavioural dispositions (and their practical attitudes towards success or failure in doing so) (2008, 322). Moreover, we think it defensible to consider the operation of implicit bias in terms of character, since (as we will see) the operation of implicit biases interact with agents' values in various ways. And, even if an epistemic error is at issue, this does not render questions of character irrelevant: the mistakes individuals make are often reflective of who they are (their values, with respect to what they are scrupulous, say).

The operation of implicit bias *can* be thought of in terms of character, then; but should it be? Besser-Jones's comments direct us to the important question of the extent to which individuals can exercise control over the expression in behaviour and judgement of their own implicit biases. Are these processes and the behavioural dispositions they produce the kind of things that individuals can regulate or control so as to bring their actions into line with their considered evaluative commitments? If not, then the manifestation of implicit bias starts to look more like the spasm of a hand, or perhaps the intrusion of compulsive or phobic thoughts—uncontrollable, and not attributable to the agent in a way that enables us to evaluate her, or her evaluative commitments, on the basis of such behaviours. Crucial in answering this question, then, is assessing whether individuals have control over the expression of implicit biases. We start to address this question in the following section.

5.2 Control Conditions and Implicit Bias

It has been commonplace to contrast implicit associations with *controlled* processing.[5] The idea that implicit biases are not under the agent's control has contributed to and underpinned the claim that individuals are not responsible for implicit biases, and that they don't 'stand for' who the agent is. This is bound up with the nature of such biases as 'implicit': 'without the consciousness of having an implicit race bias, it seems difficult or impossible to exert control to correct it' (Cameron et al. 2010, 275). But this is too simple. Notions of control proliferate in the philosophical literature,[6] and to ascertain whether individuals are able to exercise control over their implicit biases in a way that can legitimize evaluation of them as part of one's character, we need to take care to be clear about what sense(s) of control might be at issue. In this section, we examine some candidate notions of control, as they are found in the current literature.

5.2.1 Direct control

Saul has suggested that individuals' lack of *direct* control over implicit biases should exempt individuals from moral responsibility for them: individuals 'do not [when made aware of biases] instantly become able to control their biases, and so they should not be blamed for them' (2013, 55). This sounds reasonable, but many traits and dispositions that are typically thought of as part of our characters are not under any kind of direct or immediate control, either. Indeed, the cultivation of stable dispositions to act that are underpinned by evaluative commitments has

---

[5] Dovidio, Kawakami, Johnson, and Johnson 1997.
[6] Some of the more interesting notions taken from the philosophical literature include: ultimate control (Kane 1989), regulative and guidance control (Fischer and Ravizza 1999), rational control (Smith M. 2001, Smith A. 2008), intervention control (Snow 2006), valuative control (Hieronymi 2006), indirect control (Arpaly 2003), long-range control (Feldman 2008), narrative control (Velleman 2005; he never uses the terminology, but we feel this captures the general idea), ecological or soft control (Clark 2007), fluent control (Railton 2009), habitual control (Romdenh-Romluc 2011), skilled control (Annas 2011), and dialogic control (Doris 2015).

traditionally been considered to require time and practice.[7] We submit that less direct types of control are often actually paradigmatic of the kind of control we have over aspects of our character—witness, for instance, the Aristotelian notion of habituation of virtuous traits. As such, being subject to such indirect types of control permits a mental state or disposition to count as a component of a person's character, and so to be properly the object of character-based moral evaluations.

However, even if individuals have indirect control over implicit biases there remains further unpacking of the kind of indirect control at issue. Moreover, doubts may remain about the significance of other important forms of control that we don't have over the operation of implicit biases, such that it may indeed be inappropriate to consider the agent responsible for their influence. We now consider three further kinds of control that, arguably, individuals lack with respect to implicit biases.

5.2.2 Unified agency and reflective control

Levy argues that 'agents should be excused responsibility for actions caused by implicit attitudes' (2011, 17). One central idea that supports this claim, from Levy, is that implicit attitudes have an associative structure, and as such cannot play a role in unifying the agent. On Levy's account, being an agent—being an individual with evaluative commitments that structure one's plans and projects—requires being able to manifest a kind of 'diachronic unity'. Diachronic unity requires being able to plan and pursue projects, which in turn requires that one's attitudes must be norm-governed such that they can satisfy certain desiderata like avoiding inconsistency and meeting rationality requirements of means-ends reasoning. Explicit attitudes and beliefs are governed by these sorts of norms, and are a kind of 'rule-based processing' (Levy 2011, 13), which enables individuals to bring their evaluative commitments into a coherent structure, and plan according to them. In this way, we can see 'where the agent stands' over time. But Levy argues that the associative, non-inferential structure of implicit biases (and other implicit associations and processes) simply means that they are not so governed, and so not the kind of state that can underpin this

---

[7] For detailed evaluation of this control condition for moral responsibility in relation to implicit bias, see Holroyd 2012.

sort of unification.[8] Since they are not under the agent's control in a way that enables the unification of agency and the expression, over time, of who the agent is, they are not the proper objects of evaluative assessments, nor relevant to the evaluation of the agent's character.

We disagree for two reasons. First, we see no reason to suppose that implicit, associative processes in general, as a kind of mental structure, cannot contribute to the unification of an agent. Consider for example the findings from Moskowitz and Li (2011): individuals who were actively committed to 'egalitarian' goals (goals of treating individuals fairly) were better able to regulate the expression of negative implicit biases. This 'active commitment' involved being strongly committed, in reports on explicit beliefs, to such egalitarian values, and having the specific goal of treating people fairly activated. As goal activation can be automatic, this need not involve conscious strivings or effort. Because the regulation was not due to conscious effort (subjects were placed under cognitive loads to prevent this), the results indicate that automatic implicit processes, outside of the awareness of reflective agency, are serving to bring behaviour into conformity with explicit values. If this is right, then there are cases in which non-inferential, associative, processes seem to be able to play a role in unifying agency. (See also Devine et al. (2002), who also hypothesize that in individuals strongly committed to fair treatment, preconscious and automatic regulatory systems inhibit the expression of implicit bias.)

Second, even if we accept Levy's claim that such states disrupt or fail to contribute to unified agency, this by itself does not entail that such states are not candidates for moral evaluation in an agent who meets some threshold of unity by other means. For example, it is implausible that behavioural dispositions, in isolation or on their own, would achieve Levy's required kind of unity. Rather, beliefs and commitments that structure these behavioural dispositions are also needed to achieve that unity. But this does not mean that, once an agent meets the threshold of unity and is able to pursue projects coherently over time, their behavioural dispositions remain outside the scope of moral evaluation. Analogously, we can happily accept the claim that implicit biases, operating in isolation and on their own, do not themselves have or provide the

---

[8] It is not uncontroversial that implicit processing is associative (see Mandelbaum 2015), but we grant this assumption for the purposes of argument.

structure required for unified agency. This, however, does not entail that the operation of those implicit biases contribute *nothing* to who the (otherwise unified) agent is, or that they cannot be the target of evaluation. Consider an individual's associations concerning gender and leadership: many have been found to have stronger associations between men—rather than women—and leadership qualities (see Valian 2005). This association alone could of course not provide the unity Levy requires for agency. (It is hard to see how any association by itself, implicit or otherwise, could do that.) But once the agent meets the threshold of unity that makes her qualified for normative evaluation in general, this component of her cognitive make-up also becomes a viable target of assessment, and we can consider whether it reflects well or badly on her.

5.2.3 Alienation and evaluative control

One might still find something troubling in the idea that certain actions are influenced by processes (e.g. negative implicit biases) which conflict with explicit attitudes (commitment to fair treatment), and which one is unable to bring into line with one's explicit attitudes. That is, one might worry that implicit biases are not subject to the sort of 'evaluative control' that we have over other parts of our cognitive structures.[9] One might insist that if an agent's action or judgement 'is not responsive... to the beliefs, values, and so on of the agent, then the person has lost control over it' (Levy 2011, 5) and therefore that action or judgement cannot be indicative of where she stands as an agent—it is not part of her character.

The cases of implicit bias that have garnered the most attention are those in which the individuals' explicit attitudes come apart from her implicit associations. For example, a person has explicit attitudes endorsing anti-discrimination, whilst being influenced by implicit associations between black men and negative stereotypical associations. In such cases, actions driven by the person's implicit biases appear to be candidates for actions which are out of control, in exactly this sense: they are unresponsive to the agent's explicit evaluative attitudes (at least her considered evaluative attitudes), and in that respect she is alienated from her implicit attitude.

---

[9] See also Smith 2008.

The notion of *alienation* has been used to capture this psychological state of affairs, where a person is alienated from certain states or processes that are present in her psychological make-up. The notion has also loomed large in 'real-self' views of moral responsibility, where some have argued that 'alienation' can (in at least some cases) exculpate because those alienated states or dispositions are not part of the 'real self'. However, we see no good reason to suppose that alienation entails that the states from which the agent is alienated should not be part of our evaluation of that agent. As Besser-Jones claimed in relation to Mark and Jane, it is not only that Jane has implicit biases, but also *that she is alienated from them* that should be reflected in our evaluation of her character (as less bad in this respect than Mark—but, we add, less good than some third character who neither has nor manifests implicit race bias). Here we also find ourselves sympathetic to aspects of Josh Glasgow's treatment of alienation from implicit bias. Focusing on a case of dissociated implicit and explicit attitudes, Glasgow identifies such implicit attitudes as ones from which the agent is alienated. Nonetheless, asking us to reflect on our own judgements about our relationship to those attitudes from which we are alienated, Glasgow strongly asserts that, whilst confident in his alienation from the implicit biases he harbours, and 'wholeheartedly disavow[ing] such nonsense', he would not doubt their presence, nor that he is culpable for their presence: 'alienation is not sufficient for exculpation' (forthcoming). In short, while *being alienated from* one's implicit biases is relevant to the evaluation of one's character, it does not completely absolve one from *having* or *being influenced by* those implicit biases.

Whilst primarily concerned with moral responsibility, Glasgow here holds two distinctive claims: a) that implicit biases are not part of the agent's moral character (due to alienation, or lack of evaluative control), and b) that nonetheless, the presence of those biases can influence the moral evaluation of her and her actions.[10] We agree with Glasgow that moral evaluation is appropriate. However, we reject the idea that lack of evaluative control (the sort of 'alienation' identified here) entails that implicit biases are not part of 'who the agent is'. In the following section (5.3), we articulate a kind of control that suffices for considering implicit biases as part of moral character.

[10] See also Stump 1996.

5.2.4 Intervention control

So far, we have examined claims about the lack of direct control over implicit biases, about their associative structure that does not underwrite unified agency, and about the fact that agents are often 'alienated' from the implicit biases they may be influenced by. We have argued that none of these considerations provides sufficient reason to suppose that implicit biases are not part of an agent's character, and so should be left out of evaluations of 'who she is' and 'what she stands for'.

However, a further concern may remain: if implicit biases influence behaviour and judgement without the agent being able to prevent them, then we should not consider the influence of implicit biases in behaviour—such behavioural dispositions—as part of the agent's character. These behavioural dispositions should be considered more like an agent's disposition for her hand to spasm under certain circumstances—something outside of her control, and not therefore attributable to her. We might identify the worry here in terms of a lack of 'intervention' or 'inhibition' control—the agent's ability to inhibit certain actions that are not expressive of her core values and moral commitments (see Levy 2011, 16). Nancy Snow articulates the notion of inhibition or intervention control in her discussion of virtuous agency and its relation to the automatic processing involved in the pursuit of virtuous goals. Snow notes that whilst automatic processes can be initiated and run without the guidance of reflective deliberation, they are nonetheless attributable to the agent insofar as she has intervention control over them. An agent exercises intervention control when she intervenes in an instance of behaviour that is unfolding smoothly and relatively unthinkingly on its own (such as cycling while on 'autopilot mode')—either inhibiting that behaviour or redirecting it (2006, 549).

A question that this raises is whether individuals have the ability to intervene in, and bring under reflective control, the manifestation of their own implicit biases. Surely if one cannot in any way prevent the expression of implicit biases, one is not properly morally evaluable for those expressions?

Some empirical studies indicate that there is indeed trouble lurking here; attempts to consciously suppress implicit biases are notoriously problematic, and an individual's lack of awareness of the extent to which she is influenced by implicit biases seems to threaten her ability to inhibit their influence.[11]

Accordingly, we are willing to concede that understood thus, individuals will often lack intervention control over implicit biases. However, we believe—and argue in the next two sections—that this articulation of 'intervention control' is too narrow, focusing only on the ability to inhibit implicit processes by bringing them directly and immediately under reflective control. To make our case, we articulate a model that draws together more extensive resources for intervening in behaviour and bringing one's actions and judgements into line with one's evaluative commitments. We argue that this model of control can underpin the idea that implicit biases should legitimately be included in the evaluation of an agent's character, before articulating (in section 5.5) how this prompts us to revise the notion of self-regulation and character development.

5.3 Clark on Ecological Control

In this section we develop an account of control according to which implicit biases are (or can be brought) under an agent's control. We also argue that in light of this account of control, implicit biases can be thought of as part of a person's character, and are thus relevant to the moral evaluation of that character. We draw on and develop Andy Clark's notion of 'ecological control', using Clark's articulation of this idea as our point of departure to simplify our own exposition, and because he has done so much to unpack and defend it. We situate the model within Clark's larger picture before going on to develop and apply it in the context of empirical research on implicit biases.

5.3.1 Motivating the idea

What is it to exercise ecological control in cognition and action? Clark elucidates it as follows:

---

[11] See Galinsky and Moskowitz 2000; and Saul 2012 for pursuit of the question of whether this unawareness should lead us to quite radical sceptical conclusions. On the other hand, empirical findings from Monteith and Voils (1998) indicate that at least sometimes individuals are aware that their actions are not in conformity with their ideals, and able to attribute this to implicit biases.

Ecological control is the kind of top-level control that does not micro-manage every detail, but rather encourages substantial devolvement of power and responsibility... And it allows (I claim) much of our prowess at thought and reason to depend upon the robust and reliable operation, often (but not always) in dense brain-involving loops, of a variety of non-biological problem-solving resources spread throughout our social and technological surround. (Clark 2007, 101)

One well-known element of Clark's model is alluded to here, namely his commitment to the idea that the boundaries of minds, and even selves, are fluid, and need not coincide with the biological boundaries of the organisms they animate (see Clark and Chalmers 1998; cf. Sterelny 2003, 2010). Clark holds that this is especially true of human beings, who exploit and incorporate features of the physical structure of their own bodies and surrounding environment into their strategies of acting and pursuing goals, thus exemplifying the type of ecological control in which he is interested. Various processes employed by 'ecological controllers' incorporate features of their bodies and of the external world, integrating them into 'whole new unified systems of distributed problem-solving' (Clark 2007, 103).

Ecological control is devolved, distributed, diffuse, decentralized, often spread out over time, and typically not accompanied by the kind of rich consciousness-awareness characteristic of higher-level and reflective cognition. This type of control is obviously involved in some lower-level physiological systems. However, Clark claims it is not restricted to 'the "autonomic" functions (breathing, heart-beat, etc.)' but instead holds that 'all *kinds* of human activities turn out to be partly supported by quasi-independent non-conscious sub-systems' (Clark 2007, 110). Indeed, ecological control often involves the effective coordination and calibration of such subsystems: corralling, nudging, tweaking their coordinated operation in the service of a particular goal, rather than micromanaging every detail of each individual component. Consider the simple act of reaching out our hand to pick up a coffee mug. While this may seem simplicity itself, and a behavior under near complete conscious control, Clark argues that even in this case the appearance is misleading, and that 'fine-tuned reaching and grasping involves the delicate use of visually-received information by functionally and neuro-anatomically distinct sub-systems operating, for the most part, outside the window of conscious awareness' (Clark 2007, 109). Even in this mundane case, much of the control of behaviour is distributed throughout the 'non-conscious circuitry that guides the most delicate shape-and-position sensitive aspects of reach and grasp' (Clark 2007, 109–10).

So pathways of ecological control—'loops' of influence, as Clark and others sometimes call them—are mediated by *sub-personal* structures and subsystems of which the organism is not directly aware or in immediate, direct, control at the *personal* level. Ecological controllers often exploit the features of those sub-personal structures and subsystems to their advantage, to simplify problem-solving and fine-tune performance in the service of achieving their personal goals and complying with their personal values. (Clark uses the personal/sub-personal distinction, but the terminology originates with Dennett 1969, see also Elton 2000.)

As mentioned above, though, Clark holds that these kinds of sub-personal structures and subsystems need not be confined to the organism's skin. Organisms who employ ecological control to manage their behaviour (of whom humans are the example par excellence) often do so by reshaping, even incorporating, elements of their extra-bodily environment into the process of fine-tuning their performance. Loops of ecological control can extend into the environment and back again. Humans do not just exploit the structure they *find* outside their own bodies and heads, but rather take an active hand in *shaping* and *organizing* that environment in such a way that it, too, helps them to fine-tune actions, solve problems, realize their intentions, and express their values. In other words, one central feature of human agency involves supplementing the internal sub-personal mechanisms that guide behaviour by engineering their world, calibrating 'external' sub-personal structures so that they help simplify cognition and bring out the kinds of behaviours and outcomes to which they aspire. A particularly compelling example of this is the effort people put into organizing their offices, to do things like maximize productivity, manage their own moods (or at least ward off despair!) and generally make things epistemically easier on themselves. As Clark points out, in organizing an office, an individual attunes her surroundings to her own particular epistemic needs. In taking such measures, individuals seek to structure and stabilize their environments in ways that 'simplify or enhance the problem-solving that needs to be done' (Clark 2007, 115).

A crucial aspect of the notion, as developed by Clark, is that one goal that people might attempt to achieve using ecological control is to *further* calibrate the operation of specific sub-personal mechanisms. We might shape our external environments as a means to more effectively manipulating sub-personal operations. Here we see the recursive use of control to enhance and heighten control itself. An agent can do this by fine-tuning the role of subsystems which in turn help produce dispositions and behaviours that can better fulfil her more distal goals, thus allowing her to better behave in ways that more precisely reflect her intentions, and more crisply conform to her considered ideals and values. Ultimately, a person can calibrate subsystems that guide behaviour until eventually they operate, on their own, in precisely the way she wants them to operate, even when she is not consciously and explicitly attending to them.

5.3.2 Developing Clark's model

With the idea of ecological control outlined, an ambiguity in our presentation of it so far can now be teased out. Sometimes, what we call the *exercise* of ecological control involves executing actions or parts of actions without the guidance of reflective, deliberative control. A professional tennis player exercises ecological control, for example, when instinctively responding—without deliberate, reflective, thought—to a baseline shot in tennis. However, individuals can *take* ecological control of something when they reflectively decide to manipulate their mental states or environment, so as to shape their cognitive processes, thus enabling the exercise of ecological control in the future. Given this distinction, what we are calling 'taking' ecological control does require that the agent is at least sometimes able to reflectively control their behaviour. So we acknowledge that the capacity for and occasional exercise of this more deliberate and reflective kind of control is necessary for evaluable action, although its exercise on any one occasion is not.

We mentioned that one way of *taking* ecological control is by calibrating subsystems, and one way to do that is to *practise*. Rehearsal is a common way to deliberately hone a skill, calibrating the sub-personal structures that implement it, making the whole process routine enough that eventually intentions can be expressed smoothly, automatically, and without deliberation, and the performance of the fine-tuned, goal-directed behaviour is natural, easy, and unthinking. This kind of agency can involve and is often accompanied by reflective control—the ability to reflectively decide upon a high-level course of action and carry it out—but with a view to ultimately obviating the need for reflective agency (or much of it) over lower-level, component parts of the behaviour being practised. In other words, one of the uses of ecological control is that it can be used to attain what Railton (2009) calls *fluent agency*. Once achieved, high-level intentions consciously formed at the personal level can be fluidly enacted via pathways of ecological control mediated by those previously calibrated sub-personal mechanisms, without each individual step being directly controlled or consciously attended to along the way (and perhaps without need for reference to intention; see Romdenh-Romluc 2011). As Clark notes, examples of this use of ecological control can be drawn from sport: 'This is no surprise, I am sure, to any sports player: it doesn't even seem, when playing a fast game of squash, as if your conscious perception of the ball is, moment-by-moment, guiding your hand and racket' (Clark 2007, 17). But as we will see (in section 5.4.3), the particular line of thought can be extended from sports to other domains, and from the sub-personal subsystems that underlie behaviour to those that underlie evaluation and judgement.

Another way of taking ecological control is to co-opt aspects of what is intuitively thought of as our external environment, shaping it so that it can better guide our cognitive processes in a way congenial to our goals and values. In short, beyond the distinction between exercising and taking ecological control, there are several ways in which we can exert ecological control over mental processes. And, as we set out in the next section, there are ways in which we can take and exercise ecological control over implicit biases.

5.4 Ecological Control and Implicit Bias

Implicit biases are troublesome not just because they can contribute to morally problematic outcomes, but also because of their psychological profile. They pose a problem for moral evaluation because they are not introspectively accessible, and so can coexist unknown and alongside explicit attitudes to the contrary; because they can operate outside of conscious awareness; are associative, not under our direct evaluative control, and once activated their expression in judgement and behaviour is difficult to directly manage or completely suppress. But, as we argued in section 5.2, none of these features suffices to exempt it from moral evaluation. Here, we address two questions: first, are implicit biases susceptible to ecological control (do we exercise ecological control, and can we take ecological control)? Second, is ecological control sufficient (or part of a set of jointly sufficient conditions) for moral evaluation?

Whilst not subject to the kinds of control we considered in section 5.2, empirical work has shown that implicit biases are 'malleable' in a number of ways. This empirical research has investigated the most effective ways of impeding the influence of implicit biases, and revealed that some strategies work while others don't (and still others seem to make matters worse). It has also shown that intuition and common sense tend to be a poor guide to which strategies are likely to be successful. But most importantly it has shown that there is a very real sense in which a person can exert control over her implicit biases. We hold that Clark's notion of ecological control provides a useful way to think about the nature of that control. We identify three different kinds of ecological control that might be exercised in relation to implicit biases. Drawing on the distinction introduced above, we present the first two as concerning instances in which individuals might reflectively *take* ecological control, to better enable their actions to conform to their values. The third example of *exercising* ecological control indicates that individuals' actions can draw on implicit processes so as to be influenced by and calibrated with their values, even when intentional strategies have not been implemented to ensure this.

5.4.1 Environmental props consciously employed for guiding cognitive processes

Clark emphasizes that ecological control can involve the 'offloading' of cognitive structures onto the world beyond the boundaries of the skin (recall the example of structuring one's office to facilitate one's professional activities). One might use similar means to help mitigate one's implicit biases as well. For instance, early studies (Dasgupta and Greenwald 2001) showed that the influence of some implicit racial biases could be weakened simply by exposing participants to pictures of admired black celebrities and other counter-stereotypical images. So, a person might rein in the expression of her own implicit racial biases by putting up pictures of admired black celebrities around her office, thus taking indirect, ecological control over those biases so that her judgements and actions more accurately express her character and values. A person might engineer her 'external' epistemic environment in other ways to ensure that her intentions and values are more fluidly expressed in her actions and judgements, and not distorted by the operation of implicit biases. For instance, if one is (justifiably) worried about implicit biases corrupting the assessment of candidates in a job search, one can take measures to remove information from application dossiers that may trigger those implicit biases in the first place.

5.4.2 Cognitive props consciously employed for guiding cognitive processes

Another promising strategy for mitigating the influence of implicit biases has been investigated under the name of 'implementation intentions' (Webb, Sheeran, and Pepper 2012). For example, an individual seeking to exert control over her implicit biases might deliberately repeat to herself, 'If I see a Black face, I will think "safe",' practising this line of thought enough that it becomes routine and automatic, thus defeating her implicit racial bias. One might draw an analogy to Clark's discussion of a sports player who practises, calibrating the operation of sub-personal subsystems to bring them in line with intentions, and thus developing a certain kind of fluent and unthinking control. In the case of implicit biases a person does not practise, say, a backhand tennis stroke or the subtle biomechanics required to throw a curveball, but rather rehearses a psychological process aimed at forming a particular kind of counter-bias association. Once successfully formed, that new association will be able to bring the way she makes snap judgements into line with her more thought out intentions, thus better reflecting her character and values.

5.4.3 Automatic processes as props unconsciously employed for guiding cognitive processes

Following Clark, we have argued that some features of our environment can shape our cognitive processes, and can be manipulated so as to influence the subsystems that will produce judgements and actions. We also hold that automatic features of our mental processes can be manipulated in similar ways, and to similar ends. Recall the finding, mentioned above (Moskowitz and Li 2011), that individuals who were actively committed to egalitarian goals (without consciously reflecting on such goals themselves) manifested less implicit racial bias in experimental testing. The explanatory hypothesis for this effect was that certain goals automatically block other competing goals (goals such as speed and efficiency, which have been found to encourage the reliance on implicit associations). The agent's values and goals themselves, then, can play a role qua mechanisms that influence and calibrate the subsystems that run without reflective or direct control. This is a case of one element of a person's psychological economy influencing another. The agent's values 'keep in check' the operation of implicit bias, such that pursuing certain values is one way of exercising ecological control even when one is not actively monitoring one's actions with respect to whether they promote (or depart from) those values. Crucially, this can be so without the agent expressly intending, at any point, to put in place mechanisms for this purpose. One can exercise ecological control, then, without having reflectively taken (in senses 5.4.1 and 5.4.2 above) ecological control.

There is much more that can be said here (indeed, the literature on implicit biases and how to influence them is growing at a tremendous rate), but for present purposes we can simply point out that the idea that an agent's implicit biases are beyond her control in any relevant sense is simply false. Whilst implicit biases themselves are rarely under our direct, evaluative, or intervention control, empirical studies indicate that the kind of ecological control that we exercise in many actions and cognitions can, in many ways, be extended to implicit biases as well. While some of these strategies for controlling implicit biases may look exotic, we hold that another virtue of Clark's discussion is that he articulates a notion of control that seems to capture something at the core of many of these strategies, whilst making clear that use of this kind of control is actually quite mundane. It is a type of control that underlies a vast swathe of human behaviour and problem-solving.

This observation supports our second claim, that susceptibility to ecological control is sufficient for evaluation, and that in virtue of their susceptibility to this kind of control, implicit biases and actions influenced by them are proper targets of character-based evaluation. We believe our discussion renders this claim plausible by showing that there is nothing unusual about the processes implicated in implicit biases, and that denying they are the proper objects of moral evaluation would commit the proponents of this claim to far wider scepticism about the moral evaluation of our cognitive states and actions than they seem to acknowledge.[12] Unless some further way in which such processes

---

[12] Nomy Arpaly 2003, for instance, has argued that automatic actions of tennis players are apt targets for evaluation; see also Doris 2002, 2009.

differ from our other cognitive processes can be identified, denying that such states are evaluable as part of 'who the agent is' will entail denying that many of our commonplace actions and judgements are apt candidates for character-based evaluation also. Whilst embracing scepticism is always an option, we do not believe that it would be charitable to attribute this to our interlocutors.

5.4.4 Two challenges

There are two further challenges to address. The first challenge to this conclusion asks whether all kinds of control that might fall under the rubric of 'ecological control' are sufficient for biases (that are potentially controllable in these ways) to be evaluable. To see the worry here, note that some of the methods of ecological control we identified (conscious use of environmental props) fall into the category of the 'negative programme' of character development, described by Webber in his chapter in this volume. The negative programme involves acknowledging our susceptibility to the influence of implicit biases (and other forms of situational manipulation), and aiming to mitigate or eliminate those influences (changing the environment to prime for counter-stereotypical exemplars, say). Is it really possible, Webber's challenge goes, to try to counteract every possible bias one might be susceptible to (race, age, gender, height, class, educational background, and so on and so on)? If not, then is it really fair to take such biases into account when we evaluate individuals, finding it to their discredit should some such influences persist—especially in the absence of comprehensive and easily accessible information about how to combat all forms (and potential interactions) of such bias?

We argue that it is reasonable to maintain that implicit biases can be part of the target of character-based evaluation, even if such information is not (yet!) readily accessible, and even if it would be extremely demanding to undertake the negative programme in relation to each bias. Firstly, the fact that it would be very demanding does not mean that it would not be to the agent's credit to undertake such a project, and to their discredit to the extent that they have failed to do so. But secondly, and most crucially, it is worth noting that the second two strategies for ecological control that we identify—consciously employing cognitive props, and the role of automatic processes unconsciously employed in regulating implicit biases—fall under what Webber describes as the 'positive programme' of character development. This programme consists of the entrenchment of attitudes and dispositions to act well. Ecological control strategies of this variety are properly thought of as part of a positive programme of developing cognitive and motivational habits that enable agents to be robustly resistant to implicit biases. It is precisely because the susceptibility to implicit bias is bound up with the strength of agents' habits and commitments that such dispositions are apt candidates for character-based evaluation.

The second challenge asks whether, given the extent that an individual's dispositions are dependent upon these kinds of 'props', those dispositions should be considered part of that individual's character at all. Don't we give up on the notion of character altogether once we recognize how fragile those character trait-like dispositions are, and how dependent they are on the support of such environmental resources? We think not. Rather, we respond by pointing out that while this challenge may seem decisive to those in the grip of a common picture of what character amounts to, it is not the only picture, and perhaps not the best one. Rather, our view fits quite nicely what Maria Merritt (2000) calls the Humean model of character. She distinguishes the Aristotelian model of character, on which an individual's dispositions are 'firm and unchanging' and are motivationally sufficient to produce virtuous action, from the Humean model that she prefers (in no small part because she holds it is better equipped to withstand the situationist critiques of virtue ethical theories). Merritt shows how the Humean model permits stability of character to be supported by a range of mechanisms that prominently include social relations and environmental settings (2000, 377–80). By her lights, the normative task is then to create the social and environmental factors that best support stable dispositions to act well. In this, we see ourselves as fellow travellers with Merritt, and assert that our discussion of character in this paper is best understood on the Humean model she champions. And so in our view, what falls within the scope of character evaluations is not only the behavioural dispositions implicated in implicit bias themselves, but also the agent's sensitivity (both conscious and otherwise) to the kinds of environmental settings that permit those dispositions to take hold—or those which function as effective regulatory mechanisms in serving the agent's endorsed goals and values.

In sum, then, we hold that since a person can exert intervention and ecological control over implicit biases, there is a real sense in which whether or not they influence an individual's behaviour is very much a reflection of that person's character. Thus, the behavioural dispositions implicated in implicit biases, and the behaviours they influence, are an appropriate subject matter for character-based evaluation.

5.5 Character and Self-Regulation with Ecological Control

We have argued that it is possible for individuals to exercise control over their implicit biases on the model of ecological control—devolving the task of mitigating the influence of implicit bias to parts of their environment, or to mechanistic or automatic cognitive responses. In this section, we make an important qualification of this claim, and tease out two important implications of our conclusion.

5.5.1 Ecological control and epistemic conditions

We have argued that an individual *can* take and exercise ecological control over her implicit biases—it is possible for her to do so—and so she cannot, on grounds of lack of control, maintain that her implicit biases are not evaluable.

However, our conclusion is vulnerable to the following objection: we claim that it is possible for individuals to exercise such control (see sections 5.4.1–3) over implicit biases. But whether, for any individual, she can in fact exercise ecological control depends on whether she is aware of these possibilities (and indeed, aware of the phenomena of implicit bias, and that she may be affected by it). So the mere possibility of having ecological control is not sufficient for implicit biases to be considered as 'part of the agent' and hence morally evaluable. In addition to the control conditions, epistemic conditions must also be met as well.

For present purposes, we are willing to accept that ecological control can permit moral evaluation only if other conditions also obtain. (Indeed, the authors' opinions differ on whether epistemic conditions are necessary. One of us believes that awareness of implicit bias is not required, because awareness of all processes involved in the production of action cannot be a condition on that action being evaluable (Holroyd

2012), and because normative conditions about what individuals should know rather apply (Holroyd 2015). The other believes that they are, but that these epistemic conditions are sensitive to context in various ways, including the social role occupied by the individual in question, as well as the contents of her external epistemic environment (see Kelly and Washington forthcoming).)

However, this dispute can be set aside: our key claim is that a certain argumentative move cannot be made. That move is to deny that implicit biases are part of who the agent is—or that they can be evaluated for being influenced by them—because the agent lacks control over such mental entities. We have identified an important sense in which agents *can* have control over such mental entities. If implicit biases are rogue states beyond moral evaluation, then, it is not because they are beyond the scope of the agent's control.

If this is endorsed, then we believe there are two further implications for our understanding of control, character, and self-regulation.

5.5.2 Intervention control on an ecological model

Recall Snow's idea that even if one lacks reflective, direct control over one's cognitions and behaviours, they remain morally evaluable if one retains intervention control—the ability to exert influence on autonomously running processes by stopping them or redirecting how they shape action. According to this understanding of intervention control, individuals lack it in relation to implicit biases—it is very difficult to prevent behavioural manifestation of implicit bias via direct reflective control. The job interview panellist cannot effectively intervene on the operation of implicit biases as they influence cognition, simply by thinking: 'Oops, there it goes; better get my cognitive processes back on track and stop that biased evaluation.'

If the ecological control model is endorsed, then we claim that a broader understanding of 'intervention control' is warranted. An agent can intervene in some automatic process not by bringing it under direct reflective control at the moment of its activation, but by diverting its activation by means of some environmental or cognitive prop put in place to derail unwanted cognitive or behavioural patterns. If this more expansive understanding of intervention control is endorsed, then agents can retain control and be morally evaluable for actions even when those actions cannot be brought under direct reflective control as typically understood. Thus the range of behaviours that are candidates for evaluation as moral or virtuous action could be greater than on Snow's narrow construal of intervention control—although its full extent, and how that class might be delineated in a full account of ecological control, is beyond the scope of this paper.

5.5.3 Character development on an ecological model

We initially framed our discussion by considering whether implicit biases are properly thought of as part of 'who the agent is', and showing how this question turned on the kind of control the agent might have over the mental entities involved in implicit bias. Our main claim has been that taking ecological control is one way in which people can shape the processes and behaviours that constitute character. This claim also has implications for how to understand character development.

Our inquiry was motivated by Besser-Jones's remarks that indicated that implicit biases were a proper candidate in the moral evaluation of character. We have attempted to vindicate this claim by showing that implicit biases are appropriately understood as under the agent's control in a way that renders them objects of character-based moral evaluation. But even given her willingness to include such implicit attitudes in the set of character-constituting attitudes, we find her remarks on character development in need of some fleshing out. In her early work (2008) Besser-Jones focuses on self-regulation by means of prescriptions that remind the agent of the priority of acting well, and strategic rules for action or a decision procedure to be relied on in difficult cases.

Given the significant role that implicit processes have in influencing action, it is clear that both of these strategies will be at best partial, as they speak to the agent's regulation of wayward influences that are within the field of her cognitive attention. In her later (2014) work, Besser-Jones articulates two more strategies that might enable the development of virtuous character even in the face of challenges presented by automatic processes that can hinder the pursuit of virtuous goals. The first strategy involves the articulation of a hierarchical structure of goal-directed activity that will help translate abstract ideals into sequences for concrete actions in fulfilment of those goals. This, in turn, will set up feedback loops that will facilitate *evaluating* whether those actions are in fact serving those goals (2014, 150–2). The second type of strategy for developing virtue also appeals to self-regulation, this time via the articulation of plans for action which are then used to *anticipate* opportunities for acting well, and helping ensure those opportunities are seized (152–4). For example, Besser-Jones recommends the use of implementation intentions, which enable agents to be cued to situational features that should trigger goal pursuits, rather than irrelevant situational features of the sort shown to hinder acting well.

These two strategies seem much better placed to address the kinds of implicit cognitions that may both serve, or hinder, the development of good character and action upon it. However, given the concerns about implicit bias, we propose two further ways in which these strategies for the development of virtue could be supplemented.

First, in relation to the evaluation of whether action sequences are serving goals, we note that it may not always be obvious whether an agent's actions are hindering one's goals. Consider the goal of acting justly; if agents are (for various reasons) unaware that their actions are inflected with implicit bias, then it may not be apparent to them that certain actions they perform are not serving this goal. Accordingly, agents should supplement their hierarchical goal structures with active investigation into possible ways their actions might be hindering their goals which are not available to introspection.

Secondly, with respect to the plans for action, we note that Besser-Jones gives most attention to the manipulation of cognitive resources (such as implementation intentions) that help agents act in accordance with their commitments. Our discussion of ecological control, and the way that external environments can be harnessed to enable agents to better act in the service of their goals, shows the importance of supplementing these strategies with ones that utilize environmental as well as cognitive props to enable individuals to effectively take and exercise ecological control.

These friendly extensions to Besser-Jones's prescriptions are attuned specifically to how one might ensure the development of virtuous character and action in the face of challenges from research on implicitly biased cognitions.

5.6 Concluding Remarks

We have argued that there is an important sense in which individuals have control over implicit biases, and this kind of control is a sort that is commonplace in our exercise of agency. Ecological control is the structuring of one's environment and cognitive habits such that autonomous processes and subsystems can effectively fulfil one's person-level goals. We set out at least three ways in which individuals can take or exercise ecological control with respect to their implicit biases.

There are two central implications of this claim: firstly, that agents can have this kind of control means that (subject to other necessary conditions being met) such implicit attitudes can be the appropriate target of character-based evaluation. Secondly, that agents can exercise this control means that (subject to other necessary conditions obtaining) such implicit attitudes can be properly regarded as part of 'who the agent is'—part of her character, which is as a whole subject to moral evaluation. This does not, of course, preclude the agent taking up a stance of disgust or alienation towards that part of her character; that stance is part of 'who she is' too.

If one's character involves not only one's beliefs, behavioural dispositions, and attitudes towards these mental entities, but also the cognitive habits that one uses environmental and mechanistic strategies to shape, then a model of character development and regulation must also make adequate prescriptions for the exercise of ecological control.

Works Cited

Amodio, D., Harmon-Jones, E., and Devine, P. 2003. Individual Differences in the Activation and Control of Affective Race Bias as Assessed by Startle Eyeblink Response and Self-Report. *Journal of Personality and Social Psychology* 84 (4): 738–53.

Annas, J. 2011. *Intelligent Virtue*. Oxford: Oxford University Press.

Arpaly, N. 2003. *Unprincipled Virtue: An Inquiry into Moral Agency*. Oxford: Oxford University Press.

Besser-Jones, L. 2008. Social Psychology, Moral Character, and Moral Fallibility. *Philosophy and Phenomenological Research* 76 (2): 310–32.

Besser-Jones, L. 2014. *Eudaimonic Ethics: The Philosophy and Psychology of Living Well*. New York: Routledge Press.

Cameron, D., Payne, K., and Knobe, J. 2010. Do Theories of Implicit Race Bias Change Moral Judgment? *Social Justice Research* 23: 272–89.

Clark, A. 2007. Soft Selves and Ecological Control. In *Distributed Cognition and the Will*, ed. D. Spurrett, D. Ross, H. Kincaid, and L. Stephens. Cambridge, MA: The MIT Press, 101–21.

Clark, A., and Chalmers, D. 1998. The Extended Mind. *Analysis* 58 (1): 7-19.
Dasgupta, N., and Greenwald, A. 2001. On the Malleability of Automatic Attitudes: Combating Automatic Prejudice with Images of Admired and Disliked Individuals. *Journal of Personality and Social Psychology* 81 (5): 800-14.
Dennett D. 1969. *Content and Consciousness*. London: Routledge & Kegan Paul.
Devine, P., Plant, E., Amodio, D., Harmon-Jones, E., and Vance, S. 2002. The Regulation of Explicit and Implicit Race Bias: The Role of Motivations to Respond without Prejudice. *Journal of Personality and Social Psychology* 82 (5): 835-48.
Doris, J. 2002. *Lack of Character: Personality and Moral Behavior*. New York: Cambridge.
Doris, J. 2009. Skepticism about Persons. *Philosophical Issues* 19: 57-91.
Doris, J. 2015. *Talking To Ourselves*. Oxford: Oxford University Press.
Dovidio, J. F., and Gaertner, S. L. 2000. Aversive Racism and Selection Decisions: 1989 and 1999. *Psychological Science* 11: 319-23.
Dovidio, J. F., Kawakami, K., Johnson, C., Johnson, B., and Howard, A. 1997. On the Nature of Prejudice: Automatic and Controlled Processes. *Journal of Experimental Social Psychology* 33: 510-40.
Elton, M. 2000. Consciousness: Only at the Personal Level. *Philosophical Explorations* 3 (1): 25-42.
Feldman, R. 2008. Modest Deontologism in Epistemology. *Synthese* 161: 339-55.
Fischer, J., and Ravizza, M. 1999. *Responsibility and Control: A Theory of Moral Responsibility*. Cambridge: Cambridge University Press.
Galinsky, A. D., and Moskowitz, G. B. 2000. Perspective-Taking: Decreasing Stereotype Expression, Stereotype Accessibility, and In-group Favoritism. *Journal of Personality & Social Psychology* 78 (4): 708-24.
Gendler, T. S. 2011. On the Epistemic Costs of Implicit Bias. *Philosophical Studies* 156: 33-63.
Glasgow, J. forthcoming. 'Alienation and Responsibility'. In *Philosophy and Implicit Bias*, ed. M. Brownstein and J. Saul. Oxford: Oxford University Press.
Hieronymi, P. 2006. Controlling Attitudes. *Pacific Philosophical Quarterly* 87 (1): 45-74.
Holroyd, J. 2012. Responsibility for Implicit Bias. *Journal of Social Philosophy* 43 (3): 274-306.
Holroyd, J. 2015. Implicit Bias, Awareness and Imperfect Cognitions. *Consciousness and Cognition* 33: 511-23.
Jost, J. T., Rudman, L. A, Blair, I. V., Carney, D. R., Dasgupta, N., Glaser, J., and Hardin, C. D. 2009. The Existence of Implicit Bias is Beyond Reasonable Doubt: A Refutation of Ideological and Methodological Objections and Executive Summary of Ten Studies That No Manager Should Ignore. *Research in Organizational Behavior* 29: 39-69.

Kane, R. 1989. Two Kinds of Incompatibilism. *Philosophy and Phenomenological Research* 69: 219–54.

Kelly, D., and Roedder, E. 2008. Racial Cognition and the Ethics of Implicit Bias. *Philosophy Compass* 3 (3): 522–40.

Kelly, D., and Washington, N. forthcoming. Who's Responsible for This? Implicit Bias and the Epistemology of Moral Responsibility. In *Philosophy and Implicit Bias*, ed. M. Brownstein and J. Saul. Oxford: Oxford University Press.

Levy, N. 2011. Expressing Who We Are: Moral Responsibility and Awareness of our Reasons for Action. *Analytic Philosophy* 52(4): 243–61.

Levy, N. 2012. Consciousness, Implicit Attitudes, and Moral Responsibility. *Noûs*: 1–22 doi: 10.1111/j.1468-0068.2011.00853.x.

Mandelbaum, E. 2015. Attitude, Inference, Association: On the Propositional Structure of Implicit Bias. *Noûs*. doi: 10.1111/nous.12089.

Merritt, M. 2000. Virtue Ethics and Situationist Personality Psychology. *Ethical Theory and Moral Practice* 3 (4): 365–83.

Monteith, M. J., and Voils, C. I. 1998. Proneness to Prejudiced Responses: Toward Understanding the Authenticity of Self-Reported Discrepancies. *Journal of Personality and Social Psychology* 75 (4): 901–16.

Moskowitz, G. B., and Li, P. 2011. Egalitarian Goals Trigger Stereotype Inhibition: A Proactive Form of Stereotype Control. *Journal of Experimental Social Psychology* 47 (1): 103–16.

Payne, B. K. 2005. Conceptualizing Control in Social Cognition: The Role of Automatic and Controlled Processes in Misperceiving a Weapon. *Journal of Personality and Social Psychology* 81: 181–92.

Railton, P. 2009. Practical Competence and Fluent Agency. In *Reasons for Action*, ed. D. Sobel and S. Wall. Cambridge: Cambridge University Press, 81–115.

Romdenh-Romluc, K. 2011. Agency and Embodied Cognition. *Proceedings of the Aristotelian Society* 111 (1): 79–95.

Saul, J. 2012. Skepticism and Implicit Bias, Disputatio, Lecture, 5 (37): 243–63.

Saul, J. 2013. Implicit Bias, Stereotype Threat and Women in Philosophy. In *Women in Philosophy: What Needs to Change?*, ed. F. Jenkins and K. Hutchinson. Oxford: Oxford University Press, 39–60.

Smith, A. 2008. Control, Responsibility, and Moral Assessment. *Philosophical Studies* 38: 367–92.

Smith, M. 2001. Responsibility and Self-Control. In *Relating to Responsibility: Essays in Honour of Tony Honore on his 80th Birthday*, ed. P. Cane and J. Gardner. Oxford: Hart Publishing, 1–19.

Snow, N. 2006. Habitual Virtuous Actions and Automaticity. *Ethical Theory and Moral Practice* 9: 545–61.

Sterelny, K. 2003. *Thought in a Hostile World*. New York: Blackwell.

Sterelny, K. 2010. Minds: Extended or Scaffolded? *Phenomenology and the Cognitive Sciences* 9 (4): 465–81.

Stump, E. 1996. Persons: Identification and Freedom. *Philosophical Topics* 24: 183–214.

Valian, V. 2005. Beyond Gender Schemas: Improving the Advancement of Women in Academia. *Hypatia* 20 (3): 198–213.

Velleman, D. 2005. The Self as Narrator. In *Autonomy and the Challenges to Liberalism: New Essays*, ed. J. Christman and J. Anderson. New York: Cambridge University Press, 56–76.

Webb, T., Sheeran, P., and Pepper, J. 2012. Gaining Control over Responses to Implicit Attitude Tests: Implementation Intentions Engender Fast Responses on Attitude-Incongruent Trials. *British Journal of Social Psychology* 51 (1): 13–32.

6

Instilling Virtue

Jonathan Webber

Two debates in contemporary philosophical moral psychology have so far been conducted almost entirely in isolation from each other despite their structural similarity. One is the debate over the importance for virtue ethics of the results of situational manipulation experiments in social psychology. The other is the debate over the ethical implications of experiments that reveal gender and race biases in social cognition. In both cases, the ethical problem posed cannot be identified without first clarifying the cognitive structures underlying the problematic phenomena. In this chapter, I argue that the two kinds of phenomena share a basic cognitive structure, which is well articulated by the findings of the empirical psychology of attitudes, especially if these findings are understood in the context of the cognitive-affective system theory of personality. On the basis of this joint construal of situationism and implicit bias, I argue that the negative programme of ethical improvement that many philosophers recommend in response to one or other problem is unrealistic. Instead, we should consider more seriously the prospects of the positive programme of ethical improvement recommended by Aristotle, the direct aim of which is to instil deeply in ourselves the values at the heart of each of the virtues.

6.1 Situational Manipulation and Implicit Bias

The richest and most robust demonstration of situational manipulation in social psychology remains Stanley Milgram's investigation into the ease with which people can be persuaded to inflict what appear to be potentially lethal electric shocks on what appears to be a fellow volunteer. By varying the experimental set-up, Milgram showed that subtle situational differences made a significant difference to the degree to which subjects did as they are asked (Milgram 1974). Indeed, a recent analysis of Milgram's personal archive makes clear that Milgram employed such situational manipulation to design his experiment in the first place. Through a series of pilot studies, he refined the instructions given to the subjects, their sensory access to the effects of the shocks on their victim, the design of the shock generator itself, and various other details of the experiment, with the express aim of finding a surprising headline result. Having found a structure that would produce such a surprising result, Milgram published this version of the experiment first, subsequently referring to it as the 'baseline condition' when publishing results of other versions of the experiment (Russell 2011).

Does it matter, scientifically, that Milgram refined his experiment until it achieved his desired results? Does it matter that he designated one version the 'baseline condition' purely because its results were most likely to attract attention? It depends on the lesson that one wants to draw from the data. The results of the 'baseline condition' should not be taken in isolation. Taken together, the variations of the experiment might provide important evidence concerning the details of human motivation. There is certainly one general truth that they and the pilot studies clearly reveal: that the subjects' response to the morally most important aspect of the situation, the requests to inflict high levels of electric shock on another person, vary significantly with the other aspects of the situation, many of which seem to be of no moral importance at all.

Research into implicit bias probes more deeply into the cognitive architecture that generates this situational variation of behaviour. One such experiment found subjects to hold much stronger cognitive associations between white people and positive evaluation than between black people and positive evaluation. A series of words appeared on a screen and subjects were asked to press one of two keys to classify each word into one of two categories. They were asked to make their judgements as quickly as possible, but not so fast as to allow mistakes. Some of the words (such as 'crash', 'happy', 'peace', 'rotten') were to be categorized according to whether they are pleasant or unpleasant. These were mixed with names (such as 'Ebony', 'Jed', 'Katie', 'Lamar') that were to be categorized as typically names of black people or typically names of white people. The subjects themselves were white. Their reaction times were much faster when the button for indicating pleasant words was also the one used to indicate that a name is typically of a white person than when the button for indicating pleasant words was also used to indicate that a name is typically of a black person (Greenwald et al. 1998, Experiment 3).

Moreover, a subsequent replication of the experiment found these cognitive associations to correlate strongly with biases in the way subjects behaved towards a black experimenter and a white experimenter. In particular, the bias in cognitive associations correlated with differences in the amount of time the subjects spent talking to each experimenter, the proportion of that time the subjects spent actually facing the experimenter, and the physical distance they set between themselves and each experimenter. These behavioural biases were evident to the experimenters in the discussion as well as to external observers (McConnell and Leibold 2001).

For both kinds of experiment, it has been shown that subjects would explicitly disavow the attitudes implied by their behaviour. Of the many subjects who had obeyed his experimenter to a high level of electric shock, Milgram found that very few subsequently claimed that they had done the right thing in the circumstances (Milgram 1974, ch. 5). When the 'baseline' version of the experiment was explained to diverse groups of people and they were asked to predict how they themselves would behave, most said they would stop the experiment when the shock levels were still very low (Milgram 1974, ch. 3). The original experiment into cognitive associations of names of black people and white people with positive evaluation asked the same subjects explicit questions about their attitudes to black people and white people, about the causes of discrimination, and about the value of multiculturalism. Many subjects' responses indicated no racial preference or a mild preference in favour of black people even though the implicit association test had indicated a preference for white people in those same subjects. The experimenters concluded that the results should be taken as 'indicating the pervasiveness of unconscious forms of prejudice' (Greenwald et al. 1998, 1475).

6.2 Evaluative Judgements and the Cognitive-Affective Personality System

How should we understand the disparity evident in both the Milgram experiment and the implicit association experiment between the attitudes indicated by the subjects' behaviour and the attitudes indicated by their explicit judgements? What is the moral problem that this disparity poses? One answer to these questions distinguishes between a person's evaluative beliefs and their behavioural dispositions. Evaluative beliefs, on this account, are reflectively held and are reported in explicit avowals of belief and in conscious judgements about what one should do, but our behaviour is governed by these beliefs only to the extent that it results from conscious deliberation. The more intuitive and automatic aspects of our behaviour manifest our behavioural dispositions. Given this account of action, the moral task presented by the disparity between behaviour and evaluative judgement is the task of training one's behavioural dispositions to bring them into line with one's evaluative beliefs (Besser-Jones 2008).

An alternative account denies that people have evaluative beliefs that remain consistent across contexts. Not only behavioural responses are dependent on seemingly irrelevant aspects of the context in which they are made, on this view. The same is true of explicit, conscious, deliberative evaluative judgements. The influence these details have over judgement, as with their influence over behavioural responses, need not be noticed by the subject and might not be endorsed if brought to the subject's attention. One form of this account rests on the idea that mental states each have a degree of accessibility, measured by the time it takes to be brought to bear on cognition. The more rapidly one makes a judgement, the fewer relevant considerations are going to be taken into account. The more slowly and effortfully one deliberates, the more one brings into play relevant beliefs and desires that have lower degrees of accessibility. On this view, the moral task is to ensure that one makes well-considered judgements when it matters, perhaps by adopting the strategy of imagining justifying one's judgement to an audience whose values are unknown to oneself (Merritt 2009).

Both accounts seem consistent with the cognitive-affective system theory of personality, which is the dominant theory of the cognition generating behaviour across situations. This theory was developed to account for the stability in an individual's behaviour across repetitions of the same situation as well as the variation in that individual's behaviour across situations that differ in subtle details, a stability and variation which together make the individual's 'behavioural signature that reflects personality coherence' (Mischel and Shoda 1995, 251). It is not just an individual's set of mental states themselves that determine their behaviour, since 'it is the organisation of the relationships among them that forms the core of the personality structure and that guides and constrains their impact' (Mischel and Shoda 1995, 253). Each mental state is associated with many others and these connections vary in strength. They are formed through experience and strengthened through use. The cognition that generates behaviour is a flow of activity across this network of cognitive and affective states, constrained by the stimuli presented by the environment. Because the system develops only slowly, the resulting behaviour is likely to be the same on two occasions where the situation is the same. But where a detail of the situation is different, this may result in a different flow of activity through the personality system and thus a different behavioural outcome.

This theory was developed to account for behavioural patterns. But if this is the right picture of personality generally, rather than simply of behaviour, then we ought to be able to understand evaluative judgements in terms of it as well. There seem to be two ways in which this personality system might generate evaluative judgements. One corresponds to the view that such judgements remain consistent across contexts. If this is right, then the judgements in question manifest stable evaluative beliefs, such as the belief that people of different ethnicities are equal. Such a belief would be a mental state within the personality system. Alternatively, we might understand evaluative judgements to be generated by the personality system in much the same way as behaviour. Since the number and strengths of a mental state's associations determine the speed with which it influences cognition, a given evaluative judgement will depend on the amount of time devoted to seriously deliberating about the issue.

The cognitive-affective personality system was proposed as a 'framework within which to conceptualise and conduct research to understand the intra-individual dynamics of personality and their expression' (Shoda and Mischel 1996, 415). One way to develop this research is to consider which of the two accounts of evaluative judgement is correct. Do evaluative judgements express beliefs that are themselves stable units within the personality system, or are they situationally variable products of the personality system? We will see that this question can be answered by augmenting the personality system theory with the findings of attitude psychology.

6.3 Moral Choice Blindness

Current research into 'moral choice blindness' casts doubt on the idea that moral beliefs are generally stable. In one experiment, subjects were asked to complete a two-page survey that asked how much they agreed with a series of moral statements by giving a score on a numerical scale. During the course of the survey, some of the statements they had responded to were switched for their negations. After the survey had been completed, subjects were asked to work through each statement and justify the response they had given. Experimenters were interested in whether subjects would notice that some of the statements had been negated, or whether they would offer reasons in favour of the opposite view to the one they had originally expressed. If subjects were expressing stable moral beliefs, we would expect them not to then justify the opposite of the view they expressed. But if they do go ahead and justify the opposing view, then it seems that they are not expressing a stable moral belief at all.

The switch of statements was very well designed. The survey was on two pages of paper attached to a clipboard. The statements on the first page were actually printed on a separate piece of paper invisibly glued to the page. On the back of the clipboard, in exactly the right place, was a patch of stronger glue, so that when the subject turned to the second page the statements from the first page stayed on the back of the clipboard, revealing a different set of statements underneath. Some of the statements in this set were the same as the ones that had been glued over them. Some were the negations of those statements. The experimenters recorded the switch as having been detected if the subject spontaneously corrected for it by changing their response rather than defending it, or if the subject expressed any suspicions about the statements in the post-experimental discussion, or if the subject could correctly identify which statements had been reversed once they had been told how the experiment worked. Even with this generous range of forms of detection, the majority of subjects did not detect any change to the statements (Hall et al. 2012).[1]

Two conditions are necessary for a subject to fail to detect the change in statement and blithely justify the opposite of the view they originally expressed. One is that the subject does not remember the original statement. The other is that the subject's judgements on the topic are not consistent across situations. For if the subject did hold a stable view on the issue that the statement concerned, then the subject should express that same stable view when they first complete the survey and when they are asked to justify the responses on the page in front of them. The two situations in which the subject is asked to express a view on this topic differ only in one respect. In the second situation only, they are provided with false evidence concerning the view they expressed moments earlier. For the majority of the subjects, those who did not detect the switch, this difference in situation is enough to negate the judgement that they express. In terms of the cognitive-affective personality system, the two situations caused different sequences of activity through the network of mental states leading to different judgements being expressed.

What of those who did detect the switch? Perhaps detection was due to the subjects holding stable views on the matters that the switched statement concerned. This would explain the consistency in judgement across the two situations. In the second situation, the subject would recognize that the view expressed on the page is not their own view, so would assume that something had gone wrong, perhaps that they had misunderstood the question first time around. In terms of the cognitive-affective personality system, there are two ways in which such a stability of judgement might occur. One is that the judgement simply expresses a particular mental state in the system, a moral belief that remains constant irrespective of its position in the network. The other is that the judgements in both cases were generated by the personality system as a whole, with the difference between the two situations being insufficient to cause a different outcome from this cognition.

---

[1] A film of the survey being used can be seen at: http://www.lucs.lu.se/cbq/.

However, stability of judgement across situations is not the only possible explanation of detection in this experiment. For it was a short survey and subjects were asked to justify their responses as soon as they had finished it. So it remains possible that those who detected the switch did so simply because they remembered the original statement. This leaves us with two candidate explanations of the experiment overall. One is that some of the subjects had stable moral beliefs where others did not. The other is that none of the subjects expressed stable moral judgements, but some subjects were better than others at remembering the statements. Either way, the experiment presents evidence against the idea that moral judgements generally express stable moral beliefs.

6.4 Strength and Influence in Attitude Psychology

Which of these two explanations of the moral choice blindness experiment is correct? Empirical research into the nature and influence of evaluative attitudes suggests that some subjects had sufficiently stable attitudes concerning the topic of the switched statements to detect the switch, but other subjects did not. An attitude's stability over time is a matter of the 'strength' or firmness with which that attitude is held. This is distinct from the attitude's content. For example, you might hold a positive attitude towards democracy as a political system. The overall content of this attitude is the degree to which you approve of democracy, though the content can also be characterized in more detail to include what you think of various aspects of democracy and various different democratic systems. Attitude psychologists reserve the term 'strength' for a different dimension of the attitude. This is the degree to which the attitude is embedded in your cognitive system. An attitude that is strong in this sense is not easily changed by persuasion or reconsideration.

One classic experiment concerning the effects of attitude strength measured the relation between subjects' attitudes towards Greenpeace and their response to an opportunity to donate to Greenpeace (Holland et al. 2002). At the first stage of the experiment, subjects completed a lengthy questionnaire, which included questions about their attitude towards Greenpeace. They were asked how much they approved or disapproved of Greenpeace, how certain they were of their attitude towards Greenpeace, how important this attitude was to them personally, whether this attitude is central to their self-image, and whether this attitude reflects values they hold to be important. The first of these questions measured the attitude content, the other four measured its strength or firmness. Subjects returned a week later for an entirely unrelated experiment. After that experiment was over, they were paid for their participation. The payment consisted of a set of coins. They were then offered the opportunity to donate some of the money to Greenpeace and were asked to complete a short questionnaire about Greenpeace. The first question on the questionnaire asked how much of their payment they had donated to Greenpeace, ensuring that subjects made the donation before completing the rest of the questionnaire, and the efficacy of this was confirmed by observation. One of the later questions asked the subjects to evaluate the work of Greenpeace on a scale of 1 to 10.

Subjects whose attitudes towards Greenpeace were strong, or firmly held, when measured at the start of the experiment acted in line with those attitudes when offered the chance to donate to Greenpeace a week later. Those with strong attitudes in favour of Greenpeace donated, whereas those with strong attitudes against did not. By contrast, there was no significant relation between the attitude reported at the start of the experiment and the response to the opportunity to donate to Greenpeace among those subjects whose attitudes towards Greenpeace did not score highly on the strength measures at the start of the experiment. Moreover, the results of the second attitude measure, taken immediately after the opportunity to donate, show that those whose attitudes had scored highly on the strength measures a week earlier tended to report the same attitude at this point. Subjects who had originally reported weak attitudes, on the other hand, did not tend to report the same attitude at this point. Indeed, the attitude they reported at this point reflected whether or not they had just donated to Greenpeace, which in turn was unrelated to their original attitude report.

This experiment illustrates a finding that attitude psychology has gradually converged upon, that strongly held attitudes consistently manifest in judgements about their objects and in behaviour, whereas weakly held attitudes do neither. The experimenters explain this in terms of the structures of attitudes. A strong attitude, they argue, is a persisting state, but a weak attitude is constructed at the time at which it is needed

(Holland et al. 2002). The mental states that a weak attitude is constructed from will vary with the occasion, since their relative levels of accessibility vary according to their recent employment in cognition and since the amount of time and cognitive resources used to construct the attitude will vary.[2] In terms of the cognitive-affective personality system, attitude strength is determined by the strengths of the associative connections between the mental states that compose the attitude. When these are sufficiently strong, the set of mental states will continually influence cognition together as a whole. But mental states linked by connections that are not stronger than most connections in the system will influence the flow of cognition individually, each according to its own range and strength of connections.

6.5 Attitude Strength and Consistent Judgement

We can understand the moral choice blindness experiments in terms of this relation between attitude strength and consistency of evaluative judgement across situations. If your attitude towards democracy, for example, is firmly held, then you are unlikely to be tricked into thinking that you have just expressed the negation of that attitude. In a moral choice blindness experiment where a switched statement concerned democracy, you would be likely to detect the switch. If the statement concerned some topic on which you do not hold a strong attitude, however, you would construct your response at the time on the basis of the available relevant beliefs and desires. When presented with your purported response to such a statement and asked to justify the response, if you did not remember that this was not in fact your response, then you

---

[2] It is sometimes reported that attitude psychology has found that where explicitly endorsed attitudes correlate with behaviour, this is generally due to the attitude having been formed to justify prior behaviour rather than the other way around (e.g. Knobe and Leiter 2007, 102). Although this is true, it ignores experimental investigation into why attitude is shaped by behaviour in many cases while in other cases behaviour is shaped by attitude. Danny Axsom and Joel Cooper provided striking evidence that the difference lies in attitude strength in 1985. (For discussion of this experiment in relation to Aristotle's theory of trait habituation, see Webber 2013, §4.) The more recent experiment concerning attitudes towards Greenpeace confirms this finding and adds that consistency of attitude expression in judgement over time is likewise a matter of attitude strength.

will again construct and explain an attitude, but this time one of the most salient mental states drawn on in constructing the attitude would be the false belief about your response to the statement moments earlier. So the mental states drawn upon in the attitude construction will feature those most closely and strongly associated with the content of that purported response. These will be the reasons you then give.

A detail of the experiment supports this interpretation. The survey asked subjects whether they held strong moral opinions in general and whether they were politically active. Responses to the first of these did not correlate with whether the subject detected the statement negation. This is consonant with the explanation in terms of attitude strength, for one's answer to this general question seems unlikely to correlate with strength of attitude on the specific topics that the negated statements concerned. There was, however, some correlation between detection of statement negation and the second question. More specifically, this correlation held for one group of subjects but not the other. For there were two versions of the survey. One presented highly general moral statements, such as 'even if an action might harm the innocent, it can still be morally permissible to perform it'. The other presented more specific statements, such as 'the violence Israel used in the conflict with Hamas is morally defensible despite the civilian casualties suffered by the Palestinians'. Subjects who considered themselves politically active and who were given the more specific moral questions were significantly more likely than any other subjects to detect the statement negation. This is unsurprising. Politically active people are more likely to hold strong attitudes on the moral aspects of specific political issues, but it does not follow that they are likely to hold strong general moral attitudes. Indeed, such a person might express agreement with a general moral statement on the basis of strong attitudes concerning specific applications of it, but when presented with evidence that they disagree with the general statement might justify this in terms of strong attitudes concerning other specific applications.

We can understand the Milgram experiment and the implicit bias experiment in the same way. Before one has encountered the Milgram experiment, one is extremely unlikely to have a strong attitude concerning how one ought to behave in precisely that situation. When asked to predict how one would behave in the experiment, therefore, one constructs an attitude from relevant mental states. When actually in the experiment, one also judges and acts on the basis of attitudes constructed at the time. Many subjects in the experiment do construct the attitude that people predict they would construct. This is manifested when the subjects argue with the experimenter, seek confirmation that their actions are causing no harm, and even briefly refuse to continue. But each prompt from the experimenter requires the subjects to construct their attitudes anew. As it does so, each prompt also changes the relative levels of accessibility of the mental states drawn on to construct the attitude. For this reason, a subject is likely to vacillate between judging that the experiment should stop and judging that it can continue. Neither judgement, moreover, is wholehearted. Each attitude constructed incorporates considerations in favour of continuing and considerations against.

Do the explicit measures that are compared with the results of the implicit association test record persistent strong attitudes or weak attitudes? Although the original experiment found that the implicit test results were often contradicted by the same subject's explicitly reported attitudes, a subsequent replication with a minor alteration eliminated this divergence. In the original experiment, the explicit questions followed the implicit test (Greenwald et al. 1998). In the replication, this order was reversed (McConnell and Leibold 2001). This suggests that the explicit measures generally recorded weak attitudes that were dependent on the situation. Since the reaction time differences measured by the implicit association test are imperceptible to the subject, the test often leaves the subject with the false impression that they have treated black and white faces equally in what is clearly a scientific measure of their attitudes. Since weak attitudes tend to confirm recent behaviour, as we saw in the Greenpeace experiment, these subjects are likely to report attitudes consonant with their false belief that they have just treated these two ethnic groups equally. When the question is asked before the implicit association test is taken, on the other hand, the weak attitude constructed is likely to manifest the same associations and accessibility levels as are then manifested in the test itself.[3]

---

[3] The authors of the replication study hypothesize that having taken the implicit association test might increase the role of self-presentation effects in answering the explicit questions (McConnell and Leibold 2001, 440–1). Since the explicit measure was thoroughly anonymized, the authors must have in mind the presentation of one's self to oneself. But

If this is right, then neither of the two construals of situationist and implicit bias experiments that we began with is correct. One of these construals held that our behavioural dispositions are not always in line with our evaluative beliefs, which assumed our explicit moral judgements to be consistent across situations. The other construal denied this assumption, portraying moral judgements as varying with some details of the situation. What the attitude strength and moral choice blindness experiments suggest, however, is that those of our explicit moral judgements that express firmly held attitudes are thereby consistent across situations, whereas others are constructed when needed from resources that vary across situations. Moreover, the strong attitudes that manifest in consistent judgements also manifest in consistent behaviour. So the moral task these experiments pose is neither one of bringing behavioural dispositions into line with evaluative beliefs nor one of undertaking strategies to ensure careful deliberation in morally important situations. It is to ensure that one holds the right moral attitudes sufficiently strongly that one's judgements and actions will express them consistently.[4]

6.6 The Negative Programme of Moral Improvement

How should one aim to ensure that one's moral attitudes are not only correct but also sufficiently firmly held to manifest in consistent judgement and behaviour? What practical ethical guidance is the best response to the cognitive structures that explain situational manipulation and implicit bias? One kind of response would be to prescribe a negative programme of moral improvement. The aim would be to identify the features of situations that lead one to judge and act in morally problematic ways, then undertake strategies to prevent these features from having this malign influence. This is a negative programme because it aims to negate the morally negative influence of particular aspects of situations.

---

they do not explain why the explicit measures themselves would not have this effect to a sufficient degree to shape one's responses to them even without having taken the implicit association test.

[4] This is the idea of virtue ethics and situational variation ascribed to Plato, Aristotle, and the Stoics by Rachana Kamtekar (2004, 277–86).

Such recommendations are not uncommon as responses to both situationist experimental results and the implicit bias experiments.

One form of this response recommends that we simply avoid situations that might lead us to behave badly (Doris 2002, 147–8). This might be sage advice for some kinds of situation, but the scope for this kind of control is clearly very limited. A more promising form of this response is the converse recommendation to preserve and promote the features of situations that support morally desirable behaviour (Kamtekar 2004, 490–1). For example, if one's behaviour towards a particular ethnic group is biased by strong negative associations in one's cognitive system, then one can alter one's environment in ways that are likely to weaken these associations or strengthen more positive ones to counteract them. The efficacy of such a strategy is strikingly illustrated by 'the Obama effect': implicit measures of white people's cognition in response to images of black people found a significant decrease in evidence of negative associations as a result of the widespread media coverage of Barack Obama's first presidential campaign (Plant et al. 2009).

Other forms of the negative programme dispense with the idea of managing one's situation and instead focus on shaping one's cognitive system more directly. One such strategy is to aim to alter one's pattern of cognitive associations with some particular situational feature through regularly forming the desired associations in action or in conscious imagination (Mischel and Shoda 1995, 261; Snow 2006, 556, 560). Alternatively, one can formulate and rehearse intentions to behave in a particular way in response to particular situations (Mischel and Shoda 1995, 261; Kamtekar 2004, 487–8; Besser-Jones 2008, 328–9). In terms of the cognitive-affective personality system, these strategies aim to forge and strengthen particular pathways through the architecture that generates judgements and behaviour, so that when the relevant situations arise one's cognitive system tends towards producing the outcomes that one has trained it to produce.

However, this negative programme might seem inordinately demanding. A very wide variety of subtle situational cues can influence our judgements and actions. Although the experimental literature on implicit bias tends to focus on responses to women and to black men there is no reason to assume that such biases are limited to these categories. The negative programme of moral improvement should include all the biases relating to the full range of ethnic and religious identities we encounter. Moreover, there is evidence of widespread biases concerning an individual's height and weight (e.g. Marini et al. 2013). It seems plausible that there are further biases concerning aspects of social background indicated by a speaker's accent. Once all of these are taken into account, the negative programme seems rather daunting. But it may be even more so, since there remains the question of how these biases interact. Must a white person's bias concerning Oriental women, for example, simply be a function of distinct biases concerning Oriental people and concerning women? Or is it a specific bias that would require its own strategy for overcoming? The same question arises about the interplay of these biases and the classic situational manipulations. Do ethnicity and gender feature in our perceptions of authority figures or passive bystanders in the same way that they feature in our perceptions of students in a seminar room?

Even if these issues were to be resolved satisfactorily, so that a full set of strategies could be formulated for counteracting one's most morally problematic implicit biases and situational weaknesses, and even if it were accepted that this set of strategies was not overly demanding, then there would still remain the further question of how one can ensure that this programme of strategies will actually be carried through. This is most obvious in the case of the strategy of avoiding certain situations. The problem here is not that one might find oneself in such a situation for reasons beyond one's control. It is rather that when one is making a decision that determines whether one enters that situation, one might at that point be subject to situational influences or implicit biases. On a larger scale, a full programme of strategies for counteracting unwanted influences is itself an intended sustained pattern of behaviour that seems vulnerable to the kinds of influence it is intended to counter. The negative programme, that is to say, seems to preserve a vestige of the idea that our behaviour manifests our reflectively endorsed beliefs. We need to take more seriously the finding that simply deciding to adopt a certain mode of behaviour, or to pursue a range of strategies, is not enough to ensure that we actually do so. Our strategies can be derailed by the influence on our cognition of the subtle features of our situations, of our biases concerning the people we deal with, and of the demands of our everyday lives.

6.7 The Positive Programme of Moral Improvement

How can we deal with the problems of situational manipulation and implicit bias without our strategies for doing so being undermined by the same aspects of cognition that produce these problems? The findings of attitude psychology afford an answer to this question. To pursue some behavioural strategy, it is important that one habituates in oneself a sufficiently strong attitude in favour of that strategy. One's judgements about whether to expend effort in pursuit of this strategy will remain consistent across situations only if they manifest a firmly held attitude. If they are merely constructed out of the most accessible relevant beliefs and desires each time, they will vary with the relative accessibility of one's mental states, which in turn will vary with the situation one is in, the situations one has recently experienced, and one's recent cognitive activity. Indeed, these factors will determine whether one even consciously thinks of the strategy on a given occasion when it could be pursued.

Once we see this problem in terms of attitude strength, however, it becomes clear that the negative programme is not the only way to address the practical problems of situational manipulation and implicit bias. For the influence that a strong attitude has on cognition and behaviour is not restricted to situations in which some feature of the environment is directly related to the attitude. Attitude strength determines the attitude's general degree of accessibility to cognition. The stronger it is, the more accessible it is, the greater its influence over cognition generally. For this reason, a strong attitude can shape cognition and behaviour in ways that are not responses to the manifest features of the situation (Webber 2013, §4). In order to reduce one's susceptibility to situational manipulations and implicit biases, therefore, one can aim to instil in oneself a few firmly held moral attitudes, such as attitudes in favour of fairness or against discrimination. With a sufficiently high degree of accessibility, these general attitudes should serve to counteract the influence of situational manipulations and implicit biases. Unlike the negative programme of moral improvement, the aim of this programme would be to identify and embed in one's cognition the attitudes that tend one towards the right behaviour. This is a positive programme of moral improvement, which relies on the holistic nature of the cognitive-affective personality system.

This proposed programme of moral improvement echoes Aristotle's account of habituation. Character traits develop, according to Aristotle, through critically reflective practice. This habituation serves two ethical purposes. One is that it embeds one's values into one's behavioural cognition sufficiently firmly that one will judge and act in ways that manifest those values even in the face of temptations to do otherwise (2002, 1152a25-33). The other is that it refines one's understanding of the nature and demands of those evaluative commitments. One learns what justice really is and what it requires through repeatedly thinking about what justice requires in particular situations (2002, 1104a5-10). In terms of attitude psychology, the first of these purposes is served by strengthening the attitude and the second by refining the set of mental states that compose that attitude. In the context of the cognitive-affective personality system, these are processes of strengthening the associative connections between the relevant mental states, connections that strengthen each time they are used. The positive programme of moral improvement, therefore, would carry out the Aristotelian recommendation of habituating the ethical virtues.[5]

Because this programme would be focused on instilling a few basic traits, it would not face the problems that affect the negative programme. The task of instilling such basic values as justice, considerateness, and generosity does require ongoing critical reflection on one's own behaviour in relation to the demands of these values, but this is significantly less demanding than the reflection required to identify all of one's significant situational weaknesses and cognitive biases. In the positive programme, moreover, that reflection itself is the central technique for instilling virtue, though it may be supplemented by other techniques, whereas in the negative programme the reflection is merely an inquiry that informs one's strategies for self-improvement. This less demanding nature of the positive programme means that it is less

---

[5] Peggy DesAutels (2012) also suggests a positive programme of counteracting implicit biases. Her suggestion is grounded in a different area of cognitive science. Whether her account of the generation of implicit bias is compatible with the one detailed in this paper is too complicated a matter to be properly addressed here.

susceptible to being derailed by situational pressures, cognitive biases, and everyday life. For these have their greatest influence on the rapid cognition underlying everyday decision-making. The slower, more careful, and only occasional deliberative reflection required by the positive programme is not generally susceptible to them. Moreover, as the programme progresses one's tendency towards critical reflection in the light of the values one is trying to instil will itself be strengthened.

At present, there is no direct empirical confirmation of this theoretical prediction that one can reduce susceptibility to situational manipulation and implicit bias by habituating the requisite attitudes. Research into situational effects has developed independently of attitude psychology. Research into prejudice and stereotyping began in the context of attitude psychology, but soon developed independently of the main path of development of attitude psychology.[6] However, there are experimental findings that support confidence that such empirical confirmation could be found. Research into the efficacy of goals is particularly suggestive in this regard, because goals share with attitudes the feature of having a dimension of strength or firmness as well as a dimension of content.

In one such experiment, subjects were shown a series of words, each preceded by a picture of a woman or a man, and asked to pronounce the word. If a picture of a woman had activated concepts stereotypically associated with women, then the subject should be able to pronounce any stereotypical words more quickly. Subjects had been tested for whether they strongly held the goal of treating women equally with men. The experiment found that a strong goal of egalitarianism towards women prevented the activation of stereotypical associations in response to pictures of women. Moreover, the speed at which the subjects responded indicates that the egalitarian goal had this effect without the subject's conscious intent (Moskowitz et al. 1999).

This goal of egalitarianism towards women is more general than the goal of treating women equally with men if they are of a particular

---

[6] For the history of this divergence and a detailed argument in favour of reintegrating attitude psychology with the psychology of prejudice and stereotyping, see Maio et al. 2010.

ethnicity, or a particular range of body shapes, or in particular social roles or situations, but less general than the positive programme recommends. Perhaps at least some of the subjects held this goal because they were committed generally to egalitarianism, but the experiment did not test for this. A more recent experiment tested the effect on stereotyping of a broader egalitarian goal, defined as 'treating people equally regardless of their ethnicity, gender, race, physical appearance'. This experiment did not measure how firmly each subject was already committed to this value, but manipulated the subjects so that this value became temporarily highly accessible for some, much less accessible for others. It found that subjects for whom this general egalitarianism was highly accessible did not make stereotypical associations in response to images of black people, whereas those subjects for whom this value was not highly accessible did. Again, the speed of the experiment makes it impossible for this stereotype inhibition to be the result of conscious thought (Moskowitz and Li 2011).

Precisely how the idea of a goal employed in these experiments is related to the conception of an attitude emerging from attitude psychology is a matter that cannot be properly addressed here. Nevertheless, these results do suggest that direct empirical support could be found for the theoretical prediction that strengthening the right attitudes reduces the automatic activation of problematic associations. The design and analysis of such experiments would need to be grounded in an integrative conceptual approach to the findings of these divergent research areas. Debates over the ethical implications of situational manipulation and of implicit bias, and indeed over the prospects for virtue ethics more generally, would benefit greatly if such experiments concerning the positive programme of character development were to be undertaken.[7]

---

[7] This paper was developed through presentations at the Ethics and the Architecture of Personal Dispositions conference at the Sorbonne in July 2012, a workshop of the Leverhulme Implicit Bias and Philosophy project at University of Sheffield in July 2012, the Bristol–Cardiff Ethics Symposium in November 2013, and a conference of the Jubilee Centre for Character and Values in January 2014. I am grateful to the organizers and participants of those conferences for discussion. I am also grateful to Mark Alfano, Alberto Masala, Clea Rees, and an anonymous referee for comments on an earlier draft.

Works Cited

Aristotle. 2002. *Nicomachean Ethics*. Trans. Christopher Rowe. Introduction by Sarah Broadie. Oxford: Oxford University Press.

Axsom, Danny and Joel Cooper. 1985. Cognitive Dissonance and Psychotherapy: The Role of Effort Justification in Inducing Weight Loss. *Journal of Experimental Social Psychology* 21: 149–60.

Besser-Jones, Lorraine. 2008. Social Psychology, Moral Character, and Moral Fallibility. *Philosophy and Phenomenological Research* 76: 310–32.

DesAutels, Peggy. 2012. Moral Perception and Responsiveness. *Journal of Social Philosophy* 43: 334–46.

Doris, John. 2002. *Lack of Character: Personality and Moral Behavior*. Cambridge: Cambridge University Press.

Greenwald, Anthony, Debbie McGhee, and Jordan Schwartz. 1998. Measuring Individual Differences in Implicit Cognition: The Implicit Association Test. *Journal of Personality and Social Psychology* 74: 1464–80.

Hall, Lars, Petter Johansson, and Thomas Strandberg. 2012. Lifting the Veil of Morality: Choice Blindness and Attitude Reversals on a Self-Transforming Survey. *Plos One* 7: e45457.

Holland, Rob W., Bas Verplanken, and Ad van Knippenberg. 2002. On the Nature of Attitude-Behavior Relations: The Strong Guide, The Weak Follow. *European Journal of Social Psychology* 32: 869–76.

Kamtekar, Rachana. 2004. Situationism and Virtue Ethics on the Content of Our Character. *Ethics* 114: 458–91.

Knobe, Joshua, and Brian Leiter. 2007. The Case for Nietzschean Moral Psychology. In *Nietzsche and Morality*, ed. Brian Leiter and Neil Sinhababu. Oxford: Oxford University Press, 83–109.

McConnell, Allen, and Jill Leibold. 2001. Relations among the Implicit Association Test, Discriminatory Behavior, and Explicit Measures of Racial Attitudes. *Journal of Experimental Social Psychology* 37: 435–42.

Maio, Gregory, Geoffrey Haddock, Russell Spears, and Antony Manstead. 2010. Attitudes and Intergroup Relations. In *The Sage Handbook of Prejudice, Stereotyping and Discrimination*, ed. John Dovidio, Mies Hewstone, Peter Glick, and Victoria Esses. London: Sage, 261–75.

Marini, Maddalena, Natarajan Sriram, Konrad Schnabel, Norbert Maliszewski, Thierry Devos, Bo Ekehammar, Reinout Wiers, Cai HuaJian, Mónika Somogyi, Kimihiro Shiomura, Simone Schnall, Félix Neto, Yoav Bar-Anan, Michelangelo Vianello, Alfonso Ayala, Gabriel Dorantes, Jaihyun Park, Selin Kesebir, Antonio Pereira, Bogdan Tulbure, Tuulia Ortner, Irena Stepanikova, Anthony G. Greenwald, and Brian A. Nosek. 2013. Overweight People Have Low Levels of Implicit Weight Bias, but Overweight Nations Have High Levels of Implicit Weight Bias. *Plos One* 8: e83543.

Merritt, Maria. 2009. Aristotelian Virtue and the Interpersonal Aspect of Ethical Character. *Journal of Moral Philosophy* 6: 23–49.

Milgram, Stanley. 1974. *Obedience to Authority: An Experimental View.* New York: Harper and Row.

Mischel, Walter, and Yuichi Shoda. 1995. A Cognitive-Affective System Theory of Personality: Reconceptualizing Situations, Dispositions, Dynamics, and Invariance in Personality Structure. *Psychological Review* 102: 246–68.

Moskowitz, Gordon, Peter Gollwitzer, Wolfgang Wasel, and Bernd Schaal. 1999. Preconscious Control of Stereotype Activation through Chronic Egalitarian Goals. *Journal of Personality and Social Psychology* 77: 167–84.

Moskowitz, Gordon, and Peizhong Li. 2011. Egalitarian Goals Trigger Stereotype Inhibition: A Proactive Form of Stereotype Control. *Journal of Experimental Social Psychology* 47: 103–16.

Plant, E. Ashby, Patricia Devine, William Cox, Coey Columb, Saul Miller, Joanna Gople, and Michele Peruche. 2009. The Obama Effect: Decreasing Implicit Prejudice and Stereotyping. *Journal of Experimental Social Psychology* 45: 961–4.

Russell, Nestar. 2011. Milgram's Obedience to Authority Experiments: Origins and Early Evolution. *British Journal of Social Psychology* 50: 140–62.

Shoda, Yuichi, and Walter Mischel. 1996. Toward a Unified, Intra-Individual Dynamic Conception of Personality. *Journal of Research in Personality* 30: 414–28.

Snow, Nancy. 2006. Habitual Virtuous Actions and Automaticity. *Ethical Theory and Moral Practice* 9: 545–61.

Webber, Jonathan. 2013. Character, Attitude and Disposition. *European Journal of Philosophy*. DOI: 10.1111/ejop.12028.

7

Does the CAPS Model Improve Our Understanding of Personality and Character?

Christian B. Miller

Over the past forty years, Walter Mischel, Yuichi Shoda, and Jack Wright have developed a version of the social-cognitive approach to the study of personality in great detail. Their 'cognitive-affective personality system' or 'CAPS' model, as it has become known, is now one of the leading approaches to understanding personality in psychology today.[1] In addition, it is receiving increased attention in philosophical work on character, as evidenced by two important recent monographs by Russell (2009) and Snow (2010) which use the CAPS model to develop a positive account of character traits in the face of skeptical challenges by Harman (1999, 2000, 2009) and Doris (1998, 2002, 2010).

The goal of this chapter is to offer the first detailed critical assessment of the CAPS model from a philosophical perspective. I will argue for the following claim: *using technical language, the CAPS model re-describes and finds supporting evidence for basic platitudes of commonsense folk psychology.*

In order to explore this claim, in the next section I first outline some of these 'basic platitudes,' and then in the subsequent section show how the

---

[1] Hence the focus of this paper will be on the CAPS model specifically, rather than all versions of the social-cognitive approach. Given limitations of space, I omit discussion of alternative versions such as that developed by Bandura 1978, 1986, 1999. For a range of social-cognitive views, see the papers in Cervone and Shoda 1999b.

central ideas associated with the CAPS model—such as cognitive-affective units, if...then...behavioral contingencies, intraindividual behavioral signatures, and so forth—straightforwardly follow from them. The third section will focus specifically on the CAPS model and traits, before I conclude in section four with a brief discussion of whether, if my claim is correct, it represents a strength or a weakness of the CAPS model.

7.1 Some Commonsense Assumptions

The following six claims are perfectly ordinary and standard assumptions from our ordinary lives which are captured in commonsense thinking about the mind. Here is the first one:

(i) We have a vast array of different mental states, including beliefs, wants, wishes, hopes, intentions, and so forth. They can be very broadly classified as beliefs and desires.[2] These mental states can function as plans, goals, convictions, norms, aspirations, and so forth. They are used, among other things, to shape our interpretation of the world, and to bring about changes in the world. Whether we can affect change in the world is limited by our abilities, and for some actions we are not able to perform them.

Nothing much should need to be said here. I think I have certain beliefs and desires, and so do you. Some of them have contents which involve planning for the long-term future, whereas others involve short-term goals, or norms about how to act. Some of my mental states are commonplace, and some of them are highly unique to me. Some of them I am able to carry out in action (such as the desire to write this chapter), whereas others I am not able to realize (such as my desire to be a fully virtuous person, or that there be world peace).

Here is the second assumption:

(ii) Many of our mental states are not active or occurrent at every moment. They are dispositional states which can *become* activated.

Prior to writing this sentence, I had not consciously thought today about the fact that $7 + 5 = 12$. Nevertheless I still have this belief even when

---

[2] I am not committing myself to the claim that all of what goes on in our mental lives falls under the heading of either beliefs or desires. Rather it is customary to divide all mental states *with intentional objects* into these two categories.

I am not thinking about it, and so do you. Hence it is true to say of me that I believe that 7 + 5 = 12, even though it has not come across my radar screen all day.

The third assumption is that:

(iii) Relevant information from the situations we are in and from other parts of our minds can activate our mental states. What counts as 'relevant' is a matter of the particular content of our mental states themselves.

When I see a snake slithering by, that can activate my fear of getting bitten. The fact that I have this state of fear with respect specifically to snakes is what makes that particular information highly relevant. In contrast, information that the laundry is finished is not relevant to the content of this particular fear, although it certainly is relevant to various other mental states. Similarly, when I think back on a broken promise, that can activate feelings of guilt over what I did. When the room gets suddenly dark, that can activate my belief that the power has gone out. These are all perfectly familiar observations.

Fourth:

(iv) Certain of our mental states tend to cluster together, and so be mutually activated. Which mental states these are, and how strongly their interconnections are, varies from person to person. But all of us have a number of different clusters of interrelated mental states, pertaining to different facets of our lives.

When I see the snake, that activates in me my fear of getting bitten. It also tends to activate various beliefs about how to not get bitten, such as by running away, or by standing perfectly still, or by hitting the snake. Through some psychological process, a desire to run away might be activated. And so forth. The point is that this cluster of mental states tends to hang together and so get activated in my mind, whereas a belief that 7 + 5 = 12 is not part of that cluster. At the same time, this cluster of mental states is not held by everyone; other people do not get afraid of snake bites at all, or if they do, they adopt different avoidance strategies.

According to the fifth assumption:

(v) Given that these are clusters of interrelated mental state *dispositions*, then barring some significant change to the cluster, they should tend to function similarly when activated in similar ways, other things being equal.

Hence the next time I come across a snake, I will probably also be fearful, form the same beliefs, and desire to run away, while not thinking about how 7 + 5 = 12.

Finally:

(vi) Since relevant information from the situations we are in and from other parts of our minds can activate our individual mental states (claim (iii)), relevant information can also activate the clusters of interrelated mental states as well. Each cluster has specific kinds of information that tend to activate it, and so for any given cluster, it may *not* be activated during a variety of different situations a person comes across in a given day. Or if it is activated regularly during the day, it may not always be activated with the same intensity.

My cluster of mental states associated with a fear of snakes, beliefs about how to avoid them, and a desire to run away, will obviously be activated in certain highly specific situations, and (I can report) is as a matter of fact rarely activated at all. The cluster of mental states associated with satisfying feelings of hunger, on the other hand, tends to be activated much more frequently every day. This cluster is sensitive to various pieces of relevant information, such as how hungry I am, how much money I have, what the nearest food options are, whether it is important to maintain a diet, and so forth. Given changes in these or other variables, I may or may not directly attempt to find the nearest food option or attempt to eat now as opposed to later.

This completes my presentation of these six basic assumptions. Note that, while they may have been stated in more abstract or academic language than many people might use, the ideas themselves are perfectly ordinary and familiar, as the examples following each of them tried to show. Hence I am *not* claiming that the six assumptions are statements you would expect to be made by the ordinary person on the street. But I am claiming that the basic ideas behind each of them, once clearly explained and illustrated using simple examples like my fear of snakes, should be quite amenable to most people. So barring a powerful reason to reject them, I think we should accept that these six claims are intuitive and commonsensical assumptions that any psychological theory of personality and behavior should have among its first principles.

Of course, nothing about these assumptions tells us what the specific mental states *actually are* which exist in each of our minds. None of them tells us, for instance, whether people have a basic desire to help other people or instead a basic desire to harm other people. Rather, these assumptions just concern the general existence and functioning of our mental states, and not their specific contents. This point will be important at the end of the chapter.

7.2 The CAPS Approach

Let me now return to Mischel's version of the social-cognitive theory of personality. I intend to show that the central tenets of the CAPS model simply involve repackaging these ordinary assumptions using more sophisticated technical vocabulary.

(a) Cognitive-Affective Units. The conceptual starting point of the CAPS model is with what Mischel has called 'cognitive-affective units' or 'cognitive social learning person variables.'[3] The idea is to take the focus in studying personality away from broad or global traits, and put it squarely on a given person's capacities and specific psychological states or processes.[4] Here are the five cognitive-affective units Mischel initially outlined in 1973:[5]

Construction competencies
Encoding strategies and personal constructs
Behavior-outcome and stimulus-outcome expectancies in particular situations
Subjective stimulus values
Self-regulatory systems and plans

Now these might sound like new categories, but closely examining Mischel's characterization of each one of these variables tells a different story. For instance, the 'expectancies' are just ordinary instrumental beliefs, i.e., beliefs about the best means in order to attain a given end. They "guide the person's selection (choice) of behaviors from among the enormous number which he is capable of constructing within any situation."[6] For instance, if I desire to avoid the snake, then my instrumental belief might be that the best way to avoid the snake is to run away. Similarly, 'stimulus values' are just "his stimulus preferences and aversions. This unit

---

[3] For further discussion, see Mischel 1973; 1984, 353; 2004, 4–5, 11; 2009, 284; Mischel and Mischel 1976; Mischel and Peake 1982, 749; Shoda and Mischel 1996, 416; Mischel and Shoda 1998, 237–8; Shoda 1999a, 165–71; and Mischel et al. 2002, 53.

[4] As Mischel writes, "The proposed cognitive social learning approach to personality shifts the unit of study from global traits inferred from behavioral signs to the individual's cognitive activities and behavior patterns, studied in relation to the specific conditions that evoke, maintain, and modify them and which they, in turn, change" (1973, 265).

[5] Mischel 1973, 265, 275. For an updated version, see Mischel and Shoda 1995, 252; 1998, 238; 2008, 211; Shoda and Mischel 1996, 416; and Mischel 1999b, 47.

[6] Mischel 1973, 269. See also Mischel 1973, 269–72; Mischel and Mischel 1976, 191–3; Mischel and Shoda 1995, 252; 1998, 238; Cervone and Shoda 1999a, 19; and Shoda 1999a, 167–8.

refers to stimuli that have acquired the power to induce positive or negative emotional states in the person and to function as incentives or reinforcers for his behavior."[7] In other words, this category just refers to plain old desires, such as my desire to avoid the snake. 'Self-regulatory systems and plans' ends up referring to goals, rules, and plans, which are just specific kinds of beliefs and desires.[8] Finally, the first two categories refer not to specific kinds of mental states, but rather to general capacities and abilities, i.e., to our basic dispositions to perform certain kinds of mental and physical actions and to interpret, encode, identify, and categorize incoming information.[9]

What should be clear, then, is that these categories introduce technical terms to label familiar phenomena from ordinary thinking. They are already captured in the first of the six assumptions.[10]

(b) If... Then... Situation-Behavior Contingencies. Another well-known feature of the CAPS model is the claim that each individual's personality can be represented by various 'if-then situation-behavior contingencies.'[11] The 'ifs' are situations, and the 'thens' are behavioral outputs.[12] In other words, the idea is that there are true conditional statements linking the situations a person encounters with the resulting behaviors. Furthermore, on the CAPS model these are not highly specific conditionals, such as "If student X comes to my office, then..." and "If

---

[7] Mischel 1973, 273. See also Mischel 1973, 272–3; Mischel and Mischel 1976, 193; and Mischel and Shoda 1995, 252; 1998, 238.

[8] Mischel 1973, 273–5. See also Mischel and Mischel 1976, 193–6; Mischel and Shoda 1995, 253, 259; 1998, 238; Cervone and Shoda 1999a, 19; and Shoda 1999a, 165–7.

[9] Mischel 1973, 265–9. See also Mischel and Mischel 1976, 187–90; Shoda et al. 1993, 1023, 1029; Mischel and Shoda 1995, 253; 1998, 238 and Shoda 1999a, 168.

[10] See also the examples in Mischel and Shoda 1995, 255; 1998, 237; Shoda 1999a, 166; and the discussion in Cervone and Shoda 1999a, 18–19.

[11] For relevant discussion, see Mischel 1968, 189; 1984, 360–1; 1999a, 459; 1999b, 43, 50; 2004, 8, 11, 16; 2007, 266, 269–70; 2009, 284; Wright and Mischel 1987, 1161–4; Shoda et al. 1993, 1029; 1994, 675, 677; Mischel and Shoda 1995, 249; 1998, 243; 2008, 215; Vansteelandt and Van Mechelen 1998, 758–9; Shoda 1999a, 159–64; Cervone and Shoda 1999a, 21; Caprara and Cervone 2000, 80; Shoda and LeeTiernan 2002, 259; Zayas and Shoda 2009, 281; Andersen and Thorpe 2009, 163; and Smith et al. 2009, 187, 194.

[12] Typically this is how the conditionals are stated. But Mischel and Shoda also note that there are if... then... relations in which either one or both of the relata are mental states. See Mischel and Shoda 1995, 251–2; 1998, 240; 2008, 219, 229; Shoda 1999a, 164; and Mischel 1999b, 52; 2004, 16. In some places the idea of using category structures in both relata has been explored. See, e.g., Wright and Mischel 1987, 1161; and Shoda et al. 1993. Wright and Mischel (1987, 1161) also consider different strengths in the linking relationship between the relata, i.e., whether it is a probabilistic relation or not.

student Y comes to my office, then..." Rather they are broader conditionals which will allow for some coherence in behavior across situations (on which more below). Finally, these contingencies vary from person to person—two people can be in the same nominal situation, and yet act in very different ways. The CAPS view can explain this variability in terms of differences in their cognitive-affective units—different people can have different particular units, and furthermore they can be activated, can be accessible, and can be related to each other in different ways from one person to the next.[13]

The main evidence that Mischel, Shoda, and Wright have offered for there being such true conditionals derives from an extensive study of children's behavior at a summer treatment camp.[14] There participants were observed by a team of seventy-seven trained counselors for an average of 167 hours of behavioral observation per child during the six-week summer program. Levels of verbal aggression, for instance, were measured in different situations, and in the situation "when teased or provoked by a peer," one child exhibited a standardized z-score of roughly +1.0 (where 0 is the mean), whereas another child had a score of roughly -2.0.[15] So for the second child, his personality could be partially understood as: if teased by a peer, then unlikely to exhibit verbal aggression.[16]

This terminology of 'if...then...situation-behavior contingencies' is another label for an ordinary phenomenon. Dispositions ground the truth of conditional statements. So if I have the disposition to fear snake bites, then it is true of me that if I see a snake, then I will exhibit fearful emotional behavior in my facial and other body language (subject to all the usual qualifications about background conditions and holding

---

[13] For more on individual differences in the CAPS model, see Shoda et al. 1994, 676; Mischel and Shoda 1995, 253; 1998, 237–40; 2008, 211–12; Shoda and Mischel 1996, 418; Mischel et al. 2002, 53; and Mischel 2004, 11; 2009, 284, 286.

[14] For relevant data from this camp, see Mischel 1984, 361–2; Wright and Mischel 1987; and Shoda et al. 1993; 1994. For a recent study by Shoda and colleagues using youth baseball players and coaches, see Smith et al. 2009.

[15] See the figures in Shoda et al. 1994, 678. These z-scores are the standardized deviations from the mean score for this sample of participants. They can be understood as rank orderings for that group, behavior, and situation.

[16] In addition to verbal and physical aggression, they also studied withdrawal, friendliness, compliance, and prosocial behavior. For relevant discussion, see Mischel 1984, 359–61; Wright and Mischel 1987, 1164–8; Shoda et al. 1993, 1025; 1994, 677; Mischel and Shoda 1995, 249; 1998, 244–5; and Shoda and LeeTiernan 2002, 245.

other things equal). So if we have any mental state dispositions *at all* which pertain to behavior, then they will ground true if... then... conditionals. Furthermore, if we have *clusters* of mental state dispositions which pertain to behavior, then they will ground their own if... then... conditional statements. If I see a snake, then it is highly likely that I will run away—this is a familiar conditional which is 'made true' by a particular cluster of beliefs and desires which are connected to each other and which concern snake bites. In other words, because of these specific beliefs and desires and their relations, it is true of me that if I see a snake, then it is highly likely that such-and-such behavior will follow. Finally, individual differences are to be explained in terms of whether people possess the same mental state dispositions, and if they do, whether they have them to the same strength and relate them to other mental states in the same way.

So the idea of 'if... then... situation-behavior contingencies' also follows straight away from commonsense assumptions.[17]

(c) Nominal versus Psychologically Salient Features of Situations. This aspect of the CAPS model is always highlighted prominently, and has recently been made much of in the philosophy literature on character too.[18] While it is hard to draw the distinction precisely, a common approach is to say that the 'psychologically salient features' or 'active ingredients' are "the features of the situation that have significant meaning for a given individual or type, and that are related to the experienced psychological situation—the thoughts and affects and goals that become activated within the personality system."[19] So what is psychologically salient is a function of the person's relevant cognitive-affective units, i.e., the relevant thoughts, affects, and goals. Nominal characteristics of a

---

[17] For passages where this is especially apparent, see Mischel and Shoda 1995, 251, 253, 255; 1998, 238–9; 2008, 211–12; Shoda and Mischel 1996, 417, 420; Shoda 1999a, 164, 173; and Mischel 1999b, 46; 2009, 286. For a roughly similar observation, see Johnson 1999, 446.

[18] See, e.g., Mischel 1968, 64, 67, 189–90, 285, 300; 1973, 259–61, 263; 1999b, 43–4, 46; 2004, 15; 2007, 266; 2009, 284; Mischel and Peake 1982, 749; Shoda et al. 1993, 1024–5, 1029; 1994, 685; Mischel and Shoda 1995, 248; 1998, 247–8; 2008, 218; Shoda and Mischel 1996, 421–2; Shoda 1999a, 163; Cervone 1999, 323–6; Mischel et al. 2002, 51; Mendoza-Denton et al. 2007, 215; Zayas and Shoda 2009, 280–1; and especially Shoda et al. 1994, 675–6; and Shoda and LeeTiernan 2002. For discussion in the philosophy literature, see Brandt 1988, 78; Flanagan 1991, 291; Sreenivasan 2002, 50, 57–60; Doris 2002, 76–85; Solomon 2003, 52; Kamtekar 2004, 470–3; Upton 2009, 178; Lukes 2009, 293; Russell 2009, chs 8–10; and Snow 2010, ch. 1.

[19] Mischel 2004, 15.

situation (also sometimes labeled simply as 'nominal units of situations' or 'nominal situations') are generic features such as the physical location, time, or event, e.g., being in the office, eating dinner, doing homework at night, talking on the telephone with Jane, watching television, etc.

The idea is that any given person might react to a variety of different features in a given nominal situation, and furthermore react to those features in different ways. So, for instance, the children in the summer camp studies were observed in different situations understood in terms of their psychologically salient features, such as whether they were being teased or provoked, to see how they would react. It was found that for some of them, being teased was connected to cognitive-affective states of aggression in a variety of nominal situations, and for others it was not. Similarly, to take another example, a person might be very sensitive to perceived criticism by others, which triggers defensive psychological strategies. Such a person could think that he is being criticized on separate occasions at the office, home, parties, and so forth, and have the same strategies be activated as a result. So the claim of the CAPS model is that studies of personality should pay close attention to what features are psychologically relevant for the participants in question, and not just to the nominal situations. And what is psychologically relevant for an individual is a matter of his or her cognitive-affective units and the relationships between them.[20]

Again, I think we should all agree with this. As noted earlier:

(iii) Relevant information from the situations we are in and from other parts of our minds can activate our mental states. What counts as 'relevant' is a matter of the particular content of our mental states themselves.

Some people are afraid of snakes, and so observing a snake slithering by is highly relevant information that might not be captured in a description of the situation as 'in the garden.' For other people, though, it is completely irrelevant. The difference comes down to their mental

---

[20] See Mischel 1973, 263; 2004, 15; Mischel and Shoda 1995, 248; 1998, 248; Shoda 1999a, 163; and Shoda and LeeTiernan 2002. The claim goes back all the way to Mischel's 1968 book: "Assessing the acquired meaning of stimuli is the core of social behavior assessment..." (1968, 190). There are various ways of identifying the psychologically salient features of situations. For the different approaches that were used with the summer camp children, see Shoda et al. 1993; 1994. See also the discussion in Shoda et al. 1994, 685; and especially Shoda and LeeTiernan 2002, 247.

states—some have a fear of snakes, and others do not. Given this difference in their mental states, naturally different features of the same nominal garden situation are going to be relevant to them. Commonsense agrees.

(d) Intraindividual Behavioral Signatures and Cross-Situational Consistency. These prior claims offered by the CAPS model can be put together to introduce the concept of an 'intraindividual behavioral signature.' This label refers to the pattern of behavior that one person (hence 'intra' individual) exhibits in multiple situations, where the situations are distinguished by their psychologically relevant features. For instance, each summer camper was observed over the course of multiple situations to record patterns of aggressive behavior. Other situations included "when approached by a peer" and "when warned by an adult counselor."[21] In general, for any given person her behavioral signature can be represented using a profile with situations on the x-axis and some measure of behavior on the y-axis. For two examples of actual profiles (rather than my fictional ones) see the next subsection.[22]

Using the idea of intraindividual behavior signatures, the CAPS model can say something about cross-situational consistency. Whereas the situationist view might leave us with a picture of human beings as highly inconsistent and fragmented, this model claims that there can be a kind of cross-situational consistency with respect to the same psychologically salient features of various nominal situations. In other words, 'the office' and 'the gym' might not seem to have much in common, but a person might exhibit similar levels of behavior in both in virtue of picking up on the same features in each. At other times, when those features are not present in the office or gym, the same person might act in a different way. With their data collected from the summer camp, Shoda and company found that the consistency correlation for verbal aggression in response to the same psychologically salient feature ('peer teased') in two independent camp activities was 0.40, for this feature and whining it was 0.45,

---

[21] Shoda 1999a, 160.

[22] For more on the ideas of behavioral signatures and profiles in the CAPS model, see Shoda et al. 1994, 675–8; Mischel and Shoda 1995, 249, 251, 255, 258; 1998, 242, 245; 2008, 208, 224, 228, 233; Shoda and Mischel 1996, 419; Mischel 1999a, 459; 1999b, 44; 2004, 8, 10–11, 16, 2009, 285; Shoda 1999a, 160; 1999b, 366; Cervone and Shoda 1999a, 21; Caprara and Cervone 2000, 80; Shoda and LeeTiernan 2002, 245, 264; Mischel et al. 2002, 51; Fournier et al. 2009; and Smith et al. 2009.

and for this feature and compliance it was 0.39.[23] These are quite high correlations, suggesting that the participants were acting consistently in their verbal aggressiveness in these two situations when they picked up on, say, the whining that was going on in both of them. Furthermore, "as the number of shared features decreased, the consistency of individual differences in behaviors also decreased."[24] And this is what we would have expected on this approach—the more dissimilar the situations are in the participants' own eyes, the less consistent their particular idiosyncratic patterns of behavior will be across those situations.

So a person's behavior can exhibit a form of cross-situational consistency in virtue of adjusting and adapting to what cognitive-affective units are being activated in a given moment. As Mischel writes, "people behave in ways that are consistent with the meanings that particular situations have for them."[25] Even if these patterns do not exhibit high consistency correlations across nominal situations and can seem to be fragmented to outside observers, they can reflect a stable and intelligible underlying system of cognitive-affective units. Thus the CAPS model "predicts that the person's behavior in a domain will change from one situation to another—when the *if* changes, so will the *then*—even if the personality system were to remain entirely unchanged."[26]

These claims are again in line with commonsense. Our behavior does vary from one situation to another in virtue of the psychologically relevant features in each (at least as far as intentional actions are concerned which are done for motivating reasons, rather than mere reflex movements which are not the focus of this chapter). For someone like me, the presence of the snake in the garden is going to be relevant and be highly correlated with fleeing behavior, and so too in a different nominal situation when I am in the office and a snake gets in through the cracked

---

[23] Shoda et al. 1994, 682.   [24] Ibid., 681.

[25] Mischel 2007, 266. Similarly, "individuals are characterized by distinctive and stable patterns of behavior variability across situations" (2004, 7).

[26] Mischel and Shoda 1995, 257, emphasis theirs. See also pp. 258–9. For further elaboration of the CAPS approach to cross-situational consistency, see Mischel 1984, 360–1; 1999b, 43–4; 2004, 7, 15; 2007, 266–7; 2009, 284; Mischel and Peake 1982, 749; Shoda et al. 1993, 1024–5, 1027–8; 1994, 675–6, 684; Mischel and Shoda 1995, 255–7; 1998, 248; 2008, 218; Cervone and Shoda 1999a, 10–11, 21–2; Cervone 1999, 315–29; 2005, 442–3; Caprara and Cervone 2000, 110, 118–21; Shoda and LeeTiernan 2002, 266; Mischel et al. 2002, 53; and especially Shoda 1999a, 169–71.

window—there again this feature of the situation is highly relevant to my fleeing behavior and explains why I am being cross-situationally consistent. More generally, we might each have many different clusters of mental states, but each of those mental states is itself sensitive to its own relevant incoming information, and can be activated and issue in relevant behavior in a wide variety of nominal situations.[27] This follows from the commonsense assumption (vi).

(e) *Stability of Behavioral Signatures*. A given person's behavioral signature is expected to exhibit a fair amount of stability over time, barring significant changes in his mental life. Figure 7.1 shows an example for one student which draws on data Mischel and Philip Peake collected on the contentiousness of participants at Carleton College.[28]

Similarly, Figure 7.2 displays the profile Shoda, Mischel, and Wright found for the verbal aggression shown by Child #28 at the summer camp in three situations and two times.[29] While the child's level of verbal aggression differs significantly from one kind of situation to the next, he exhibits roughly the same pattern in these situations at two different times.[30]

This should not come as a surprise. We have clusters of mental state dispositions, and they tend to persist with us over time. When they are activated in the same way at different times, they are going to tend to function in a similar manner. As I said:

(v) Given that these are clusters of interrelated mental state dispositions, then barring some significant change to the cluster, they should tend to function similarly when activated in similar ways, other things being equal.

---

[27] For various passages using sophisticated language to express what amounts to this commonsense platitude, see Shoda et al. 1994, 684; Mischel and Shoda 1995, 255–7; 1998, 243; Shoda and Mischel 1996, 418; Mischel 1999b, 43, 50; Mischel et al. 2002, 53; and Mischel 2004, 11. For a roughly similar observation, see Johnson 1999, 448.

[28] Shoda 1999b, 366. See Mischel and Peake 1982.   [29] Shoda 1999a, 160.

[30] More generally, Shoda and company found that for the fifty-three children who encountered all five situations with sufficient frequency that were being studied, the stability coefficients in their intraindividual profiles were 0.19 for prosocial talk, 0.28 for whining, 0.41 for compliance, and 0.47 for verbal aggression (1994, 679).

For further discussion of stability, see Mischel 1968, 36, 135, 281–98; 1984, 362; 1999b, 43; 2004, 6–8; 2009, 285; Mischel and Peake 1982, 749; Shoda et al. 1993, 1023; 1994, 675–85; Mischel and Shoda 1995, 253; 1998, 242–5; 2008, 208, 219, 224, 229; Shoda 1999a, 160; Shoda and LeeTiernan 2002, 249–56; Mischel et al. 2002, 52; and Smith et al. 2009.

THE CAPS MODEL, PERSONALITY, AND CHARACTER 167

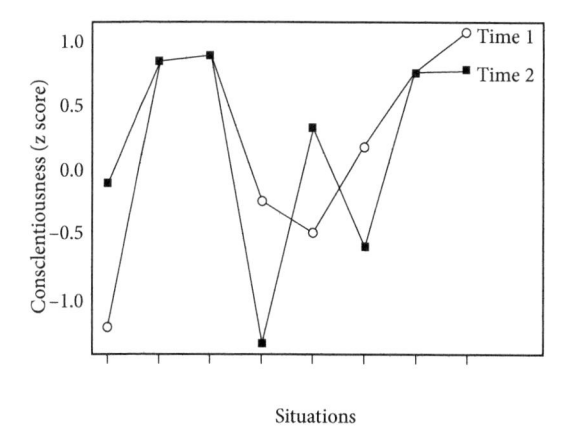

Figure 7.1. A conscientiousness profile for one student at two times (from Shoda 1999b).

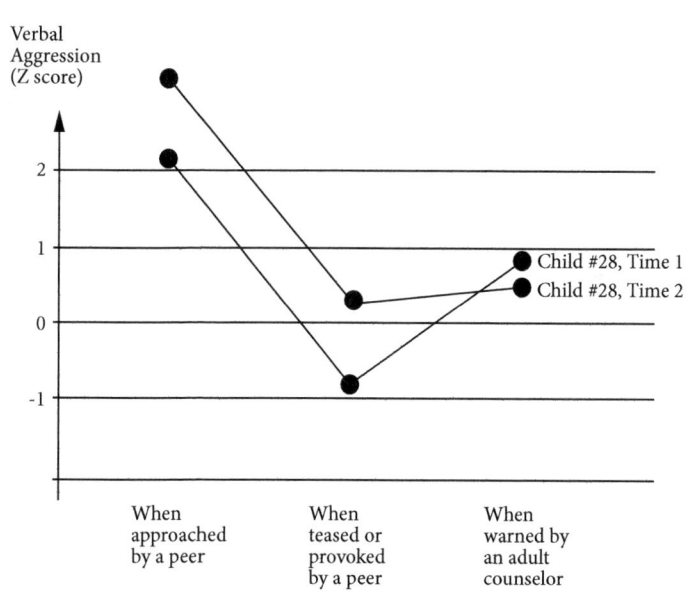

Figure 7.2. A verbal aggression profile for one child at two times (from Shoda 1999a).

(f) Aggregation. The CAPS model rejects the idea that aggregation of a particular kind of behavior (e.g., friendly or courageous behavior) performed by a person in many different situations can tell us the whole story about personality. Briefly, the aggregation approach concedes that consistency correlations for behaviors in a few situations are often low and not helpful for the purpose of predicting what the person will do next in a new situation. But the approach also argues that such correlations can increase significantly when many situations are taken into account. For instance, high correlations are expected when the average of measures of a person's honesty or conscientiousness on even days of a year are correlated with the same person's average score on odd days during that same year. As Seymour Epstein summarizes the view, "It may be concluded that within-subject reliability coefficients provide evidence for a relatively high degree of stability of the organization of variables within most individuals when the data are derived from sufficient observations but provide no such evidence when the data are derived from single observations."[31]

Now advocates of the CAPS model accept that aggregation data is important and useful for a number of purposes. Thus, as Shoda and his colleagues note, the model "recognizes the existence of broad overall average individual differences at the aggregate level with regard to which most people can be compared on most dimensions... such overall average differences are highly informative..."[32] But CAPS advocates tend to not be satisfied *just* with aggregation data across numerous situations. In particular, they reject Epstein's claims that "most single items of behavior have a high component of error of measurement and a narrow range of generality," and that, "Single items of behavior, no matter how carefully measured, like single items in a test, normally have too high a component of error of measurement to permit demonstration of high degrees of stability."[33] Rather, for them, aggregation data

---

[31] Epstein 1979, 1110. For more on the aggregation approach, see Epstein 1979; 1983; Mischel and Peake 1982; and Ross and Nisbett 1991, 107–9.

[32] Shoda et al. 1994, 685. See also Mischel and Peake 1982, 738, 747–8; Shoda and Mischel 1996, 421; Mischel 2004, 3; and Cervone et al. 2007, 7.

[33] Epstein 1979, 1097 and 1121. Similarly they would reject Jack Block's claim that "The reliability of many of the measures employed in personality research... is often poor, unnecessarily so. It makes no sense to use measures so unreliable that subsequent intercorrelations among measures are constrained to be close to zero" (1977, 40).

gives us insight into only *one* aspect of personality, and in addition an individual's specific actions are important data too. Each item of behavior is often not 'noise' or 'error' to be aggregated away, but rather a reflection of the person's underlying cognitive-effective units.[34]

Commonsense would seem to agree here too. If we have mental state dispositions, and if when they become activated they form occurrent mental states which can subsequently cause relevant behavior, then that behavior is important and reveals something about one's personality. It is evidence that can be used to attempt to identify just what these mental state dispositions are, and with that information in hand, observers can know what I believe and desire in this area of my life, and so try to predict when such mental states might be activated again even in different nominal situations.

7.3 The CAPS Model and Traits

So far the claims made by the CAPS model seem to me to be very plausible, and that is because they follow from commonsense platitudes about how the mind works. However, there is one important topic where advocates of CAPS can sometimes present a confusing picture. And it so happens that it is also the topic which is the central concern of this volume, namely the existence and nature of traits (of which the virtues would form a proper subset).

In a number of places, Mischel and company make claims which seem to suggest that they are willing to accept the existence of trait dispositions. For instance, they say that "Dispositions, no matter how conceptualized, are key aspects of the personality construct" and that "Recognition of the limitations of traditional global trait and state theories does not imply that people have no dispositions..."[35] Unfortunately, though, the relevant passages are usually too brief to offer a

---

[34] For further discussion of CAPS and aggregation, see also Mischel 1973, 258; 1984, 358–9; 1999a, 459; 1999b, 41–2; 2004, 6; 2007, 268; Mischel and Peake 1982, 731–9, 747–8; Shoda et al. 1994, 684–5; Mischel and Shoda 1995, 247–51, 257, 260; 1998, 243–4; 2008, 222–4, 228; Shoda and Mischel 1996, 420–1; Shoda 1999a, 159; 1999b; Cervone and Shoda 1999a, 4; Cervone 1999, 323; Caprara and Cervone 2000, 78, 80; Shoda and LeeTiernan 2002, 242; Mischel et al. 2002, 51; Cervone et al. 2007, 7; and Smith et al. 2009, 187.

[35] Mischel and Shoda 1998, 233 and Mischel 1984, 356. See also Mischel 1973, 262–4; 1999a, 456 and Mischel and Shoda 1995, 257, 263.

detailed positive account. But in an extensive treatment of the issue, Wright and Mischel (1987) did distinguish between and assess three views of traits. It is worth briefly reviewing each of these approaches.[36]

The *causal view* claims that traits are dispositions understood as stable mental attributes or structures had by a person which, when activated, causally give rise to relevant thoughts and (in many cases) behavior. Advocates of the view typically expect this trait-generated behavior to be cross-situationally consistent, although that is not a necessary feature of the view. The causal view is historically the most famous and popular position about trait dispositions, especially in philosophy, and is the kind of approach I have employed in my own work as well. It accepts a realist view about dispositions, claiming that there actually are such properties which are had by people who instantiate them.[37]

In contrast, the *summary view* (or act-frequency view) claims that traits are not causal entities and do not exist as mental properties of a person's mind, but rather are just summaries of behavior. They pertain solely to actual frequencies of a person's behavior, play no role in explaining that behavior, and are not expected to be cross-situationally consistent.[38]

Finally, the *conditional view* also denies that trait dispositions exist. Dispositional statements, however, are not summary statements about the general tendencies of persons, but rather statements about probabilistic conditionals or if...then...relations between situations and behaviors.[39] On this view,

an attribution of a personality disposition (e.g., aggressive) is an implicit subjunctive statement about what a person would be likely to do under appropriate conditions (e.g., when frustrated, when aversively stimulated), not necessarily what he or she will do on average. The fundamental unit of a disposition is therefore not the unconditional probability of trait-relevant behaviors, $p(B)$, as in a summary view; rather it is the conditional probability

---

[36] For a similar set of three views, see Zuroff 1986, 996–7. I discuss each of these views in more detail in Miller 2014, ch. 1.

[37] For more see Wright and Mischel 1987, 1160; as well as Miller 2014, ch. 1.

[38] For more see Wright and Mischel 1987, 1160; Buss and Craik 1983; and Wiggins 1997; as well as Miller 2014, ch. 1.

[39] Or put metaphysically instead of semantically, the conditional view "instead posits that a disposition is itself a set of condition-behavior relations" (Wright and Mischel 1987, 1162).

of a certain behavior or category of behaviors given a certain condition or set of conditions has occurred, $p(B\backslash C)$.[40]

This is the view that Wright and Mischel end up accepting about trait dispositions in that particular paper.[41]

In an earlier paper Mischel seems to clearly endorse the summary view.[42] And then in a 1999 paper, Mischel seems instead to accept a causal view after all. For instance, he accepts the existence of a 'processing disposition' which is a "characteristic social cognitive-affective processing structure that underlies, and generates, distinctive processing dynamics within the personality system."[43] In other words, a processing disposition is made up of one or more clusters of cognitive-affective units.

Here I do not want to get bogged down in textual interpretation; perhaps there are ways to make these different passages fit with each other, or perhaps Mischel's view has simply evolved over time from one position to the next. Instead what I want to do here is argue that the causal view is perfectly consistent with the CAPS model. In fact, I will argue for an even stronger claim—that it is problematic for the CAPS model to accept *anything other than* the causal view.

One way to argue for the causal view is to enter into a larger discussion of realist versus anti-realist views about dispositions in general. Clearly this is not the appropriate place for such a discussion. Besides, others have argued for realist views far better than I can, to the point where that approach seems to be gaining the upper hand at least in the philosophy

---

[40] *Ibid.*, 1161. The editors have noted that this passage, as stated, may be consistent with the causal view of dispositions. I am not sure that it is, but in any event the passage is not quoted here as an expression of the *entire* conditional view, but rather only the positive claims being made about trait attributions that the conditional view would combine with a negative claim denying the actual existence of such dispositions. Hence on this view, "the dispositional attribution *that child is aggressive* refers to a cluster of condition-behavior contingencies such as *if* (frustrated or threatened or punished) *then sometimes* (physically aggressive or verbally abusive or impulsive)..." (*ibid.*, 1162, emphasis theirs). It does not refer to a dispositional property of aggressiveness with causal powers.

[41] For much further elaboration, see *ibid.*, 1161–2. See also Newman and Uleman 1989, 163–4 for related discussion.

[42] Mischel 1973, 262, 264. See also Mischel 1968, 42, 68–9, 72, 189; Cervone 1999, 316, 331; Cervone and Shoda 1999a, 9; Caprara and Cervone 2000, 16–17; and Mischel and Shoda 2008, 235.

[43] Mischel 1999b, 52. See also 1999b, 46, 52–3, 56; and Mischel and Shoda 2008, 217, 233. I am grateful to Nancy Snow for calling the Mischel 1999b paper to my attention.

literature.[44] Instead, all I will try to show here is that, *given the other commitments of the CAPS model*, the advocate of that model should not only accept that there are trait dispositions, but also understand them as having causal powers and as being grounded in a person's mind.

The line of reasoning here is fairly simple.[45] The CAPS model already accepts that there are mental state dispositions, i.e., dispositions to form beliefs and desires which are labeled as 'cognitive-affective units.' Short of adopting a form of behaviorism or some other unconventional and highly controversial view, the advocate of a CAPS model should readily agree that these mental state dispositions can be relatively enduring psychological structures in a person's mind and, when activated, play a causal role in giving rise to occurrent beliefs and desires and (thereby) behavior. In other words, we are caused to act the way we do, at least in significant part, thanks to our beliefs and desires, and what occurrent beliefs and desires we happen to have at a given moment depend on what we are disposed to believe and desire. Furthermore, these mental states are not activated 'unconditionally' or in a way that is 'situation free'; rather each mental state disposition has its own unique activating conditions, whether in the form of information about the present situation or other mental states in the person's mind (or both). Hence these dispositions ground the truth of 'if... then...' conditionals, as already explained earlier in this chapter. Given my disposition to fear snakes, it is true of me that if I see a snake, then I will exhibit signs of the emotion of fear.

The advocate of the CAPS model also accepts that there are *clusters* of interrelated mental state dispositions, which when activated tend to give rise to multiple occurrent mental states together.[46] These mental states

---

[44] For a helpful overview of this debate, see Mumford 1998. For specific criticism of anti-realism about traits, see Brandt 1970.

[45] See also Mumford 1998, 182; Kamtekar 2004, 472, 477; Adams 2006, 131–8; Badhwar 2009, 279; Russell 2009, xii, 172, 292–3, 330; Sosa 2009, 279; and Lukes 2009, 292.

[46] As Mischel and Shoda write, "cognitive-affective representations and affective states interact dynamically and influence each other reciprocally. It is the organization of the relationships among them that forms the core of the personality structure and that guides and constrains their effects" (2008, 211; see also 212, 219, 233). Similarly Vivian Zayas and Shoda write that "Understanding the effects of situations means understanding how *sets* of cognitions and affects are activated and influence behaviors" (2009, 281, emphasis theirs). See also Caprara and Cervone 2000, 109. Note that the authors here are committing themselves to more than the claim that multiple cognitive-affective units can be involved in the generation of a particular action. As the first quote makes clear, these units also

can in turn show up in behavior as part of that person's behavioral signature. Plus, these mental states are not fleeting—as the model itself holds, a person's behavioral signature tends to be stable over time in the same situations, which in turn is explained in terms of stable and persisting mental state dispositions. And they are conditional too, just like their individual mental state dispositions are. Given the cluster of mental states associated with my disposition to fear snakes, it is also true of me that if I see a snake, then I will believe that the best thing to do is to run, and I will likely start to do so. Finally, some individuals have similar clusters of mental state dispositions, and so it makes sense to talk about there being 'types' of people who "share certain key psychological processes."[47]

But then once the CAPS model accepts that people have clusters of interrelated mental state dispositions, then the causal view seems unavoidable. For then trait dispositions can simply be *identified with* these clusters.[48] So they will have causal powers, given that mental state dispositions have causal powers, and they will be grounded in mental structures in a person's mind. At the same time, they are not the broad, 'situation free' traits that have been the subject of much controversy in psychology in discussions of situationism; they are highly conditional trait dispositions which ground the truth of all kinds of if . . . then . . . conditionals.

I suspect that some psychologists might be tempted to reject a causal view of trait dispositions because it might be thought that the view is committed to the widespread possession of empirically inadequate

---

"interact dynamically" and "influence each other reciprocally," and there is an "organization of the relationships among them." In the same paper, Mischel and Shoda also describe each person's "characteristic set of cognitions, affects, and behavioral strategies in an organization of inter-relations that guides and constrains their activation" (2008, 233). Thanks to the editors for inviting me to clarify this point.

[47] Shoda et al. 1994, 683. See also Mischel and Shoda 1995, 257; 1998, 242, 249; 2008, 216, 226; Mischel 1999b, 52; 2004, 14–15; 2007, 271; Cervone and Shoda 1999a, 20; Mischel et al. 2002, 53.

[48] In several places Mischel and company seem to do precisely this. For instance, in one place 'personality traits' and 'dispositions' are "defined by a characteristic cognitive-affective processing structure that underlies, and generates, distinctive processing dynamics. The processing structure of the disposition consists of a characteristic set of cognitions, affects, and behavioral strategies in an organization of interrelations that guides and constrains their activation" (Mischel and Shoda 1995, 257, emphasis removed). This appears to exactly mirror the reasoning in the text above, including even the causal language of 'generating.' See also Mischel 1999a, 456; and Roberts 2009, 140.

broad, situation-free traits. But nothing of the kind follows logically. One can accept the causal view and endorse only highly narrow or local traits.[49] Or one can accept the causal view and endorse my unconventional view of mixed traits.[50] Or, most important for my purposes here, one can accept the causal view and endorse everything else the CAPS model wants to say.

Hence I conclude that the CAPS model should be amended to accept the claim that traits of at least certain kinds do exist, are empirically adequate, have causal powers, and are grounded in enduring mental structures in our minds.

7.4 Final Thoughts on the CAPS Model

Of course there is more to the CAPS model than what I have highlighted above. The work by Mischel, Shoda, and Wright alone is extensive, and has also generated a vast literature.[51] However, in reviewing that literature I have not found any central claims of the view, such as the ones presented above, which are not already captured by our commonsense understanding of how the mind works. Hence I stand by my claim at the start of this chapter that *using technical language, the CAPS model redescribes and finds supporting evidence for basic platitudes of commonsense folk psychology.*

Suppose this claim is correct. What should we make of it? More precisely, is the close connection between the CAPS model and commonsense folk platitudes a significant strength or weakness of the model? I do not believe there is any straightforward answer to this question. But let me make an initial attempt at highlighting some of the costs and benefits as I see them.

On the positive side, the existing data that has been published as support for the CAPS model can thereby also provide significant empirical support for various strands of our commonsense outlook. Indeed in the contemporary philosophical literature on character traits, there have been a number of attempts to show that commonsense assumptions are

---

[49] For more on local traits, see Doris 2002. [50] See Miller 2013; 2014.
[51] See, e.g., the papers in Cervone and Shoda 1999b.

often unreliable.[52] The CAPS model can be used to marshal a response and provide welcome backing for certain commitments of our folk psychology.

Furthermore, I have not said anything to question the *truth* of the CAPS model. Indeed, barring the variety of different ways we just saw about how to understand the writings of Mischel and company on the nature of trait dispositions, I largely *agree* with the basic points the model is making. So the model is both useful for various argumentative purposes, and also quite plausible in its own right. What then could be said negatively about it?

To see, let me quote at length the remarks of the psychologist John Johnson in a 1999 commentary in the *European Journal of Personality*:

> One limitation of the CAPS model is its failure to advance our scientific understanding of personality dynamics beyond how we already understand human action from common sense. As far as I can tell, the labeling and re-labeling of desires, beliefs, and abilities has simply reflected the psychological jargon popular at that point in history ... I am surprised and somewhat depressed about the enthusiasm for the CAPS model, but not because the model is wrong. The problem is that settling for this model indicates that we are content to merely re-label common sense concepts with jargon, as opposed to developing a truly scientific model of personality dynamics.[53]

Johnson is focusing specifically on the component of the CAPS model having to do with cognitive-affective units. But I think his claims can be expanded to apply to the rest of the view.

The concern here has to do with the contribution of the view to discovering the best scientific theory of personality. There are a number of criteria that any scientific theory should satisfy, other things being equal, such as internal consistency, simplicity, and explanatory value. Here I want to highlight two in particular, and suggest that the CAPS model does not deliver much in these respects.

The criteria have been nicely articulated by the psychologist Jack Block: "They should demonstrate a superior usefulness in prediction or in economy of conceptualization over competing sets of constructs."[54]

---

[52] For relevant discussion, see Harman 1999; 2009; Doris and Stich 2005; and Webber 2007. I am grateful to the editors for helpful comments here.
[53] Johnson 1999, 449–50. For additional discussion, see Alston 1975, 29 n. 2 and Johnson 1999, 449.
[54] Block 1995, 188.

But I have already suggested throughout this chapter that the CAPS model does not appear to make any contribution in these respects. It does not seem to exhibit an "economy of conceptualization" over commonsense theorizing about action. Perhaps this would be a different story if, for example, talk of 'cognitive-affective units' provided a novel and parsimonious way of categorizing our mental life so that psychological research could progress in a more organized and fruitful manner. But as I suggested at the start of section 7.2, these labels really just correspond directly to commonsensical categories like 'desires' and 'instrumental beliefs.'

Similarly with respect to Block's second criteria, the CAPS model also does not appear to provide additional theoretical insight or explanatory resources beyond what careful reflection on our commonsense platitudes already suggests. I tried to show this throughout section 7.2. If that is right, though, it also follows that the model would not seem to be able to generate new predictions that would not have already been expected by careful reflection on the commonsense approach.[55]

In a particularly revealing passage, Mischel describes the CAPS model as follows: "CAPS was cast as a meta-theory of the person as an organized, coherent system, designed to facilitate and invite questions about how the specifics of its multiple constituent components and subsystems and processes interact and exert their influences."[56] This, I think, is exactly right. The model is better understood (in my opinion) as more of a background framework or 'meta-theory' with general principles from which to *start* developing an actual, detailed account of personality, and so, by application, of character traits. But it is not an actual theory of personality itself with categorizational, exploratory, or predictive advantages over commonsense theorizing.[57]

---

[55] In conversation (July 3, 2012), Mischel claimed that the CAPS model makes two predictions in particular that take us beyond commonsense: (i) it predicts that there will be stable average levels of different types of behavior, and (ii) it predicts that for a given person there will be stable if... then behavioral signatures. My earlier discussion in this chapter, on the contrary, is meant to suggest that these predictions fall out of the commonsense assumptions from section 7.1.

[56] Mischel 2004, 13. See also Mischel and Shoda 1995, 259; 2008, 213; Cervone 2005, 436; and Mischel 2007, 271; 2009, 186.

[57] For more on the distinction between meta-theories versus theories of personality, see Cervone 2005, 432, 436.

THE CAPS MODEL, PERSONALITY, AND CHARACTER 177

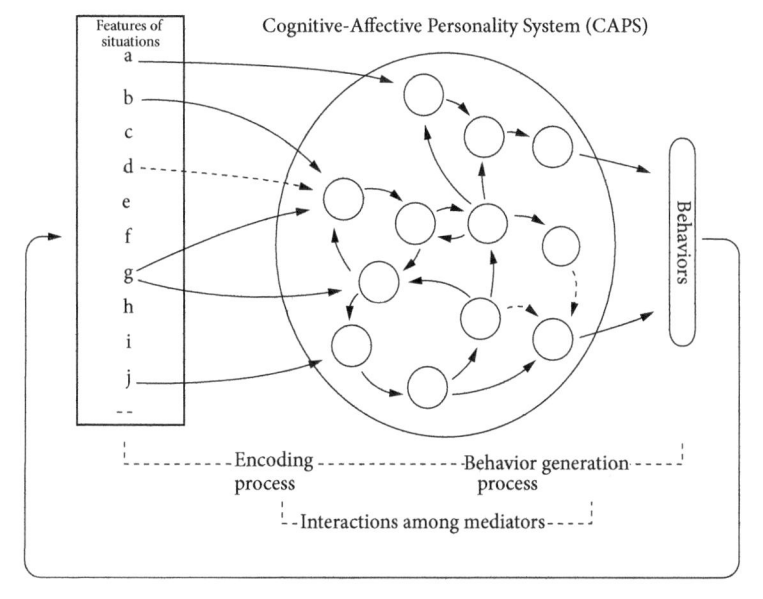

Figure 7.3. Reprint of **Mischel and Shoda** 1995, Figure Four.

To spell out a bit more the distinction between CAPS as a meta-theory versus an actual account of personality, Figure 7.3 reproduces the now famous Figure 4 from Mischel and Shoda's 1995 paper, which first presented the CAPS model in detail. As a depiction of the CAPS model understood as a meta-theory, it is important that the circles at the center of the figure are left empty. An actual CAPS-based account of personality for some particular domain, such as cheating, would build upon the meta-theory by proceeding to spell out what the cognitive-affective units *actually are* that causally mediate between the situational features that are construed as relevant to cheating and actual cheating behavior. Examples of such units could include a desire to cheat so long as there is no chance of getting caught, or a belief that cheating in all situations is morally wrong. Furthermore, such a CAPS-based account of cheating would have to be tailored to each person individually. Because each person's particular collection of cognitive-affect units (and their causal interrelations) will be idiosyncratic to that individual, great care must be taken using a CAPS approach to start with the messy details of a person's psychological life.

In a 2009 paper, Mischel discusses the same figure, and his remarks are worth quoting at some length:

> Before mailing the CAPS manuscript to *Psychological Review*, Shoda and Mischel intensely debated whether to fill or leave empty the many circles that interconnect and interact within CAPS (as shown in Figure 4 of Mischel & Shoda, 1995...)... The circles were left empty to make absolutely clear that CAPS was designed as a coherently organized meta-system with regard to contents. The hope was and remains that CAPS might become not the Mischel–Shoda model of personality but a general framework for building a more cumulative, integrative science of persons... The open circles are an invitation to other researchers to fill them as needed for their goals and substantive questions, regardless of the domain they were researching.[58]

It is the CAPS model understood as a meta-theory in just this sense that has been the focus of this chapter, and indeed of much of the published work in psychology on the CAPS model.

Interestingly, some recent work has begun to explore how researchers might go about filling in the "open circles." Here I briefly mention three examples:[59]

(i) The long quote above is taken from Mischel's contribution to a 2009 special issue of the *Journal of Personality* devoted to applying the CAPS model to racial/ethnic relations. Research in this issue explored, among other things, the cognitive-affective units associated with construing and encoding racial information, as well as the nature of the motivation to control prejudice.

(ii) In a very rich 2006 paper, Kristof Vansteelandt and Iven Van Mechelen focused on anger and sadness, and articulated a number of causal pathways between features of situations and cognitive-affective units on the one hand, and between cognitive-affective units and behaviors on the other. For instance, they varied whether a negative event affected a person weakly or strongly, whether someone else was involved in the event or not, whether the cause of the negative event was the other person, yourself, or no person, and whether the person who is the cause has or does not have control over the negative event. Among many other results, they found that seven different personality types emerged.

---

[58] Mischel et al. 2009, 1366. [59] Thanks to the editors for alerting me to these papers.

Members of all these types would report feeling anger and sadness in response to all the possible kinds of negative events; however, the personality types differed depending on the kinds of angry/sad responses displayed (such as bottling up anger versus showing it, or feeling sad versus feeling abandoned).[60]

(iii) In a recent paper, Shoda and his colleagues (2013) used the CAPS model to explore stress and coping processes in nonclinical participants, and ultimately to devise an individualized treatment approach. One interesting feature of this work was that they created signatures for each participant which measured their self-reported stress levels across twenty-four different potentially stressful features of situations. Each individual had a distinctive signature, as we would expect; for example, "Participant 9 was particularly vulnerable in situations characterized by feeling excluded and feeling inferior. On the other hand, relative to other features and relative to other participants, Participant 9 was comparatively unaffected by situations characterized by feeling exhausted."[61]

Having hopefully clarified the status of the CAPS model as a background framework or meta-theory, let me end by highlighting the two things that I believe need to happen next in order to allow researchers to fruitfully employ the model in better understanding each person's personality and specifically his or her character traits. First, psychologists need to do much more to discover what the cognitive-affective mental states *actually are* that form clusters in our minds that lead to a kind of consistent behavior across time and situations.[62] What, for instance, are the mental states that would plausibly explain why Child #28 exhibits a high degree of verbal aggression in the first situation, but not in the second one? As we have just seen, a few recent papers have begun to carry out this task, but clearly psychologists are only scratching the surface of what needs to be done.

Secondly, once psychologists get a good grip on at least some of these mental states and their causal relationships, then philosophers and other

---

[60] Vansteelandt and Van Mechelen 2006, 887.   [61] Shoda et al. 2013, 557.
[62] For relevant discussion, see Mischel and Shoda 1995, 259; Shoda et al. 1994, 685–6; and Cervone 2005, 436.

normative theorists working on character can come along and *evaluate* them. On moral grounds, for instance, are the clusters of mental states that most people have moral virtues or vices (or neither)? On prudential grounds having to do with our long term self-interest, are the clusters that most people have beneficial for them or not? And so forth for the various ways in which people can be normatively evaluated.

In my own research, I have tried to carry out both of these tasks in a preliminary manner. First, I have tried to fill in some of the details about what the clusters of interrelated mental state dispositions actually are for most people that pertain specially to the domains of helping, harming, lying, and cheating. And secondly, I have evaluated these mental state dispositions using a variety of different moral standards, and found them to qualify as neither the basis for any moral virtue nor the basis for any moral vice. These two steps constitute, in my opinion, the kinds of advances we need to move deeper than mere commonsense.[63]

Works Cited

Adams, Robert. 2006. *A Theory of Virtue: Excellence in Being for the Good.* Oxford: Clarendon Press.

Alston, William. 1975. Traits, Consistency and Conceptual Alternatives for Personality Theory. *Journal for the Theory of Social Behaviour* 5: 17–48.

Andersen, S. and J. Thorpe. 2009. An IF-THEN Theory of Personality: Significant Others and the Relational Self. *Journal of Research in Personality* 43: 163–70.

Badhwar, Neera. 2009. The Milgram Experiments, Learned Helplessness, and Character Traits. *The Journal of Ethics* 13: 257–89.

Bandura, A. 1978. The Self-System in Reciprocal Determinism. *American Psychologist* 33: 344–58.

Bandura, A. 1986. *Social Foundations of Thought and Action: A Social Cognitive Theory.* Englewood Cliffs: Prentice Hall.

---

[63] I am grateful to Alberto Masala and Jonathan Webber for inviting me to be a part of this volume, and for their very detailed and helpful comments, as well as those by an anonymous reviewer. Thanks as well to the audience at the Sorbonne conference on personality, especially Walter Mischel. This paper is derived from my 2014, ch. 5. Support for this work was funded in part by a grant from the John Templeton Foundation and by a grant from the Templeton World Charity Foundation. The opinions expressed in this paper are my own and do not necessarily reflect the views of the Templeton Foundations.

Bandura, A. 1999. Social Cognitive Theory of Personality. In *The Coherence of Personality: Social-Cognitive Bases of Consistency, Variability, and Organization*, ed. D. Cervone and Y. Shoda. New York: The Guilford Press, 185–241.

Block, J. 1977. Advancing the Psychology of Personality: Paradigmatic Shift or Improving the Quality of Research? In *Personality at the Crossroads: Current Issues in Interactional Psychology*, ed. David Magnusson and Norman Endler. Hillsdale: Lawrence Erlbaum, 37–63.

Block, J. 1995. A Contrarian View of the Five-Factor Approach to Personality Description. *Psychological Bulletin* 117: 187–215.

Brandt, Richard. 1970. Traits of Character: A Conceptual Analysis. *American Philosophical Quarterly* 7: 23–37.

Brandt, Richard. 1988. The Structure of Virtue. *Midwest Studies in Philosophy* 13: 64–82.

Buss, D. and K. Craik. 1983. The Act Frequency Approach to Personality. *Psychological Review* 90: 105–26.

Caprara, G. and D. Cervone. 2000. *Personality: Determinants, Dynamics, and Potentials*. Cambridge: Cambridge University Press.

Cervone, D. 1999. Bottom-Up Explanation in Personality Psychology: The Case of Cross-Situational Coherence. In *The Coherence of Personality: Social-Cognitive Bases of Consistency, Variability, and Organization*, ed. D. Cervone and Y. Shoda. New York: The Guilford Press, 303–41.

Cervone, D. 2005. Personality Architecture: Within-Person Structures and Processes. *Annual Review of Psychology* 56: 423–52.

Cervone, D. and Y. Shoda. 1999a. Social-Cognitive Theories and the Coherence of Personality. In *The Coherence of Personality: Social-Cognitive Bases of Consistency, Variability, and Organization*, ed. D. Cervone and Y. Shoda. New York: The Guilford Press, 3–33.

Cervone, D. and Y. Shoda. 1999b. *The Coherence of Personality: Social-Cognitive Bases of Consistency, Variability, and Organization*. New York: The Guilford Press.

Cervone, D., Shoda, Y., and Downey, G. 2007. Construing Persons in Context: On Building a Science of the Individual. In *Persons in Context: Building a Science of the Individual*, ed. Y. Shoda, D. Cervone, and G. Downey. New York: The Guilford Press, 3–15.

Doris, John. 1998. Persons, Situations, and Virtue Ethics. *Noûs* 32: 504–30.

Doris, John. 2002. *Lack of Character: Personality and Moral Behavior*. Cambridge: Cambridge University Press.

Doris, John. 2010. Heated Agreement: *Lack of Character* as Being for the Good. *Philosophical Studies* 148: 135–46.

Doris, John and Stephen Stich. 2005. As a Matter of Fact: Empirical Perspectives on Ethics. In *The Oxford Handbook of Contemporary Analytic Philosophy*, ed. F. Jackson and M. Smith. Oxford: Oxford University Press, 114–52.

Epstein, S. 1979. The Stability of Behavior: I. On Predicting Most of the People Much of the Time. *Journal of Personality and Social Psychology* 37: 1097–126.

Epstein, S. 1983. Aggregation and Beyond: Some Basic Issues on the Prediction of Behavior. *Journal of Personality* 51: 360–92.

Flanagan, Owen. 1991. *Varieties of Moral Personality*. Cambridge: Harvard University Press.

Fournier, M., D. Moskowitz, and D. Zuroff. 2009. The Interpersonal Signature. *Journal of Research in Personality* 43: 155–62.

Harman, Gilbert. 1999. Moral Philosophy Meets Social Psychology: Virtue Ethics and the Fundamental Attribution Error. *Proceedings of the Aristotelian Society* 99: 315–31.

Harman, Gilbert. 2000. The Nonexistence of Character Traits. *Proceedings of the Aristotelian Society* 100: 223–6.

Harman, Gilbert. 2009. Skepticism about Character Traits. *The Journal of Ethics* 13: 235–42.

Johnson, J. 1999. Persons in Situations: Distinguishing New Wine from Old Wine in New Bottles. *European Journal of Personality* 13: 443–53.

Kamtekar, Rachana. 2004. Situationism and Virtue Ethics on the Content of Our Character. *Ethics* 114: 458–91.

Lukes, Steven. 2009. Comment: Do People Have Character Traits. In *Philosophy of the Social Sciences: Philosophical Theory and Scientific Practice*, ed. C. Mantzavinos. Cambridge: Cambridge University Press, 291–8.

Mendoza-Denton, R., S. Park, and A. O'Connor. 2007. Toward a Science of the Social Perceiver. In *Persons in Context: Building a Science of the Individual*, ed. Y. Shoda, D. Cervone, and G. Downey. New York: The Guilford Press, 211–25.

Miller, Christian. 2013. *Moral Character: An Empirical Theory*. Oxford: Oxford University Press.

Miller, Christian. 2014. *Character and Moral Psychology*. Oxford: Oxford University Press.

Mischel, W. 1968. *Personality and Assessment*. New York: John J. Wiley and Sons.

Mischel, W. 1973. Toward a Cognitive Social Learning Reconceptualization of Personality. *Psychological Review* 80: 252–83.

Mischel, W. 1984. Convergences and Challenges in the Search for Consistency. *American Psychologist* 39: 351–64.

Mischel, W. 1999a. Implications of Person-Situation Interaction: Getting over the Field's Borderline Personality Disorder. *European Journal of Personality* 13: 455–61.

Mischel, W. 1999b. Personality Coherence and Dispositions in a Cognitive-Affective Personality System (CAPS) Approach. In *The Coherence of Personality: Social-Cognitive Bases of Consistency, Variability, and Organization*, ed. D. Cervone and Y. Shoda. New York: The Guilford Press, 37–60.

Mischel, W. 2004. Toward an Integrative Science of the Person. *Annual Review of Psychology* 55: 1–22.

Mischel, W. 2007. Toward a Science of the Individual: Past, Present, Future? In *Persons in Context: Building a Science of the Individual*, ed. Y. Shoda, D. Cervone, and G. Downey. New York: The Guilford Press, 263–77.

Mischel, W. 2009. From *Personality and Assessment* (1968) to Personality Science. *Journal of Research in Personality* 43: 282–90.

Mischel, W., R. Mendoza-Denton, and Y. Hong. 2009. Toward an Integrative CAPS Approach to Racial/Ethnic Relations. *Journal of Personality* 77: 1365–79.

Mischel, W. and H. Mischel. 1976. A Cognitive Social-Learning Approach to Morality and Self-Regulation. In *Moral Development and Behavior: Theory, Research, and Social Issues*, ed. T. Lickona. New York: Holt, Rinehart, and Winston, 84–107.

Mischel, W. and P. K. Peake. 1982. Beyond Déjà Vu in the Search for Cross-Situational Consistency. *Psychological Review* 89: 730–55.

Mischel, W. and Y. Shoda. 1995. A Cognitive-Affective System Theory of Personality: Reconceptualizing Situations, Dispositions, Dynamics, and Invariance in Personality Structure. *Psychological Review* 102: 246–68.

Mischel, W. and Y. Shoda. 1998. Reconciling Processing Dynamics and Personality Dispositions. *Annual Review of Psychology* 49: 229–58.

Mischel, W. and Y. Shoda. 2008. Toward a Unified Theory of Personality: Integrating Dispositions and Processing Dynamics within the Cognitive-Affective Processing System. In *Handbook of Personality: Theory and Research*, 3rd edn, ed. O. John, R. Robins, and L. Pervin. New York: The Guilford Press, 208–41.

Mischel, W., Y. Shoda, and R. Mendoza-Denton. 2002. Situation-Behavior Profiles as a Locus of Consistency in Personality. *Current Directions in Psychological Science* 11: 50–4.

Mumford, Stephen. 1998. *Dispositions*. Oxford: Oxford University Press.

Newman, L. and J. Uleman. 1989. Spontaneous Trait Inference. In *Unintended Thought*, ed. J. Uleman and J. Bargh. New York: The Guilford Press, 155–88.

Roberts, B. 2009. Back to the Future: *Personality and Assessment* and Personality Development. *Journal of Research in Personality* 43: 137–45.

Ross, L. and R. Nisbett. 1991. *The Person and the Situation: Perspectives of Social Psychology*. New York: McGraw-Hill.

Russell, Daniel. 2009. *Practical Intelligence and the Virtues*. Oxford: Clarendon Press.

Shoda, Y. 1999a. Behavioral Expressions of a Personality System: Generation and Perception of Behavioral Signatures. In *The Coherence of Personality: Social-Cognitive Bases of Consistency, Variability, and Organization*, ed. D. Cervone and Y. Shoda. New York: The Guilford Press, 155–81.

Shoda, Y. 1999b. A Unified Framework for the Study of Behavioral Consistency: Bridging Person x Situation Interaction and the Consistency Paradox. *European Journal of Personality* 13: 361–87.

Shoda, Y. and S. LeeTiernan. 2002. What Remains Invariant? Finding Order within a Person's Thoughts, Feelings, and Behaviors across Situations. In *Advances in Personality Science*, ed. D. Cervone and W. Mischel. New York: The Guilford Press, 241–70.

Shoda, Y. and W. Mischel. 1996. Toward a Unified, Intra-Individual Dynamic Conception of Personality. *Journal of Research in Personality* 30: 414–28.

Shoda, Y., W. Mischel, and J. Wright. 1993. The Role of Situational Demands and Cognitive Competencies in Behavior Organization and Personality Coherence. *Journal of Personality and Social Psychology* 65: 1023–35.

Shoda, Y., W. Mischel, and J. Wright. 1994. Intraindividual Stability in the Organization and Patterning of Behavior: Incorporating Psychological Situations into the Idiographic Analysis of Personality. *Journal of Personality and Social Psychology* 67: 674–87.

Shoda, Y., N. Wilson, J. Chen, A. Gilmore, and R. Smith. 2013. Cognitive-Affective Processing System Analysis of Intra-Individual Dynamics in Collaborative Therapeutic Assessment: Translating Basic Theory and Research into Clinical Applications. *Journal of Personality* 81: 554–68.

Smith, R., Y. Shoda, S. Cumming, and F. Smoll. 2009. Behavioral Signatures at the Ballpark: Intraindividual Consistency of Adults' Situation-Behavior Patterns and their Interpersonal Consequences. *Journal of Research in Personality* 43: 187–95.

Snow, Nancy. 2010. *Virtue as Social Intelligence: An Empirically Grounded Theory*. New York: Routledge Press.

Solomon, Robert. 2003. Victims of Circumstances? A Defense of Virtue Ethics in Business. *Business Ethics Quarterly* 13: 43–62.

Sosa, Ernest. 2009. Situations against Virtues: The Situationist Attack on Virtue Theory. In *Philosophy of the Social Sciences: Philosophical Theory and Scientific Practice*, ed. C. Mantzavinos. Cambridge: Cambridge University Press, 274–90.

Sreenivasan, Gopal. 2002. Errors about Errors: Virtue Theory and Trait Attribution. *Mind* 111: 47–68.

Upton, Candace. 2009. The Structure of Character. *The Journal of Ethics* 13: 175–93.

Vansteelandt, K. and I. Van Mechelen. 1998. Individual Differences in Situation-Behavior Profiles: A Triple Typology Model. *Journal of Personality and Social Psychology* 75: 751–65.

Vansteelandt, K. and I. Van Mechelen. 2006. Individual Differences in Anger and Sadness: In Pursuit of Active Situational Features and Psychological Processes. *Journal of Personality* 74: 871–909.

Webber, Jonathan. 2007. Character, Common-Sense, and Expertise. *Ethical Theory and Moral Practice* 10: 89–104.

Wiggins, J. 1997. In Defense of Traits. In *Handbook of Personality Psychology*, ed. R. Hogan, J. Johnson, and S. Briggs. San Diego: Academic Press, 95–115. Originally presented in 1973.

Wright, J. and W. Mischel. 1987. A Conditional Approach to Dispositional Constructs: The Local Predictability of Social Behavior. *Journal of Personality and Social Psychology* 53: 1159–77.

Zayas, V. and Y. Shoda. 2009. Three Decades after the Personality Paradox: Understanding Situations. *Journal of Research in Personality* 43: 280–1.

Zuroff, D. 1986. Was Gordon Allport a Trait Theorist? *Journal of Personality and Social Psychology* 51: 993–1000.

8

Friendship and the Structure of Trust

Mark Alfano

8.1 Introduction

Friendship might seem like a bizarre virtue—or not a virtue at all. In Aristotle's early discussion of the virtues in the *Nicomachean Ethics*, we see courage, temperance, generosity, magnificence, magnanimity, pride, wit, and justice. These would all seem to be, in the first instance and primarily, monadic properties of individual agents. To be courageous is to be disposed to think, feel, desire, deliberate, act, and react in characteristic ways. Even if no one else is courageous, it would still be possible—though extremely difficult—for you to be courageous. Of course, if there are no threats to be opposed, you may never have a chance to manifest or express your courage. Furthermore, it would surely be easier to develop courage in the company of others who either are or strive to be courageous. And it may also be easier to develop or sustain courage when others think of you as courageous and signal those thoughts to you. But, one might think, even if none of these enabling facts obtains, it would still be possible, conceptually speaking, to be courageous.

Or consider generosity. To be generous is to be disposed to think, feel, desire, deliberate, act, and react in characteristic ways. Even if no one else is generous, it would still be possible—though extremely difficult—for you to be generous. Of course, if there were no other people who needed or wanted or would appreciate what you have, or if you were so down on your luck that you had no resources to offer, you may never have a chance to manifest or express your generosity. Furthermore, it would surely be easier to develop generosity in the company of others who are or strive to be generous (and, for that matter, grateful). And it may also be easier to develop or sustain generosity when others think of you as generous and signal those thoughts to you. But, one might think, even if none of these enabling facts obtains, it would still be possible, conceptually speaking, to be generous.

Friendship appears to be different. It seems to be, in the first instance and primarily, a dyadic relation between two people. To be a friend is to be disposed to think, feel, desire, deliberate, act, and react in characteristic ways towards a particular person, who is likewise disposed to think, feel, desire, deliberate, act, and react in those same characteristic ways towards you. If no one else is a friend, then it is conceptually impossible—not just difficult—for you to be a friend as well (*NE* VIII:2, 1155a; see Cooper 1977b, 624 and Nehamas 2010, 216). It is not just *easier* to develop friendship in the company of others who are doing so as well; it is in fact impossible to become a friend without there being someone else who also becomes a friend, namely *your* friend.

In this paper, I describe some of what I take to be the more interesting features of friendship, then explore the extent to which other virtues can be reconstructed as sharing those features. I use trustworthiness as my example throughout, but I think that other virtues such as generosity and gratitude, pride and respect, and the producer's and consumer's sense of humor can also be analyzed with this model. The aim of the paper is not to demonstrate that all moral virtues are exactly like friendship in all important respects, but rather to articulate a fruitful model in which to explore the virtues. Section 8.2 explores the relational nature of friendship, drawing on Aristotle's discussion of friendship in the *Nicomachean Ethics*. Section 8.3 catalogues four motivations for taking seriously the friendship model of virtue. Section 8.4 applies the friendship model in depth to the virtue of trustworthiness.

8.2 The Relational Nature of Friendship

Being a friend isn't just a matter of your first-order cognitive, affective, evaluative, and behavioral dispositions; to be a friend means, among other things, to have particular *de re* attitudes towards another person (your friend), and for that person to have congruent *de re* attitudes towards you (*NE* VIII:2, 1156a). That is, for you to be my friend, you need to think of me as your friend, to wish me well for my own sake, to wish me well in virtue of my good character (or, in other types of friendship, in virtue of my contributing to your utility or pleasure), and so on. Likewise, I need to think of you as my friend, to wish you well for your own sake, to wish you well in virtue of your good character (or in virtue of your contributing to my utility or pleasure), and so on.

But that is not enough. Not only must both you and I have these attitudes, but the existence of these attitudes must be mutual knowledge between us (*NE* IX:5, 1166b). If I wish you well for your own sake and in virtue of your good character, and you wish me well for my own sake and in virtue of my good character, but neither of us knows how the other feels, we are not friends. Instead, we merely harbor mutual but unrecognized good will towards one another. To be your friend, I need to know that you wish me well for my own sake and in virtue of my good character, and you need to know that I wish you well for your own sake and in virtue of your good character (*NE* VIII:3, 1156b).

In fact, even that is not enough. We could satisfy this description and yet still not be friends. If we have these attitudes towards each other, and each finds out through reliable testimony that the other does as well, it would still seem strange to say that we are friends. We might never have met each other, yet satisfy these conditions. Friends have a more intimate connection than this. I also need to know that you know that I wish you well for your own sake and in virtue of your good character, and you need to know that I know that you wish me well for my own sake and in virtue of my good character.

It's arguable that even this is not enough, and that what needs to hold is that we share common knowledge of our attitudes: I know that you wish me well for my own sake and in virtue of my good character; and you know that I know that you wish me well for my own sake and in virtue of my good character; and you know that I know that you know that I know that you wish me well for my own sake and in virtue of my good character, and so on. Or, somewhat less strongly, perhaps what's required is that there be what Lewis (2002, 56) calls a *basis for common knowledge* between us, even if only two levels of mutual knowledge are actually present. I will not press this point here, for even if all that's required is two orders of mutual knowledge (I know that you know, and you know that I know), my point still holds that friendship is an interesting virtue because it requires reciprocated *de re* attitudes and some kind of mutual recognition of the existence of this reciprocation.

Finally, friends typically harbor other, more complicated, attitudes towards one another, and react with higher-order attitudes to the presence or absence of lower-order attitudes. Roberts (2013) argues that *de re* emotional interactions are constitutive of friendship (p. 141); he explores the ways in which emotions and emotional feedback loops strengthen and desiccate such relationships as friendship, enmity, civility, and incivility. For example, consider a sister who generously and in a spirit of friendship gives her brother her own ticket to a concert that he would like to attend. He feels the emotion of gratitude for this gift, which he expresses with a token of thanks. Satisfied that her generosity has hit its mark, she is "gratified by his gratitude... And he may in turn be gratified that she is gratified by his gratitude" (p. 137). Despite the fact that this is a tiny schematic example, it plausibly contains a fourth-order emotion (he is gratified that she is gratified that he is gratified that she was generous). Such episodes are, in Roberts's view, constitutive of friendship and other normative personal relationships (pp. 140–1). Constructive feedback loops strengthen positive personal relationships but aggravate negative relationships such as enmity (leading enemies to hate, despise, or contemn each other all the more); destructive feedback loops, by contrast, undermine positive relationships (introducing distrust, contempt, or other negative emotions into extant friendships) but ameliorate negative relationships (introducing sympathy, respect, or even admiration into extant enmities).

In sum, being a friend is not just causally but constitutively dependent on there being another person who has the same virtue. It is, second, not just causally but constitutively dependent on there being another person towards whom you harbor certain *de re* attitudes, and who reciprocates them. Third, it is not just causally but constitutively dependent on your thinking of yourself as someone's friend. Fourth, it is also not just causally but constitutively dependent on there being between you and your friend at least two orders of mutual knowledge of these attitudes. Fifth, it is not just causally but constitutively dependent on you and your friend having first-, second-, and perhaps even third- and fourth-order emotions that include the other person in their content. Finally, it is not just causally but constitutively dependent on you and your friend sometimes knowing (and perhaps knowing that you know) that you are engaging in joint planning.

One might worry that these arguments press too hard on the relational aspects of friendship. Surely, one might think, I can be a friendly person even if everyone else is an asshole and either snubs or betrays my attempts at friendship. There is an important sense in which, even in such an unlucky social environment, I can still be a friendly person. This is a fair point, and one which should lead us to distinguish between the disposition or trait of friendliness or agreeableness or gregariousness, which is arguably a monadic property of an individual, and the virtue of friendship, which clearly is not. One test that seems to do a good job of drawing this distinction is to ask whether the person in question is *friendly* or *a friend*. There is a double dissociation between these. Someone might be friendly but still not have any friends. Conversely, it's possible for someone to be dispositionally grumpy or unagreeable but nevertheless to be a friend, provided one's grumpiness or unagreeableness doesn't become so pronounced that it turns into outright misanthropy and make one unsuitable to be anyone's friend. A modicum of grouchiness can even be charming.[1]

8.3 Motivating the Friendship Model

In this paper, I explore the prospects for using the features of friendship identified above as a model for trust. This exploration is motivated on four independent grounds, which I discuss below.

8.3.1 The historical motive

Of the ten books of the *Nicomachean Ethics*, fully two are devoted to discussing friendship.[2] This is twice as much attention as justice receives, and as much as all of the other moral virtues combined. Yet contemporary neo-Aristotelian treatments of virtue rarely address friendship, and give it short shrift when they do. Annas (1993, 249–60) devotes twelve of the five hundred plus pages of her book to friendship, and mentions it

---

[1] For an example, consider the case of a husband whose wife goes on anti-depressants to help her cope with her mother's recent death. The anti-depressants work too well, and she flips from being amusingly sarcastic to overbearingly cheerful. It can happen! (<http://www.slate.com/articles/life/dear_prudence/2013/04/dear_prudence_my_wife_s_personality_has_changed_since_going_on_paxil.html>).

[2] I should note that, though I draw here on what I take to be Aristotle's conception of friendship, I am not offering an interpretation of Aristotle.

only twice in her book (2011, 76, 151). Geach (1977, 80) mentions it once. Hurka (2001, 35-6, 200) mentions it in only a couple of passages. Hursthouse (1999, 11) calls friendship an "awkward exception" because it is relational. MacIntyre (1981, 123, 156-8) mentions friendship only twice. Russell (2009) barely engages friendship in his massive tome. Slote (2001) only mentions friendship in the context of broader discussions of love, community, and achievement. Snow (2008), despite the fact that her book is titled *Virtue as Social Intelligence*, never once uses the word 'friendship.' Adams (2006, 25-7, 69-92) and Roberts (2013, ch. 7) are the exceptions that make the rule.

The main topic of discussion in the contemporary literature on friendship is the extent to which various moral theories induce 'moral schizophrenia' by calling on us to be motivated by abstract principles—such as maximizing good outcomes or acting from duty—that seem incompatible with the warmth and intimacy of friendship (Stocker 1976). While this is an interesting issue, it is only tangentially related to the central questions of friendship: *What does it mean to be a friend? Is friendship a virtue? How is friendship related to trust, hope, and other attitudes? How is friendship related to more commonly discussed virtues, such as trustworthiness, generosity, and pride?* It would be surprising if this bias in the scholarship did not distort our understanding of virtue.

8.3.2 *The moral psychological motive*

If there is a consensus in moral psychology, it's that virtue-concepts are 'thick,' in the sense that they refer to properties that are at once descriptive (and explanatory) and evaluative. To call someone a liar is to make an assertion about what sorts of behavior that person tends to engage in, but also to evaluate his behavior or behavioral tendencies by a normative standard. To think of someone as temperate is to attribute some behaviors or behavioral tendencies to her, but also to evaluate her behavior or behavioral tendencies by a normative standard. If you find out that someone about whom you have an otherwise good opinion tends to lie, you will feel considerable pressure to revise your good opinion or to find some excuses for his lying. If you find out that someone you would otherwise consider temperate has repeatedly ended up vomiting wine into a gutter, you will feel considerable pressure to revise your good opinion or to find some excuse for her excesses.

Friendships seem to have the same thick character as virtues. If you are my friend, I (and, for that matter, third parties) can form well-founded descriptive expectations about how you will behave, what you will think and feel, and how you will deliberate. If I am your friend, you (and, for that matter, third parties) can explain some of my behaviors, thoughts, feelings, and deliberative processes. In addition, if you are my friend, I (and third parties) will tend to engage in characteristic evaluations. For instance, I will tend to give you the benefit of the evaluative doubt, and will—when I cannot find a way to do so—feel some pressure either to cut off our friendship or at least to scale it back. Moreover, realizing that you have inadvertently befriended a despicable person naturally engenders self-doubt: what sort of person am I, that I could befriend someone like this? What sort of person do I appear to be, that someone like this would want me for a friend? Additionally, those who think of you as a good person will, when they find that I am your friend, tend to form positive evaluations of me (if I am a stranger to them), or either positively revise their opinion of me (if they think well enough of you) or negatively revise their opinion of you (if they think ill enough of me).

In addition, it's generally recognized that virtues are threshold concepts: you can be honest enough to count as an honest person even if you've lied or cheated or stolen once in your life. You can be generous enough to count as a generous person even if in many (probably even most) cases in which you've had the opportunity to give something to someone who would enjoy or appreciate it, you did nothing. Honesty and generosity come in degrees. To count as honest or generous full stop, one needn't be at the furthest end of the spectrum: one simply needs to embody *enough* of the trait in question. Friendship also has this characteristic. I can be your friend even if we're not BFFs. Friendship comes in degrees. I can be better friends with X than with Y even though I'm friends with both X and Y. If, however, the quality of my relationship with X suffers too much, we cease to be friends at all. Where exactly to draw these lines is tricky business that I won't try to spell out in detail in this paper, but then, where exactly to draw the line between generosity and non-generosity is probably just as difficult.

Friendships thus seem to share with virtues both evaluative thickness and threshold instantiation properties; this is evidence that they belong in the same category. Exploring the features of one may illuminate the features of the other.

8.3.3 The empirical motive

As I have argued elsewhere (Alfano 2013, 2014), there are empirical grounds for doubting whether virtue as conceived in currently dominant neo-Aristotelian theories is an achievable ideal. John Doris (1998, 2002), Gilbert Harman (1999), and I (2013) have argued that most people's conduct does not seem to be structured by robust, global dispositions such as honesty—at least when they are tested in a decontextualized laboratory setting. Seemingly trivial and normatively irrelevant situational influences, such as mood modulators and ambient sensory stimuli, predict and explain people's cognitive, affective, evaluative, and behavioral responses as well as—and sometimes better than—personality variables. This is not the place to delve deeply into the dialectic between philosophical situationists and defenders of neo-Aristotelian ethics. Instead, I merely want to point out that there is suggestive empirical evidence—much of which I canvass in my (2013) book—for the phenomenon of *factitious* virtue. A factitious virtue simulates its neo-Aristotelian counterpart through the stabilizing influences of self-concept and social expectation-signaling. Someone may not be disposed to think, feel, and act as a generous person would think, feel, and act *except insofar* as she both thinks of herself as generous (self-concept) and knows both that others think of her as generous and that they know that she knows that they think of her as generous (social expectation-signaling). When this happens, she does not have the trait of generosity construed in neo-Aristotelian terms, but she does have factitious generosity.

Factitious generosity thus mirrors several of the more striking structural features of friendship. You cannot be my friend unless I think of you as a friend, and you know that I do, and I know that you know that I do. You cannot be factitiously generous unless I think of you as generous, and you know that I do, and I know that you know that I do. You cannot be a friend if you don't think of yourself as a friend. You can't be factitiously generous if you don't think of yourself as generous.[3] Thus, in addition to the historical and moral psychological

---

[3] Several other contributions to this volume, including those from Jacobs, Sifferd, Holroyd and Kelly, Webber, Athanassoulis, and Masala, agree that character may be *causally* dependent on externalia. The novel contribution of this chapter is to argue that it may be *constitutively* dependent.

motives for taking friendship seriously as a model for the virtues, we also have an empirical motive for exploring such a model. It may be possible to satisfy all of these motives by reconstructing other moral virtues on the model of friendship—as essentially and constitutively social.[4]

8.3.4 *The externalist motive*

The final motive for exploring the friendship model of virtue is the compelling evidence that has begun to pile up for the idea that many seemingly individual psychological phenomena are better understood as extending beyond the limits of the skin of the person to whom those phenomena are ordinarily attributed. In the 1970s, Kripke (1972) and Putnam (1975) popularized the idea that mental content is external, that the meaning and reference of some words is not determined solely by what's in the heads of people who use those words. In the 1980s, Nozick (1981) and Dretske (1981) introduced the notion that one's justification for a given belief might not be determined solely by what's in one's head. In the 1990s, Clark and Chalmers (1998) suggested that the mind itself might extend beyond the limits of the skin. According to their *parity principle*, if "a part of the world functions as a process which, were it to go on in the head, we would have no hesitation in accepting as part of the cognitive process, then that part of the world is (for that time) part of the cognitive process." Importantly, they think that external phenomena can only be recruited in this way if they are reliably available, typically invoked, automatically endorsed, and easily accessible. I would suggest that these conditions should be relaxed slightly, such that the external phenomena be *at least as reliable* as the relevant internal phenomena, *at least as likely and quickly* to be endorsed, and *as easily accessible*. In a similar spirit, Adams (2006, 138–43) argues that affiliations, such as being a Christian or a communist, and social roles, such as being a (good) father or a (good) teacher, may be plausibly counted as moral virtues. Sneddon (2011) argues that processes of moral reasoning, responsibility attribution, moral judgment, and even action production

---

[4] All? Perhaps not humility and modesty, which seem to involve a paradox of self-reference insofar as it's hard, though maybe not impossible, to be humble and modest if you also think of yourself as humble and modest. See Roberts and Wood (2007, ch. 9) for a discussion of this problem. I explore the possibility of such a paradox of self-reference with some of my colleagues in Alfano et al. (forthcoming).

are sometimes not just extended but *shared* by pairs or even larger groups of agents. Pritchard (2010) argues that cognitive abilities—which we might think of as intellectual virtues or parts thereof—may extend. Likewise, I have argued (Alfano forthcoming a) that the phenomenon of stereotype threat is evidence that cognitive processes extend.

The current proposal is that we should explore the extent to which this research program can be applied to virtue ethics, that is, the extent to which it makes sense to say that some or even all psychological dispositions that we might reasonably call moral virtues also extend beyond the limits of the skin of their possessors. The friendship model is a promising framework for doing so. At least when we are at our best, we try to live up to our friends' expectations; we are attuned to their reactive attitudes; we consider prospectively whether they would approve or disapprove of some course of action; we consult with them explicitly, implicitly, and imaginatively; and we revise our beliefs and values in light of their feedback. Friendship thus seems to involve the sort of functional integration that qualifies as an instance of extended character. Millgram (1987, 368; see also Cocking and Kennett 1998, 504) argues that, over the course of a friendship, each friend becomes causally, if not constitutively, responsible for the other's being who she is. Morton (2013) argues, in the same vein, that sometimes our behavioral dispositions are best governed by imagining the emotional reactions of those we love and respect to our thoughts, feelings, and plans.

Thus, we have four independent motivations—historical, moral psychological, empirical, and externalist—for exploring the friendship model of virtue. None of these is decisive, of course, nor is their conjunction. Nevertheless, I think that, together, they provide compelling reasons to give the model a chance. In the balance of this paper, that's what I do.

8.4 Trustworthiness on the Friendship Model

To begin fleshing out the friendship model, I want to concentrate on the virtue I take to be most amenable to assimilation: trustworthiness. Many philosophers have noticed that friendship often involves trust. Nehamas (2010, 238), for instance, points out that "friendship is immune, or at least resistant, to slander: we know our friends well and it takes much to undermine our faith in their goodness; [friends] trust one another."

Likewise, Thomas (1987, 217) claims that one of the three most salient features of friendship is that "there is an enormous bond of mutual trust between" friends. Trustworthiness is a good prospect for assimilation to the friendship model of virtue.

Trustworthiness, as I describe it in this section, has many of the interesting structural features of friendship. It is not just causally but constitutively dependent on there being another person who has a congruent virtue (trustingness). Second, it is not just causally but constitutively dependent on there being another person towards whom you harbor certain *de re* attitudes, and who reciprocates with their counterparts. Third, it is not just causally but constitutively dependent on your thinking of yourself as trustworthy. Fourth, it is also not just causally but constitutively dependent on there being between you and your trustor at least two orders of mutual knowledge of these attitudes. Finally, trustors and trustees are connected by characteristic first-, second-, and even third- and fourth-order emotions, such as the emotion of trust itself, as well as assurance, betrayal, outrage, repentance, forgiveness, and others.

8.4.1 The cunning mechanism

Consider the example, due to Pettit (1995), of a driver in an unfamiliar city who relies on a local bus driver to guide him to the city center. He notices that the bus displays a sign saying 'Downtown,' and so feels comfortable following the bus. However, since he realizes that the bus driver may find his consistently stopping when the bus stops disturbing, he pulls up beside the bus at some point to explain what he's doing. At this point, he isn't just passively relying on the bus driver. The bus driver now *knows* that he is being relied on, and the car driver knows that the bus driver knows this. Having put his trust explicitly in the bus driver, there exist at least two orders of mutual knowledge of this reliance between them. As Pettit (p. 205) puts it:

> The driver knows that I am relying on him and knows that I am aware that he knows that. Perhaps the reliance even becomes a matter of common knowledge, with each of us being aware of the reliance, each being aware of this awareness, each being aware of that higher-order awareness, and so on.

Just as, when we are friends, I wish you well, and you know it, and I know that you know it, so in such a case of interactive trust, I rely on you, and you know it, and I know that you know it.

There is a further point of analogy. When we are friends, I expect our relationship to count as a reason for action for you. Perhaps you wish me well for my own sake and in virtue of my good character, but our being friends provides you an additional reason to wish me well. Just so in the case of trustworthiness:

> I may expect that the driver will be positively moved by seeing that I have made myself vulnerable and will be motivated all the more strongly to do that which I am relying on them to do: will be motivated all the more strongly to prove reliable. (Pettit 1995, 206)

I take it that it is intuitively compelling that the bus driver would or at least might be thus motivated, but why? Why exactly would the bus driver sense an additional normative reason to prove reliable just because he is being explicitly trusted? Pettit's answer (pp. 214–15) to this question is that one of the more important rewards in moral psychology is esteem. People want money, power, sex, and stuff. They also want to be well regarded—perhaps only instrumentally, but perhaps also intrinsically. When the car driver explicitly puts his trust in the bus driver, he manifests a form of a positive regard. This is, in itself, a reward to the bus driver, assuming that he cares about how he's perceived. And, since people are usually loss-averse (Tversky and Kahneman 1991), any value the bus driver attaches to the car driver's newly acquired esteem will tend to be over-valued; he will attach more negative value to losing this esteem than he attached positive value to gaining it in the first place. Although Pettit does not make this further point about loss-aversion, it fits nicely with his view.

Finally, interactive trust of this kind essentially involves certain emotional dispositions, including higher-order emotional dispositions. At the first-order level, I will feel gratitude towards the bus driver for agreeing to lead me to the city center. He may feel anxiety on my behalf or pride that I chose to trust him rather than someone else. Should he prove reliable, I will experience another episode of gratitude, which may induce gratitude in him as well. Should he prove unreliable, I may experience anger. Should he deliberately lead me astray, I will probably experience betrayal. In response to the former, he may experience guilt; to the latter, malicious glee (if he endorses his betrayal) or surprise (if he didn't realize that I might react thusly).

8.4.2 The self-concept mechanism

Along the same lines, we might point out that people also typically find self-esteem instrumentally and even intrinsically rewarding. When I signal that I think of you as trustworthy by explicitly putting my trust in you, I prompt you to revise your self-concept, to accept that you merit this trust. To the extent that you feel that you do, you will find your newly revised self-concept rewarding. And, just as loss-aversion makes it more painful to lose others' high regard than it is pleasurable to gain it, so loss-aversion also makes it more painful to give up your own high self-regard than it is pleasurable to gain it. Hence, to the extent that you find it difficult to engage in the self-deceptive psychological acrobatics needed simultaneously to maintain your own self-esteem and to betray my trust, you will be motivated to prove trustworthy.

In addition, self-concept helps to set defaults for behavior, thought, and feeling. To the extent that I think of myself as honorable, I will be more inclined to try to avenge perceived offenses, think of others' actions as impinging positively or negatively on my honor, and feel offended or honored by others' actions and inactions. My self-concept thus constrains what I am inclined to notice, deliberate about, believe, feel, and do. Just as someone who thinks of herself as X's friend will perceive, think, feel, and act in different ways from someone who does not think of herself as X's friend, so someone who thinks of himself as patient will perceive, think, feel, and act in different ways from someone who does not think of himself as patient. Consider, for example, the following lyrics from Fountains of Wayne's song, 'Michael and Heather':

> Michael and Heather on the shuttle bus
> Standing alongside the rest of us
> Michael says, "Heather, have you had enough?"
> Heather says, "Michael, you know that it's you I love."

Does Michael think of himself as Heather's lover? If he does, he'll probably construe her as answering the questions, "Have you had enough of this airport nonsense?" and responding somewhat playfully, "None of this nonsense really matters." But if he thinks of himself as merely pursuing Heather, it's likely that he'll notice a darker reading of her response. Perhaps she's not thinking about whether she's had enough of *waiting at the airport* but of *their relationship*. Perhaps she's actively considering whether to break up with him, and is treating his question as an invitation to initiate the breakup. What we think of ourselves partially determines what even occurs to us as a possibility—a possible action, a possible interpretation, and so on. By influencing each other's self-concepts, then, we indirectly influence each other's conduct.

8.4.3 The hopeful mechanism

There are still further reasons to think that trustworthiness and trustingness can be assimilated to the friendship model. For, as McGeer points out, Pettit's explanation of how trust can be self-reinforcing is not the only possible rationalization of the relevant phenomena. As she explains, the mechanism Pettit identifies is unstable because it arguably would not survive its own elevation to mutual or common knowledge:

> trustees cannot know or suspect that they are only being trusted because the trustor is relying on the likelihood of their having a desire for good opinion; for then trustees will know or suspect that trustors do not really hold them in high regard (as actually possessing trust-attracting virtues), but only imagine them to be manipulable because they possess the less admirable trait of seeking others' good opinions. Hence, trustees will lose the incentive provided by a trustor's trust to act in a trust-responsive way. (2008, 252)

If the only reason I have to trust you is that I think that by putting my trust in you I can induce you to desire the continuance of my (signal of) high regard and the continuance of your own new-found high self-regard, then, were you to discover this reason, you might lose the very motive I aimed to induce. If you realize that my show of trust wasn't motivated by high regard but by an assumption about your desire for high regard, you may cease to value my show of trust. This does not mean that the mechanism Pettit identifies is never active, but it does suggest that there may be other, more stable mechanisms that produce similar results.

One is the mechanism of self-esteem and loss-aversion, which I sketched earlier. To my knowledge, it has not been identified previously. Even if you were to discover that my expression of trust was an attempt at manipulation, if you had at that point already revised your self-concept, you would still presumably find it more aversive to go back to your old self-concept than you found it rewarding to revise in the first place.

Another mechanism, identified by McGeer, involves the attitude of hope. For her, hope essentially involves trusting beyond what the available evidence supports.[5] McGeer reminds her readers that human motivation is often complicated and confusing. Sometimes we don't know what we really desire, like, or love. Sometimes, we forget what we really value. In those cases, it's often helpful to refer to a normative lodestone, a model of conduct. She goes on:

> For help in this regard, we are sometimes encouraged to look outside ourselves for role models, finding in others' thoughts and actions laudable patterns on which to fashion our own. And this may serve us pretty well. However, something similar can occur, often more effectively, through the dynamic of hopeful scaffolding. Here we look outside ourselves once again; but instead of looking for laudable patterns in others' behaviour, what we find instead are laudable patterns that others see—or prospectively see—in our own. We see ourselves as we might be, and thereby become something like a role model for ourselves. The advantage in this is clear: Instead of thinking, 'I want to be like her,'—i.e., like someone else altogether—the galvanizing thought that drives us forward is seemingly more immediate and reachable: 'I want to be as she already sees me to be.' (2008, 248–9)

This seems like a plausible explanation of at least some trustworthiness induced by acts of trust. It also fits nicely with existing discussions of friendship, according to which friendship is an especially salubrious context for acquiring self-knowledge. This illuminates the Aristotelian dictum that a friend is another self (see also Cooper 1977a, 300). It can sometimes be easier to know and understand oneself through the reflective mirror of what a friend sees in you than through introspection. And, if the extended character thesis is on the right track, there might be no fact of the matter concerning what your character is like until it is reflected back to you in the eyes of another person. Your trustworthiness might essentially involve your knowing that another person trusts you, or even that another person trusts you in a spirit of hope. The friendship model seems to satisfy all of the criteria that Clark and Chalmers (1998) identify as necessary for extended cognition: reliability, typicality, endorsement, and accessibility. Cues of trust tend to be reliably available—certainly as reliably available as other incitements to trustworthiness. Whether someone trusts someone else is typically invoked in predicting, explaining, and evaluating behavior. When someone with

---

[5] Hope thus clashes, prima facie, with epistemic rationality. Stroud (2006) likewise argues that friendship clashes, prima facie, with epistemic rationality—another point of analogy.

whom I have an ongoing relationship of trust expects me to do something, feel a certain way, or think something, I generally endorse this expectation automatically. Finally, the expectations and sentiments of my trustors tend to be easily accessible to me. I generally know what they want me to do.

Between McGeer's hope-based mechanism and my own self-concept-based mechanism, we may account for much of the factitious trustworthiness that Pettit's model doesn't cover. Trustworthiness and trustingness might then be said to constitute an interrelated and non-reducible dyad in much the same way that your being my friend and my being your friend constitute an interrelated and non-reducible dyad. Your being trustworthy would depend not just causally but constitutively (if only in part) on my trustingness, and my trustingness would depend not just causally but constitutively (if only in part) on your trustworthiness. Your trustworthiness would depend not just causally but constitutively on my harboring certain *de re* attitudes (of reliance, trust, and hope) towards you, and on your reciprocating with their counterparts (reliability, assurance, etc.). Your trustworthiness would depend not just causally but constitutively on your thinking of yourself as trustworthy (and hence, through loss-aversion, being unwilling to betray my trust). Your trustworthiness would depend not just causally but constitutively on there being between us at least two orders of mutual knowledge of these attitudes. Finally, your and my sentiments in a trusting relationship tend to be highly attuned, to the point that they will easily generate characteristic first-, second-, and even third- and fourth-order emotions in appropriate conditions.

8.5 Conclusion

In this section, I briefly summarize the argument thus far, then offer a few remarks about my naturalistic methodology.

8.5.1 Summary of the argument thus far

I've now argued both that we have reasons to take the friendship model seriously and that there are understandable naturalistic mechanisms through which it could work. If the considerations explored in section 8.2 are on the right track, then we have four main reasons to explore the friendship model. First, doing so reconnects virtue theory with its historical roots. Second, doing so helps explain why friendship, like other virtues, is a thick concept. Third, doing so may help to overcome or sidestep the situationist challenge. Finally, doing so may help to establish useful connections with externalist discussions in philosophy of mind. Naturally, all of these connections may also work in the other direction, helping virtue theorists export their insights and arguments to ancient philosophy, moral psychology, empirically informed ethics, and externalist philosophy of mind.

Furthermore, if the explanations explored in section 8.4 are on the right track, there are at least three mechanisms that, together, help explain how trustworthiness and trustingness are interdependent as the friendship model suggests. When the cunning mechanism is activated, one person's trustworthiness depends on another person's trustingness because the trustworthy person is motivated to prove himself worthy of the trust and esteem that have been directed his way. In this case, he wants to prove to the person who trusted him that he was and is worthy.[6] When the self-concept mechanism is activated, once again, one person's trustworthiness depends on another person's trustingness because the trustworthy person is motivated to prove himself worthy of the trust and esteem that have been directed his way. In this instance, though, he wants to prove *to himself* that he is worthy, in order to hold onto his positive self-concept.[7] Either way, esteem drives him forward. When the hopeful mechanism is activated, one person's trustworthiness depends on another person's trustingness because that trustingness gives him self-knowledge, opens up some actions as genuine possibilities, forecloses other actions as beyond the pale, and instills him with vicarious confidence. These are exactly the sorts of mechanisms that characterize friendship and that make it a paramount moral good.

8.5.2 *Methodological remark*

In this paper, I've described a model of trusting relationships. Is this model descriptive or normative? Does it characterize how trust *actually*, *typically* (or at least often) works, or does it characterize how trust *ought* to work? This question is prompted by the more general concern whether, in philosophical psychology, we should aim to elaborate

---

[6] For more on this, see Wong (2006), especially ch. 4.
[7] For more on this, see Appiah (2011).

descriptive or normative models. It might seem that I've given up on normativity altogether. One might be tempted to object, with Browning's Andrea del Sarto, that "a man's reach should exceed his grasp, / Or what's a heaven for?"

In response, I want to argue that ethics, like political philosophy, would benefit from a distinction between ideal and non-ideal theory (Rawls 1999). Moreover, I want to argue that we neglect non-ideal ethical theory at our own peril. One potentially fruitful way to proceed in virtue theory is to describe in rich detail how things actually, typically (or at least often) work, then use that description as an anchor for describing how they might work better. The ideal theorist wants to describe how things could be optimally. But there are reasons to prefer baby steps.

First, because ethics is a practical domain, ethical theory (including virtue theory) should at least sometimes be a useful guide to action. If you ask me the way to Larissa and I tell you that it's at 39° 38′ 13″ North by 22° 25′ 13″ East, I haven't given you an optimal answer. Similarly, if you ask me the way to Larissa and I tell you to go *that* way for an hour and then ask someone else, I haven't given you an optimal answer. But both answers are useful, and they're especially useful in tandem. Suppose for the sake of argument that the neo-Aristotelian picture of virtue is an adequate ideal theory. That doesn't mean that it's the only thing we need to know. Suppose for the sake of argument my friendship model of virtue suggests a few steps one could take towards being more virtuous. That doesn't mean it's the only thing we need to know.

Second, ethics—especially virtue ethics—might best be construed as essentially developmental. The point of virtue is not to achieve it and then rest content in your achievement. The point of virtue is to take another step away from where you started and another step towards a better way of living.

Third, as Morton (2012) convincingly argues in the context of intellectual rather than moral virtues, perfection can be the enemy of the good. Suppose that it would be better to achieve normative ideal X than to achieve normative ideal Y. But suppose that one's reach often does exceed one's grasp—that striving for X typically or even always yields at best an approximation of X, and that striving for Y typically or even always yields at best an approximation of Y. The following argument is clearly invalid: If X is better than Y, then an approximation of X is better than an approximation of Y. Now suppose, as I suspect many orthodox virtue theorists would say, that intrinsic trustworthiness is superior to factitious trustworthiness. In other words, suppose that trustworthiness whose vehicle is the trustworthy agent is morally superior to trustworthiness whose vehicle is that agent along with someone else who trusts her. It doesn't follow that an approximation of intrinsic trustworthiness is superior to an approximation of factitious trustworthiness. That depends on how well we approximate them. The jury is still out on that question. The right attitude to take, then, is not dismissiveness but curiosity.[8]

Works Cited

Adams, R. 2006. *A Theory of Virtue*. Oxford: Oxford University Press.
Alfano, M. 2013. *Character as Moral Fiction*. Cambridge: Cambridge University Press.
Alfano, M. 2014. What are the Bearers of Virtues? In *Advances in Moral Psychology*, ed. H. Sarkissian and J. Wright. New York: Continuum, 73–90.
Alfano, M. forthcoming. *Nietzsche's Socio-Moral Psychology*. Cambridge: Cambridge University Press.
Alfano, M. forthcoming a. Stereotype Threat and Intellectual Virtue. In *Naturalizing Epistemic Virtue*, ed. A. Fairweather and O. Flanagan. Cambridge: Cambridge University Press.
Alfano, M., Robinson, B., Stey, P., Christen, M., and Lapsley, D. forthcoming. Intellectual Humility: The Elusive Virtue. *The Journal of Positive Psychology*.
Annas, J. 1993. *The Morality of Happiness*. New York: Oxford University Press.
Annas, J. 2011. *Intelligent Virtue*. New York: Oxford University Press.
Appiah, K. A. 2011. *The Honor Code: How Moral Revolutions Happen*. New York: W. W. Norton.
Aristotle. 1984. *Nicomachean Ethics*. In *The Complete Works of Aristotle*, vol. 2, ed. J. Barnes, trans. W. D. Ross and J. O. Urmson. Princeton, NJ: Princeton University Press, 1729–1867.
Clark, A. and Chalmers, D. 1998. The Extended Mind. *Analysis* 58 (1): 7–19.
Cocking, D. and Kennett, J. 1998. Friendship and the Self. *Ethics* 108 (3): 502–27.
Cooper, J. 1977a. Friendship and the Good in Aristotle. *The Philosophical Review* 86 (3): 290–315.

---

[8] With thanks for helpful discussion to Brian Robinson, Alex Madva, Asia Ferrin, John Cooper, Alexander Nehamas, Benjamin Morison, Daniel Wodak, Philip Pettit, Marcus Arvan, John Richardson, Anthony Carreras, Jon Webber, Dhananjay Jagannathan, David Morrow, David Wong, Alberto Masala, Owen Flanagan, Hallie Liberto, and Kate Manne.

Cooper, J. 1977b. Aristotle on the Forms of Friendship. *The Review of Metaphysics* 30 (4): 619–48.
Doris, J. 1998. Persons, Situations, and Virtue Ethics. *Nous* 32 (4): 504–40.
Doris, J. 2002. *Lack of Character: Personality and Moral Behavior*. Cambridge: Cambridge University Press.
Dretske, F. 1981. *Knowledge and the Flow of Information*. Cambridge: MA: MIT Press.
Geach, P. 1977. *The Virtues*. Cambridge: Cambridge University Press.
Harman, G. 1999. Moral Philosophy Meets Social Psychology: Virtue Ethics and the Fundamental Attribution Error. *Proceedings of the Aristotelian Society*, New Series 119: 316–31.
Hurka, T. 2001. *Vice, Virtue, and Value*. Oxford: Oxford University Press.
Hursthouse, R. 1999. *On Virtue Ethics*. Oxford: Oxford University Press.
Kripke, S. 1972. *Naming and Necessity*. Oxford: Blackwell.
Lewis, D. 2002. *Convention*. Oxford: Wiley-Blackwell.
McGeer, V. 2008. Trust, Hope, and Empowerment. *Australasian Journal of Philosophy* 86 (2): 237–54.
MacIntyre, A. 1981. *After Virtue*. Notre Dame, IN: University of Notre Dame Press.
Millgram, E. 1987. Aristotle on Making Other Selves. *Canadian Journal of Philosophy* 17 (2): 361–76.
Morton, A. 2012. *Bounded Thinking: Intellectual Virtues for Limited Agents*. Oxford: Oxford University Press.
Morton, A. 2013. *Emotion and Imagination*. Cambridge: Polity Press.
Nehamas, A. 2010. Aristotelian *Philia*, Modern Friendship? In *Oxford Studies in Ancient Philosophy*, ed. B. Inwood. Oxford: Oxford University Press, 213–47.
Nozick, R. 1981. *Philosophical Explanations*. Cambridge, MA: Belknap Press.
Pettit, P. 1995. The Cunning of Trust. *Philosophy and Public Affairs* 24 (3): 202–25.
Pritchard, D. 2010. Cognitive Ability and the Extended Cognition Thesis. *Synthese* 175: 133–51.
Putnam, H. 1975. The Meaning of Meaning. *Philosophical Papers*, vol. 2: *Mind, Language, and Reality*. Cambridge: Cambridge University Press.
Rawls, J. 1999. *A Theory of Justice*. Cambridge, MA: Harvard University Press.
Roberts, R. 2013. *Emotions in the Moral Life*. Oxford: Oxford University Press.
Roberts, R. and Wood, J. 2007. *Intellectual Virtues: An Essay in Regulative Epistemology*. Oxford: Oxford University Press.
Russell, D. 2009. *Practical Intelligence and the Virtues*. Oxford: Oxford University Press.
Slote, M. 2001. *Morals from Motives*. Oxford: Oxford University Press.
Sneddon, A. 2011. *Like-Minded: Externalism and Moral Psychology*. Cambridge, MA: MIT Press.

Snow, N. 2008. *Virtue as Social Intelligence: An Empirically Grounded Theory.* New York: Routledge.

Stocker, M. 1976. The Schizophrenia of Modern Ethical Theories. *Journal of Philosophy* 73: 453–66.

Stroud, S. 2006. Partiality in Friendship. *Ethics* 116 (3): 498–524.

Thomas, L. 1987. Friendship. *Synthese*, 72: 217–36.

Tversky, A. and Kahneman, D. 1991. Loss Aversion in Riskless Choice: A Reference-Dependent Model. *The Quarterly Journal of Economics* 106 (4): 1039–61.

Wong, D. 2006. *Natural Moralities.* Oxford: Oxford University Press.

9

The Psychology of Virtue Education

Nafsika Athanassoulis

9.1 Introduction

Virtue ethics, character education, and empirical psychology have had a rocky relationship. From the perspective of psychology, as far back as the 1930s Hartshorne and May's Character Education Inquiry is believed to have dealt a 'death blow' to the very idea of character education[1] from which it has yet to recover. Modern writers interested in the interplay between philosophy and psychology have also been dismissive of a possible role for character education. Gilbert Harman sets aside the very possibility of character building in a one-sentence paragraph, which, in its brevity, makes up the entire section devoted to moral education.[2] John Doris suggests that educating for virtue may well be futile as character traits lack the relevant robustness. In addition he suggests that if we accept that the virtues are rare phenomena, it becomes unclear whether there is a role for the virtuous agent in education.[3] At the same time, from the perspective of philosophy, while virtue ethics has seen a substantial revival in research interest in the last few decades, few philosophers have taken up Elizabeth Anscombe's original call for a shift of attention to moral psychology.[4] With some notable exceptions, such as the work of Owen Flanagan and Joel Kupperman, philosophers have not taken up this aspect of Anscombe's call, leaving philosophers as

---

[1] Power, Higgins and Kohlberg 1989, 127.　　[2] Harman 1998–9.
[3] Doris 2002, 121–5 and Doris and Stich 2005, 121.　　[4] Anscombe 1958.

disconnected from the empirical sciences now as we were when the paper was written in the 1950s.

In this chapter I want to take up the specific question of the relationship between moral education and empirical findings in psychology. I will argue that moral education programmes are theoretically possible and would benefit in their practical application from empirical research already in existence in psychology. I will argue that situationism does not pose a threat for moral education, properly conceived, and that, in fact, educators can and should make use of situational factors. It strikes me that much of the debate in this field is hampered by incomplete or partly inaccurate understandings of the main concepts, in addition to conflicting versions of what it is that we should be aiming for in the first place. Therefore I will start by a brief account of what morality is, what we should expect from moral character education, and which aspects of Aristotelian virtue ethics are relevant to these endeavours.

9.2 The Goals of Character Education

This section covers a large number of ideas in a very concise manner, which may leave a lot of questions unanswered. Nevertheless I have included it as it is difficult to talk about the process of moral indication without some conception of what it is that we are aiming at. If the goal of moral education is to help people become better, more moral, more virtuous human beings, we cannot fully account for how to do so unless we understand what we are aiming for. Morality has conceptual links with agency, voluntariness, and responsibility. Morality involves choice, i.e. an expression of our agency, which need not involve *conscious* deliberation but does involve an affirmation, both rational and affective, of what has been chosen. When we make moral choices we express, through these choices, aspects of ourselves and display our values, interests, and commitments through them. The reason why we hold people responsible for their moral choices, in terms of both praise and blame, is because they are an expression of who they are, an expression of their agency. These thoughts also account for the relevance of voluntariness to morality, as genuine choice requires freedom. We hold people morally responsible for what they have freely chosen to do, what they have control over.

The first relevant point for our discussion is that we should not automatically assume an overlap between the philosophical and the psychological understandings of these terms. The above, philosophical understanding of morality is not relevant to all the traits that come under the psychological inquiry into character. For example, some psychologists are interested in the prevalence of expressive movements as a character trait in a population,[5] which is a morally neutral behaviour.

The second point is that this particular conception of morality already gives us some hints as to what we should expect to find in a successful character education programme. Indoctrination and rote repetition are unlikely to foster the personal growth and independence of spirit required for meaningful moral choice. Blind rule following is not compatible with taking responsibility for one's choices, while compliance which is wholly due to fear of punishment or which is wholly motivated by the desire for external rewards is incompatible with actions that proceed from ethical values that are acted upon for their own sake. However, at the same time, this conception of morality is similarly incompatible with a values free-for-all relativism. The very idea of holding agents responsible for their moral choices supposes that these choices must in some way be defensible and open to being judged. Freedom to choose involves the freedom to get it wrong, and just because one's actions are an expression of one's deepest held beliefs, it does not mean that these beliefs cannot be criticized and found wanting. When we make moral choices we invest ourselves in the choice but the genuineness of the choice is no guarantee of its rightness.

What should we expect then from a programme of character education? There are two possible answers to this question. One suggests that we can't expect anything, because character is simply an illusion. The other assumes that character traits exist, accepts that they can be shaped, changed, and developed in accordance with an educational goal, but still retains the idea that such a project would be difficult, lengthy, and fraught with pitfalls. I will suggest that the second answer is the correct one: character education is possible, but it is a difficult project and one which is not easily captured in a transferable, simple, and easily practically applicable programme of education. One implication of this claim is

---

[5] Allport and Vernon 1933.

that there are limits to the specificity of any practical guidance in moral education. If there is a practical science of character education, to borrow an argument from Aristotle, it can only be as exact as the subject matter allows. Character education, like ethics, is an imprecise subject matter, one that does not admit to an overriding principle, one that cannot be fully captured in an easily applicable set of rules, one that requires sensitivity to context. One answer will not suit all, and adaptability and flexibility may be the key. Rather than looking for a specific set of guidelines that can be applied at a national or even international level, we should be looking at the qualities of the people who teach character education and giving them the support required to help them tailor their approach to the needs of their individual students.

There are two concerns with any attempt to over-specify the practicalities of a character education programme. The first is a temptation to expect a successful character education programme to deal with the ills of the day, whichever way these may be conceived. In this spirit there are politicians and researchers who aspire for character education to change the sexual habits of young adults, to lead them away from a life of crime and drug use, and make a difference to the rate of unemployment, often assuming that a number of social ills are the result of the moral failings of young people.[6] The more precisely these targets are laid out, the more contentious they become and it is easy for the call for moral education, a perfectly reasonable aspiration for all our children in the abstract, to be hijacked, in practice, by particular causes. The aim to educate, to better, to improve, to nurture, risks getting lost in whatever political, ideological, or personal agendas are behind the particular goals identified as the ills that education should seek to remedy.

The second is a theoretical concern. As we shall see below, the virtuous response is always contextualized, so any attempt to inculcate very specific behaviours may well backfire. For example, obedience to school authorities sounds like a reasonable goal, one that might make the lives of school teachers easier and one that might teach students to comply with established social norms and thus avoid some of the kinds of social ills education researchers are specifically concerned with. However, it is

---

[6] For example, Lickona 1996 and Kilpatrick 1992. Even those critical of this aim still accept that the aim of character education is to instil specific virtues, e.g. Doris 2002, whose immediate examples are chastity, reduction in STDs, and teenage pregnancies (p. 121).

fairly easy to imagine situations where defiance may be the correct attitude towards authority. For example, non-cooperation is the morally correct response to an unjust rule. Behaviours such as highlighting the rule's injustice, bringing attention to its unfair repercussions, and refusing to contribute to its application may well all be morally laudable responses.

Even in a less contentious context the virtues of a good student, such as diligence, obedience to authority, ability to follow instructions, and academic achievement, are not necessarily the virtues of a good person, which might rather be traits such as autonomous decision making, independence, critical thinking, and emotional maturity.[7] Over-specifying and misidentifying the goals of moral education programmes risks resulting in educational efforts that are more concerned with short-term behavioural modification than long-term character development.[8]

9.3 Situationism and Character Formation

Much of interest has already been said on virtue ethics and its response to the situationist challenge,[9] so I will only briefly highlight some ideas that will be particularly relevant to us. The relationship between the virtues and context is a complex one, with a variety of different influences playing a role. It is important to note that, according to Aristotle, the virtues are not the only character states one may possess, and that not all character states are identical. There is a big difference between the virtues as settled, reliable, and predictable dispositions, that one arrives at after years of gradual development, and the many states of character that one may go through during this development. So while the end goal, virtue, is static, in the sense that once it has been achieved it is settled, reliable, and unchanging, the road to virtue passes through a number of dynamic states.

---

[7] For example, see the work of Mischel and Peake (1982), who measure conscientiousness by considering class attendance, punctuality in handing in assignments, thoroughness of notes taken, and neatness of personal appearance. While some of these may be good qualities in a student, it is not clear that they are also the attributes of a virtuous person.

[8] For a similar view of the problems with character education since the 1990s see Cunningham 1998, 194.

[9] For the main Aristotelian responses see Athanassoulis 2000, Annas 2003, and Kamtekar 2004.

Virtue is a settled state because it involves a choice of the noble and the good. This choice has both rational and affective elements and is made in response to morally relevant circumstances in the world. That is, morally salient elements in the situation provoke a virtuous response. Virtue is static in the sense that when a virtuous response is required, the virtuous person can be relied upon to respond appropriately each time. However, the circumstances which require virtue are themselves diverse. One cannot decide in advance of the particulars of the situation what will be the virtuous response and the content of virtue cannot be determined in advance of the context that gives rise to the moral demand. So, for example, one cannot specify in advance whether the kind response is to directly help an individual in need with his immediate concerns, or to contribute to a charity that alleviates the root causes of these needs, or concern oneself with the global causes of injustice that perpetuate a system that generates these needs in the first place. But one can rely on the virtuous person to do what virtue requires each time.

The claim that virtue is stable and predictable is a complex one. This is not a point which is lost to psychologists either. For example, Cervone and Shoda write, 'Coherence across time is revealed not only in stability of action, but in meaningful patterns of change when people face changing environmental demands ... Coherence across contexts is revealed not only in stable mean levels of response, but in variations in cognition and action from one context to another.'[10] The virtuous person can be relied upon to do (and feel) the right thing each time, but what that right thing will be will vary with circumstances. Character trait stability over time is itself a dynamic concept in that its expression changes depending on what is required by different circumstances. It would be very simplistic to assume that just because a trait itself is stable, for example one is always kind, that the expression of this trait is always identical in changing circumstances, such that one always does the same thing in the attempt to be kind regardless of what the circumstances require. Character coherence does not require blind reproduction, but a more sophisticated reliability, one that tracks the shifting demands of the good.

However, since moral development is a gradual process, one that is subject to failures and regressions, there are many other states of character

---

[10] Cervone and Shoda 1999, 10.

relevant here that do not exhibit the stability of virtue. The student of virtue will have an unformed and pliable character, one whose development can be influenced by external factors. Such factors include role models, parental influence, exemplars, peer groups, educators, opportunities for the practice of morality, temptations and pressures, and so on. While virtue is context-sensitive in the sense that its *expression* is influenced by the demands of the situation, the developmental character states on the road to virtue are dynamic in the sense that their very *development* and *formation* are influenced by situational factors. This is also not a point lost on psychologists. For example, Bandura's studies of modelling show how dispositions like a tendency towards aggression go through constant modification as a consequence of interactions with the environment.[11]

The interrelationship between situations and character continues: one's character colours how one views the world, in a way that may also further encourage the expression of certain aspects of one's character. For example, the fearful person may interpret a number of elements in his interaction with others as threatening and intimidating, which in turn may push him towards defensive actions that provoke others to see him and react to him as a fearful person. A person's character leads him to view certain situations in a particular light and certain situations bring out specific elements of a person's character. This is both an Aristotelian point[12] and one found in, for example, social-cognitive approaches to personality.[13] Psychologists recognize that the same situation, e.g. a noisy party, or a particular parental style, may be perceived differently, e.g. as fun for a sociable person and as torturous for a shy person, and lead to different behaviours, e.g. compliance from a submissive child or disobedience from a rebellious child.[14]

The long process by which our emotions come into line with our reason through habituation, the development from doing 'the that' to understanding 'the because', and the progression from incontinence to continence are all examples of developmental processes in character formation. The role of moral education is to guide, shape, and control situational factors so that they exert as positive an influence as possible on these dynamic character traits. Since these character traits are

---

[11] Bandura 1997.   [12] Aristotle, *Rhetoric* 1378a 8.
[13] For a summary of such views see, for example, Mathews et al. 2009, ch. 8.
[14] Buss 1989, 1382.

undergoing constant modification as a consequence of their interaction with the environment, if we control the environment, we can encourage character development in the right direction.

9.4 Control the Situation, Shape the Character

The main insight of all this for educators is not whether behaviour is dispositional *or* situationally motivated as two mutually exclusive causes, but rather that character traits are dispositions whose development and actualization into behaviour are shaped by situations. As such this aim is also shared by some psychologists, even some coming from surprising quarters. Hartshorne and May write in the Character Education Inquiry report:

> The large place occupied by the 'situation' in the suggestion and control of conduct, not only in its larger aspects, such as the example of other pupils, the personality of the teacher, etc., but also in its more subtle aspects, such as the nature of the opportunity to deceive, the kind of material or test on which it is possible, the relation of the child to this material, and so on, points to the need of a careful educational analysis of all such situations for the purpose of making explicit the nature of the direct or honest mode of response *in detail*, so that when a child is placed in these situations there may be a genuine opportunity for him to practice direct methods of adjustment.[15]

Far from dismissing any possibility of moral education (as some commentators interpret them[16]) Hartshorne and May have specific recommendations on how it can be undertaken. Indeed, much of their discussion is a rejection of direct methods in favour of indirect methods of teaching, rather than a rejection of the possibility of teaching morality altogether.

The difference between direct and indirect methods of teaching is a blurred one, but, in general, direct refers to teacher-centred teaching, done at a definitive time and place, with specific materials for the instruction of moral character. In the next section I will defend a possible role for more direct methods of teaching, but it is important to note that Hartshorne and May's conception of the direct methods they wish to reject is not one that would be advocated by an Aristotelian in the first place. Hartshorne and May understand as direct the 'mere urging of

---

[15] Hartshorne and May 1928, 413.   [16] See for example Doris 2002, ch. 4.

honest behaviour by teachers'[17] and see themselves as arguing against the claim that pupils possess a 'secret reservoir of honest virtue'[18] which can be appealed to by educators. However, neither of these are claims that a virtue ethicist would want to defend either. Virtue does not proceed from a secret reservoir, a mysterious power, or an innate ability; we are not engendered by nature with virtue, but we have the capacity to develop virtue through habituation. Developing this capacity is a long and complex process and it would be naive to think that it can be achieved at the mere urging of others. Indirect methods of teaching are perfectly compatible with virtue ethics and indeed are the kinds of suggestions Aristotle makes for character development. Therefore there is no immediate conflict between the psychological findings on the influence of situations on behaviour and the virtue ethical claims that character can be developed and educated.

I will contend that one of the main tasks of educators is to stage manage situations to help people develop the right habits. Most personality psychologists, including for example critics of trait theory such as Mischel, accept that traits most reliably express themselves in situations that are suited to their expression,[19] therefore the task of educators is to shape situations so as to lead to the expression of the right traits. To develop the character trait of honesty, educators must provide situations that are conducive to honest behaviour; and it is by practising honest behaviour that students will develop the ability to withstand the temptations to be deceitful.[20] The more students become used to withstanding the temptations to be deceitful, the easier it will be for them to do so next time, until the force of the temptation becomes negligible and honesty becomes a disposition that flows easily and effortlessly into practice. Psychological studies from across the board in the debate over the existence of traits accept the complex relationship between traits, behaviours, and situations. For example, a study of highly aggressive children found that they displayed behaviours central to the trait of aggressiveness, such as pushing and shoving, and that these behaviours increased in response to situational pressures.[21]

---

[17] Hartshorne and May 1928, 413.   [18] Hartshorne and May 1928, 379.
[19] For example, Wright and Mischel 1987.   [20] Aristotle, NE, 1104a 33–1104b 3.
[21] Wright and Mischel 1987.

Two experimental findings are relevant here: first, it is important to recognize that a situational manipulation will have different influences in different contexts; second, it is equally important to accept that although small factors influence behaviour in radical ways, becoming aware of these influences negates their impact. I will consider each in turn.[22]

9.5 Contexts of Situational Manipulations

On the first point, the work of Arnold Buss is relevant. Buss argues that the influence of traits on behaviour and the influence of situational manipulations on behaviour depend on the kind of situation, or *context*, the agent is in. In novel, formal, and public contexts, with detailed and complete instructions, offering little or no choice, of brief duration and with narrowly defined responses, manipulations are more influential. Whereas in familiar, informal, and private contexts, with general or no instructions, offering considerable choice, of extensive duration and broadly defined responses, traits are more influential.[23] So, for example, at a dinner party, a situation which is formal, public, and ruled by social norms, manipulations are likely to have a greater influence and can derail our usual habits. Atypical behaviour on the other hand is difficult to maintain over a long period of time, or when we are relaxed, informal, and allowed free expression without the guidance of a specific set of instructions.

Buss sees the following features emerge in the study of behaviour:

1. In public and formal situations we have a tendency to be conformists. In the public eye, unsure of ourselves, we take our cues from others and therefore we become more susceptible to situational manipulations. Many experiments that confirm the importance of manipulations are carried out in formal, public, and novel settings. By contrast in familial, relaxed, at ease situations, a person's habitual tendencies are more likely to emerge.
2. Laboratory experiments usually involve precise and clear instructions, which make subjects less likely to exhibit independent

---

[22] Jonathan Webber provides further consideration of the relationship between one's beliefs and one's behaviours and how strong moral beliefs can resist the influence of situational factors in chapter 6 in this volume.

[23] Buss 1989, 1381.

personality traits. By contrast personality research tends to consider unstructured situations and observations of subjects in a natural setting more likely to promote the expression of personality traits.
3. Laboratory studies are of short duration and it is easier for subjects to conform to modes of behaviour that are not habitual as well as conceal certain tendencies. It is difficult to maintain atypical behaviour over time, so shorter studies will confirm the importance of manipulations, while longer ones will come to the opposite conclusion.
4. In a laboratory setting responses are measured precisely and such narrowly focused, specific responses are more likely to be influenced by manipulations. Aggregating responses over time brings out the importance of character traits.

Interestingly Buss's insight might explain the importance of situational manipulations in shaping behaviour in experiments such as Milgram's which are held in formal, closely controlled settings.

To further complicate matters Buss cites a number of studies that show the importance of manipulations and traits interacting. Subjects who are more self-conscious are also more likely to feel discomfort and want to leave if manipulated in a situation where they feel more socially aware.[24] Or subjects who are low in self-esteem find that their performance is severely affected by failure, whereas subjects who are high in self-esteem do not.[25]

Educators can make use of Buss's insight in two ways: first, faced with situations where manipulations are influential they can take control of those manipulations and ensure that students are exposed to the ones which encourage the best behaviour; second, faced with students who have the rudiments of the right character traits in place, educators can shape situations to offer freer expression of these character traits in order to be able to reward their manifestation in action.

An important aspect of this part of moral education is managing failure. Failure is an inevitable part of the moral life, but it needn't necessarily be a *negative* part of moral development. Failure, properly managed to ensure that it is not catastrophic, devastating, or overwhelming, can be a source of

---

[24] Fenigstein at al., in Buss 1989, 1381. [25] Brockner in Buss 1989, 1381.

self-knowledge and improvement. Shaping situations to provide appropriate tests of temptation, duress, and pressure, even when these tests result in current failures to master the temptation, to overcome the duress, and resist the pressure, can still be useful sources of knowledge, self-development, and future self-improvement, as well as sources of ammunition for avoiding failures in the future.[26] 'If we bend so easily before the winds of situational pressures, then we need opportunities during the development, if not to face the strongest winds, at least to deal with some of the complexities and pressures of real situation.'[27] It is the role of educators to manage the contexts of failure, so that rather than being overwhelming, it becomes a lesson one learns from.

Indeed it is the task of educators to influence as far as possible all the external factors that shape character, such as peer groups and role models. Experimental studies show that children who are exposed to an aggressive model become more aggressive,[28] while subjects who see others litter follow by example,[29] and subjects who see others conserve water by switching off showers follow suit.[30] Gino, Ayal, and Ariely tested whether subjects' tendency to cheat was affected by the dishonest behaviour of others and noted that the behaviour of confederates perceived by subjects as belonging to the group they identified with had a particularly strong influence. Observing an in-group peer behave unethically increased the subjects' likelihood of doing so as well, while observing an out-group peer behave unethically had the opposite effect. So not only do in-group members become direct standards for modelling behaviour, but out-group members serve as reverse role models, drawing attention by their unethical behaviour to the subjects' own ethical beliefs and thus reinforcing the subjects' ethical behaviour. Gino et al. conclude:

Our findings suggest that relatively minor acts of dishonesty by in-group members can have a large influence on the extent of dishonesty, and that techniques that help to stigmatize the bad apples as out-group members and strengthen the saliency of their behavior could be useful tools to fight dishonesty.[31]

They also mention that similar findings regarding the importance of the overall ethical climate and culture in influencing moral behaviour have

---

[26] For more on this see Athanassoulis 2012.　　[27] Lickona 1980, 130.
[28] Bandura 1965.　　[29] Cialdini et al. 1990.
[30] Aronson and O'Leary 1983.　　[31] Gino et al. 2009, 398.

been noted in larger groups and organizations.[32] It is interesting to note that these kinds of experiments that seem to confirm a role for the expression of character traits take place in conditions that conform to Buss's insight, e.g. familial, private, offering choice, and of extensive duration.

9.6 Knowledge is Power

The second experimental finding is that while small factors have impressively large influences on our behaviour, becoming aware of these factors can negate their influence. Surprised by how small and inconsequential factors easily change our moral behaviour, it is tempting to conclude that it is difficult to overcome the influence of these factors. If we become even more willing to administer what we believe to be powerful electric shocks simply because the person urging us to do so is wearing a white coat and carrying a clip board,[33] if benefiting from finding an amount as tiny as a dime is sufficient to push us into a helping mood,[34] if perfectly ordinary people only need to knowingly play act at being guards and prisoners to turn into moral monsters in a matter of days,[35] then it is easy to be led into assuming that the influence of these factors is irresistible and all-pervasive. Consider Doris who argues:

> Given how counterintuitive it is to suppose that such factors [small situational variations] powerfully influence behaviour, it is no surprise that people typically pay them little attention, and even in the unlikely event that people developed situationist suspicions in the ordinary course of things, it would be difficult for them to engage in the systematic observation required to put such suspicions to the test.[36]

However, this is theoretical speculation on the part of Doris and actual empirical evidence suggests the opposite is in fact true. The key to resisting contrary situational factors appears to be to not only become aware of them, but to become aware of their influence through a detailed debriefing that makes subjects aware of the processes that created and reinforced the beliefs and behaviours in the first place. Such 'process debriefing' results in the effect of these small but influential factors being

---

[32] Gino et al. 2009, 397.   [33] Milgram 1974.   [34] Isen and Levin 1972.
[35] Haney and Zimbardo 1977.   [36] Doris 2002, 36.

eliminated.[37] It appears that the best way to avoid the Fundamental Attribution Error is to become aware of our propensity to make it. In addition some authors report success with such methods particularly in educational contexts.[38] Practical applications of this idea include using social psychological lectures to increase rates of shoplifting reporting[39] and to increase helping behaviours.[40] So the answer to our surprise at the influence of tiny factors on our moral behaviour is twofold: firstly we should use education in order to manage these factors so that only positive ones are allowed to influence behaviour, and secondly we should become properly aware of the influence of negative ones so that their effect is eliminated.[41]

Doris may respond here that these situational factors are too numerous and too difficult to predict and the problem persists nonetheless. To an extent this is a practical question. I will accept that more empirical research is needed to determine how many complicating factors are too many, how often are particular individuals able to overcome the influence of situational factors by becoming aware of them before fatigue sets in, whether the influence of some situational factors is more resistant to becoming aware of them than others, what other contextual elements affect our ability to become aware of situational factors that affect us, etc. The empirical project is certainly complex but it is not already determined, as Doris's analysis would lead us to believe. Furthermore, its very complexity is not a theoretical threat to virtue ethics either. Virtue ethics acknowledges and turns into an advantage the complexity of the human life. We should not shy away from complicated answers, but embrace them both as a practical challenge and as a correct description of the richness of human endeavours.

9.7 The Role of the Virtuous Agent

According to an influential account of virtue ethics, the virtuous person plays a central role in the understanding of the theory as he acts as an

---

[37] Ross et al. 1975.　[38] Samuels and Casebeer 2005, 80.
[39] Klentz and Beaman 1981.　[40] Beaman at al. 1978.
[41] It is interesting to note that philosophers who are troubled by the influence of small factors and draw radical conclusions about character from such experimental data do not appear to be aware of this further evidence on process debriefing and related experiments; see, for example, Doris 2005, 657.

exemplar for virtue. This conception of the role of the virtuous person has attracted criticisms on a number of counts,[42] some of which are of particular relevance to education. For example, if the virtuous person is a role model we would need to ensure that all teachers are perfectly virtuous, which is quite a strenuous and unrealistic demand. However, as I have argued elsewhere,[43] this is a misconception of the role of the virtuous agent. Aristotle's definition of virtue as a purposive disposition, lying in a mean that is relative to us and to the situation and determined by rational principle and by that which the virtuous man would use to determine it,[44] tells us that we should not be looking at the virtuous person *directly* but at the rational principle (*orthos logos*) and at how to determine it. If virtue is rare, we may well struggle to find the virtuous person (aside from any concerns about identifying her in the first place), and if the application of virtue is context- and person-sensitive, it is not clear how we would benefit from a direct copying of her behaviour anyway. However, in a sense we should not be looking for the virtuous person as such, we should be looking for the deliberative qualities exemplified by the virtuous person. Accepting that these qualities are exemplified in an ideal degree in the virtuous person is perfectly compatible with suggesting that the same qualities exist in an imperfect manner in less than virtuous agents. The task of the educator should be to help his students develop the qualities that can be used to determine the rational principle. These qualities are moral perception and moral judgement. Doing so does not require a direct appeal to the virtuous agent. In what follows I develop some practical ideas on how this can be done with direct reference to evidence from psychology experiments.

One of the first steps in moral education is to become aware of the world as a place that imposes moral demands on us. This may seem a simple and immediate task, but I think that anyone who has spent time teaching ethics, especially in a context with practical applications like professional ethics or research ethics committee training, will know that

---

[42] For a summary see, for example, Louden1984.
[43] Athanassoulis 2012, chs 4 and 5, and with specific reference to education see Athanassoulis forthcoming.
[44] Aristotle, NE 1106b 35–1107a 3.

it is nothing but simple and immediate.[45] Students have to become sensitized to the world as a moral place, they have to come to see the world in a particular way, they need to perceive the morally relevant features of situations. Can experimental psychology confirm the suggestion that becoming sensitive to the world as morally active is a significant factor in behaving ethically?

There is quite a lot of evidence from experimental psychology to suggest that faced with moral reminders people behave a lot more ethically. While some experiments assume that religious people will behave more ethically than non-religious people and then go on to disprove this hypothesis, Malhotra found that the right question is not 'Does religion make people nicer?' but rather '*When* does religion make people nicer?'[46] Religious people are not more prone to ethical behaviour as such, instead frequent exposure to religious norms is likely to make morality more salient and therefore moral behaviour more frequent. The experiment tested the subjects' likelihood to bid on charity auctions and found significantly more responses on days when morality had been made salient, e.g. following the Sunday sermon. Nor is this the only case in point: participants who were asked to recall the Ten Commandments were significantly less likely to cheat given the opportunity, even when standing to gain financially from cheating, than the control group.[47] Such experiments suggest that students may well benefit from the presence of moral reminders in their everyday life and from learning techniques that will encourage them to remind themselves of their moral beliefs before acting.

Variations of these types of experiment also seem to suggest that setting situations up in such a way that participants identify with their actions as expressions of their agency, as actions they can be held morally responsible for, increases ethical behaviour. Priming participants to believe in determinism results in higher levels of dishonesty than priming them to believe in free will.[48] Asking participants to sign an honour code seems to operate as an ethical reminder and a personal commitment to morality which makes it less likely to cheat even in cases where

---

[45] My conviction on this point comes purely from personal experience but there is some anecdotal evidence that colleagues have similar experiences with their students, e.g. Sokol 2012, 3. For more on my views on these ideas see Athanassoulis 2012, ch. 8.
[46] Malhotra 2010, 138. [47] Mazar et al. 2008. [48] Vohs and Schooler 2008.

there is no specific cost for dishonesty.[49] Simple changes like asking participants to sign at the top of tax return forms prior to filling them in, rather than at the bottom, seem to operate both as honesty reminders and as ways of strengthening the connection between the person and his actions so that he feels immediate responsibility for his choices.[50] The experiments seem to suggest that taking ownership of our actions, strengthening the connection between what I do and what I am held responsible for, affects moral behaviour. It wouldn't require much effort to implement these insights in educational contexts.

Moral judgement has many theoretical components which I suspect could be fruitfully linked to research in psychology, among them the development of moral imagination, the interplay between cognitive and affective elements of the reasoning process, the strengthening of will-power, and so on. It is not possible to develop all these themes in this chapter so I will concentrate on one aspect of moral judgement that involves direct engagement with moral concepts and reasoning (partly in response to concerns regarding the efficacy of direct methods of moral education raised earlier). While learning by rote, indoctrination, and mere repetition of rules is unlikely to affect anyone's beliefs, values, and commitments, learning about moral concepts in an environment that encourages critical thinking, self-reflection, and active engagement with the ideas under discussion may lead students to greater self-understanding and encourage them to question their existing beliefs in favour of greater consistency and coherence in their overall views. Practical skills involved in successful moral discussions such as being able to express one's views, being able to understand other viewpoints, accurately pinpointing similarities and differences, being intellectually tenacious without being personally offensive, and so on, contribute both to one's understanding of morality and to one's character.

In a pattern that should be becoming familiar by now there exists empirical evidence which confirms the suggestion that thinking critically about morality should be a part of character education. One, admittedly small, study showed that the teacher's skills in leading moral discussions in a manner consistent with the Socratic elenchus was the most important variable in eliciting substantial, positive character change.[51] While

[49] Ariely 2012, 43–4. [50] Shu et al., cited in Ariely 2012, 46–7.
[51] Colby et al. 1977.

studies such as this one are typically small, conclusions may be drawn from them considering that they all arrive at similar conclusions. A review of character education assessment programmes concludes:

> There are nearly 100 separate studies of the effects of classroom discussions of moral dilemmas on, typically, moral reasoning development. Cumulatively, there is strong evidence that classroom moral dilemma discussions promote significant development of moral reasoning competencies. Similarly, there are many studies of the impact of cooperative learning. These studies (and reviews of the studies) demonstrate consistent significant impacts on conflict resolution skills, cooperation, and academic achievement.[52]

Finally I want to conclude by drawing special attention to the role of the teacher who acts as a particularly influential role model, and can do so without necessarily being a perfectly virtuous agent. The role of teachers as role models is clearly significant. Hartshorne and May report one particular class who stood out by far in terms of dishonesty from their peers in other classes. Intrigued by the results they retested the same group the next year, by which time they were being taught by a different teacher, only to find that the spike in dishonest behaviour was gone. Unfortunately, the influence of one teacher was enough to push an entire class into dishonesty, although, fortunately, the very same factor, a new teacher, could reverse the negative influence. By the end of the academic year, led by a different teacher, the same class had gone from being the most dishonest to being the most honest.[53]

To effect this kind of change the teacher does not have to be perfectly virtuous, but he does have to show a commitment to morality that applies to his conduct to the same extent that he expects it to apply to the conduct of his students.[54] The role of the teacher is to function as an example of *how* to think rather than provide the content of *what* to think. The process of learning how to think focuses on the road to virtue, a developmental project, rather than the end result, the virtuous agent. As such, students can learn from many aspects of their teacher's conduct, including, very importantly, his failures. Moral failures are inevitable for fragile, vulnerable creatures such as us. The correct response to the

---

[52] Berkowitz et al. 2007, 428. [53] Hartshorne and May 1928, 328.
[54] For more on this idea see Athanassoulis forthcoming.

possibility of failure is not to deny it but to use it. In an educational context it does not matter so much whether a teacher will make moral mistakes but rather how he will respond to them. For example, a constructive response to moral failure is to recognize the mistake, make amends as appropriate, and be committed to doing better next time. These are all examples one can and should be learning from.[55]

9.8 Conclusion

Doris is concerned that '[a]ny approach to virtue ethics that appropriately engages [experimental psychology] will look different, in interesting and important ways, from the many familiar renderings of virtue ethics that have preserved their empirical innocence'.[56] I hope I have shown that the opposite is true. A very familiar version of Aristotelian virtue ethics seems to stand up very well to having its claims tested by empirical psychology. We have seen numerous points of accord between a conceptually advanced virtue ethics and an empirically diverse psychology, both confirming the same ideas and providing ample ground for constructive discussion. Philosophical work on virtue ethics is complex and sophisticated, empirical work on psychology is detailed and intricate. I have tried to suggest some areas of overlap that cast doubt on the idea that the findings of one discipline have devastating effects on the foundations of the other, while at the same time trying to suggest some areas of practical application for the character education project. My suggestions are by no means comprehensive, exhaustive, or of immediate practical applicability, but they may encourage others to take up the project and develop it further, a project which should be of equal interest to philosophers, psychologists, and educators.[57]

---

[55] Alberto Masala discusses a number of the themes explored in this section in chapter 10 of this volume, including the Aristotelian claim that morality encompasses all practical life, that the cultivation of individual virtues unfolds over several practices, how different activities express facets of the same notion of human excellence, and the complicated process through which virtue and wisdom can form part of the educational experience.
[56] Doris 2005, 657.
[57] I am grateful to Alberto Masala, Jonathan Webber, and two anonymous reviewers for Oxford University Press for very helpful comments on an earlier draft of this paper.

Works Cited

Allport, G. W., and Vernon, P. E. 1933. *Studies in Expressive Movement*. New York: Macmillan.

Annas J. 2003. Virtue Ethics and Social Psychology. In *A Priori: The Erskine Lectures in Philosophy*. <http://apriorijournal.net/volume02/Annas1.pdf>, retrieved 24 July 2015.

Anscombe, G. E. M. 1958. Modern Moral Philosophy. *Philosophy* 33(124): 1–16.

Ariely D. 2012. *The (Honest) Truth about Dishonesty*. New York: Harper Collins.

Aristotle. 1994. *Art of Rhetoric*, trans. J. H. Freese. Cambridge, MA: Harvard University Press.

Aristotle. 1994. *Nicomachean Ethics*, trans. H. Racham. Cambridge, MA: Harvard University Press.

Aronson, E., and O'Leary, M. 1983. The Relative Effectiveness of Models and Prompts on Energy Conservation: A Field Experiment in a Shower Room. *Journal of Technical Writing and Communication* 12(3): 219–24.

Athanassoulis, N. 2000. A Response to Harman. *Proceedings of the Aristotelian Society* 100: 215–21.

Athanassoulis N. 2012. *Virtue Ethics*. London: Bloomsbury.

Athanassoulis, N. 2013. Educating for Virtue. In *Handbook of Virtue Ethics*, ed. S. van Hooft. Durham: Acumen, 4404–50.

Athanassoulis, N. Forthcoming. Acquiring Aristotelian Virtue. In *Handbook of Virtue*, ed. N. Snow. Oxford: Oxford University Press.

Bandura, A. 1965. Influence of Models' Reinforcement Contingencies on the Acquisition of Imitative Responses. *Journal of Personality and Social Psychology* 1: 589–95.

Bandura A. 1997. *Self-efficacy: The Exercise of Control*. New York: W. H. Freeman and Co.

Beaman, A. L., Barnes, P. J., Klentz, B., and McQuirk, B. 1978. Increasing Helping Rates through Information Dissemination: Teaching Pays. *Personality and Social Psychology Bulletin* 4(3): 406–11.

Berkowitz, M. W., Battistich, V. A., and Bier, M. C. 2008. What Works in Character Education: What Is Known and What Needs to Be Known. In *Handbook of Moral and Character Education*, ed. L. Nucci and D. Narvaez. New York: Routledge, 414–30.

Buss, A. H. 1989. Personality as Traits. *American Psychologist* 44: 1378–88.

Cervone, D., and Shoda, Y. 1999. Beyond Traits in the Study of Personality Coherence. *Psychological Science* 8: 27–32.

Cialdini, R. B., Reno, R. R., and Kallgren, C. A. 1990. A Focus Theory of Normative Conduct: Recycling the Concept of Norms to Reduce Littering in Public Places. *Journal of Personality and Social Psychology* 58: 1015–26.

Colby, A., Kohlberg, L., Fenton, E., Speicher-Dubin, B., and Lieberman, M. 1977. Secondary School Moral Discussion Programmes Led by Social Studies Teachers. *Journal of Moral Education* 6(2): 90–111.

Cunningham, C. A. 1998. A Certain and Reasoned Art. In *Character Psychology and Character Education*, ed. D. K. Lapsey and F. C. Power. Notre Dame: University of Notre Dame Press, 166–200.

Doris, J. M. 2002. *Lack of Character*. Cambridge: Cambridge University Press.

Doris, J. M. 2005. Replies: Evidence and Sensibility. *Philosophy and Phenomenological Research* 72(3): 656–77.

Doris, J. M., and Stich, S. P., 2005. As a Matter of Fact: Empirical Perspectives on Ethics. In *The Oxford Handbook of Contemporary Philosophy*, ed. F. Jackson and M. Smith. Oxford: Oxford University Press.

Gino, F., Ayal, S., and Ariely, D. 2009. Contagion and Differentiation in Unethical Behavior. *Psychological Science* 20(3): 393–8.

Haney, C., and Zimbardo, P. 1977. The Socialization into Criminality: On Becoming a Prisoner and a Guard. In *Law, Justice and the Individual in Society: Psychological and Legal Issues*, ed. J. Tapp and F. Levine. New York: Holt, Rinehart and Winston, 198–223.

Harman, G. 1998–9. Moral Philosophy Meets Social Psychology: Virtue Ethics and the Fundamental Attribution Error. *Proceedings of the Aristotelian Society* 99: 315–31.

Hartshorne, H., and May, M. A. 1928. *Studies in the Nature of Character*. New York: The Macmillan Company.

Isen, A. M., and Levin, P. F. 1972. Effects of Feeling Good on Helping: Cookies and Kindness. *Journal of Personality and Social Psychology* 21: 384–8.

Kamtekar, R. 2004. Situationism and Virtue Ethics on the Content of our Character. *Ethics* 114: 458–91.

Kilpatrick, W. 1992. *Why Johnny Can't Tell Right from Wrong: Moral Literacy and the Case for Character Education*. New York: Simon and Schuster.

Klentz, B., and Beaman, A. L. 1981. The Effects of Type of Information and Method of Dissemination on the Reporting of a Shoplifter. *Journal of Applied Social Psychology* 11(1): 64–82.

Lickona, T. 1980. What Does Moral Psychology Have to Say to the Teacher of Ethics? In *Ethics Teaching in Higher Education*, ed. D. Callahan and S. Bok. New York: Plenum Press, 103–32.

Lickona, T. 1996. Eleven Principles of Effective Character Education. *Journal of Moral Education* 25(1): 93–100.

Louden, R. B. 1984. On Some Vices of Virtue Ethics. *American Philosophical Quarterly* 21: 227–36.

Malhotra, D. 2010. (When) Are Religious People Nicer? Religious Salience and the 'Sunday Effect' on Pro-Social Behavior. *Judgement and Decision Making* 5(2): 138–43.

Mathews, G., Deary, I. J., and Whiteman, M. C. 2009. *Personality Traits*. Cambridge: Cambridge University Press.

Mazar, N., Amir, O. and Ariely, D. 2008. The Dishonesty of Honest People: A Theory of Self-Concept Maintenance. *Journal of Marketing Research* 45: 633–44.

Milgram, S. 1974. *Obedience to Authority*. New York: Harper and Row.

Mischel, W., and Peake, P. K. 1982. Beyond Déjà Vu in the Search for Cross-Situational Consistency. *Psychological Review* 89: 730–55.

Power, C. F., Higgins, A., and Kohlberg, L. 1989. The Habit of the Common Life: Building Character through Democratic Community Schools. In *Moral Development and Character Education*, ed. L. Nucci. Berkeley, CA: McCutchan, 125–43.

Ross, L., Lepper, M. R., and Hubbard, M. 1975. Perseverance in Self-Perception and Social Perception: Biased Attributional Processes in the Debriefing Paradigm. *Journal of Personality and Social Psychology* 32(5): 880–92.

Samuels, S. M., and Casebeer, W. D. 2005. A Social Psychological View of Why Knowledge of Situational Influences on Behaviour Can Improve Character Development Practices. *Journal of Moral Education*, 34(1): 73–87.

Shu, L., Mazar, N., Gino, F., Bazeman, M., and Ariely, D. 2012. When to Sign on the Dotted Line? Signing First Makes Ethics Salient and Decreases Dishonest Self-Reports. Working paper, Harvard Business School NOM Unit 2011, cited in Ariely 2012.

Sokol, D. 2012. *Doing Clinical Ethics* Dordrecht: Springer.

Vohs, K. D., and Schooker, J. W. 2008. The Value of Believing in Free Will: Encouraging a Belief in Determinism Increases Cheating. *Psychological Science* 19: 49–54.

Wright, J. C., and Mischel, W. 1987. A Conditional Approach to Dispositional Constructs: The Local Predictability of Social Behaviour. *Journal of Personality and Social Psychology* 53: 1159–77.

10

Mastering Wisdom

Alberto Masala

Virtue ethics is a philosophical tradition built upon the idea that a general moral expertise can be cultivated. Being a good person can be learned, both from experience and from good role models. Given the right circumstances, people can improve, learning from their own mistakes and deepening their understanding of life. In the language of philosophy, this process is the slow cultivation of the virtues: becoming more generous, just, temperate, wise. For all this to make sense, it must be the case that morality is analogous enough to practical skill, in order for something similar to practical training to take place. And why should this not be so? Thinking of moral goodness as learnable in this way feels very natural, for two reasons.

First, the awe generated by heroes and moral exemplars is extremely strong. It may be easy to dismiss it when calm in your room, but it becomes very serious when facing suffering or any kind of injustice. This feeling has a participatory dimension. A sense of human greatness elevates you and pushes you to contribute. We seem to need the idea that heroism and moral greatness are real and accessible, in order to be uplifted and keep hoping. While this need is not a proof, it should not be easily dismissed either: it may even be the case that we cannot ignore it, at least not consistently. Many religions have understood this point: for example, many Christians believe that everybody can aspire to sainthood, and many Buddhists believe that everyone can eventually reach enlightenment.

Second, a first inspection by common sense finds nothing excessively problematic in the process of moral learning invoked by virtue ethics.

Among other things, morality requires finesse of judgement, articulate understanding of practical reality, and proper emotional reactions. It may not be easy, but experience and the right role models can help us to improve. The psychology of moral learning does not seem mysterious. It is plain improving from life experience. Both ancient and contemporary authors on virtue have drawn heavily from this alleged support from common sense (e.g. Aristotle 2002; Annas 2011). Virtue ethics as 'just extending common sense' is a rhetorical and argumentative staple in the literature.

And yet, if we are very honest, we do not really want to become saints or heroes, and not even great human beings in some broader sense. As soon as the feeling of awe ends, cynicism pulls in. There must be a mistake somewhere. This cynicism about human greatness is not only cultural, it is not only explained by the fact that we westerners are very egalitarian, do not like anyone taking the higher moral ground, and think of society as collective goodness emerging out of individual vices. There are more principled reasons to doubt.

In this paper, I will argue that the problem is the choice of the wrong conception of practical skill as a starting point to model virtue. Virtue is indeed analogous to practical skill, but not in the sense of skill we have in mind most of the time. As it will be made clear, there is a radical difference between skill as competence, which is aimed at and defined by performance, and skill as mastery, which is aimed at and defined by the search for superior understanding. And the difference is not just an issue of attitude or motivation: competence and mastery are two completely different processes and cognitive phenomena. It is not the same thing done for different reasons, but two different things.

I am going to introduce theories of expertise and learning coming from a field in cognitive learning sciences known as 'learning for understanding' or 'learning as an expert' (Hiebert and Carpenter 1992). I will focus on the seminal work of Carl Bereiter and Marlene Scardamalia, which is the best fit for a dialogue with virtue ethics since it stresses the social and motivational conditions necessary for the quest to understand to flourish instead of the techniques to enhance understanding as much as possible that are currently employed in standard learning institutions.

I will encourage virtue ethicists to think of morality as a quest for superior practical understanding, not for better moral performance.

Morality is not well served by a competence analogy: I will show that pursuing this analogy will imply exactly the kind of cynicism about moral greatness we actually feel in our everyday lives, which is more dangerous than the one diagnosed by Susan Wolf in her famous critique of moral saints.

The moral cynicism can be spelled out in three sobering points. When the awe we do feel about heroes subsides, if we are honest with ourselves: (i) we think these great models are rare, (ii) we do not actually think we should become like them, and (iii) we are not even persuaded that imitating them in service of our more modest goal of 'decency' as persons fully makes sense. These three points directly follow from thinking of morality as a competence.

I will then explain how modelling virtue on mastery allows us to avoid moral cynicism. It will become clear that virtue and wisdom must be conceptualized in a way that is congruent with the approach of Alasdair MacIntyre in *After Virtue*. Finally, I will draw some tentative implications on ways to build wiser institutions, in the mastery approach, inspired by an integration of MacIntyre's perspective with school reform proposals put forward by Bereiter and Scardamalia. Virtue theory and cognitive learning sciences will correct and complement each other, jointly supporting an empirically informed neo-Aristotelian account of wisdom.

10.1 Competence and Mastery

How is expertise related to real performance? In the approach I am introducing here, there are two fundamentally different ways to become an expert capable of performing reliably, distinguished by the type of motivation to learn. The first is the way of competence associated with performance motivation and the second is the way of mastery defined by understanding motivation.

Performance motivation is the default type we have in mind most of the time: it anchors expertise to a specific target level of performance. We start with what needs to be done, as it were, and call expertise the ability to do it reliably. And that's it. To drive a cab you need to know the streets, so an expert cab driver will have the map of the district in his head. If you go to live in China you need to become fluent in Chinese, and since the learning space is anchored to a reference performance level, your incentive will be finding the most economic learning method to get exactly there, which leaves out inefficient ways to fluency (too much effort for the same result) as well as any method that would aim at higher learning goals. Because that would be overshooting: you do not need to read or write poetry in Chinese. Cost efficiency is the only goal.

But sometimes human beings have the intrinsic interest to understand a problem at a higher level, to see more subtleties. This can happen in isolated instances: for example, instead of just needing to use the oven to bake a pie you may want to understand better how the oven works. But learning how to operate the oven either out of incentive or out of genuine curiosity would not make a lot of difference, if we were to leave it at that. The interesting cognitive differences between performance and mastery emerges in the long term, in the same way as two different sports make for two different physical builds.

The interesting question is this: what is the difference between a significantly extended competence and a correspondingly elevated level of mastery in the same field? We will see that there are major differences at the level of how information is organized around more or less complex 'schemas' in the mind of the learner, and concerning the social model of learning and division of labour favoured by either competence or mastery. In the two following sections it will emerge that competence is cheaper in terms of cognitive resources, but also narrow, locked to the context of initial learning and difficult to transfer. Mastery is cognitively very costly but flexible, more easily transferable and generative. Socially, it favours participative settings and emulation of role models, while competence is better suited to a scenario of rigid specialization of roles with weak emulation.

10.2 Competence as Our Default Notion of Skill

Cost effectiveness and resource saving are the most basic and universal constraints for any complex self-sustaining system. Accordingly, cost-effective skill acquisition is pervasive at any scale and level of analysis, from the unconscious learning strategies of the individual to the methodologies of large learning institutions. As a result, competence is the default notion of skill both for common sense and in the scientific understanding of learning. Most often, 'competence' and 'skill' are taken to be synonymous.

How does competence building unfold in the long term? According to Bereiter and Scardamalia, it follows a process they call 'assimilative problem solving' (1993, 168).

Acquisition of practical skill requires extended practice with solving problems specific to the domain, where the notion of 'problem' is very large and includes any 'how to do' question specific to the field. If you aim at performance, problem-solving will be assimilative in the sense that you hope old strategies and knowledge work again with each new challenge. You hope that, in spite of the appearance of novelty, you will know how to deal with it. The new problem is assimilated to old ones. This would save you precious cognitive resources.

If you stress about organizing a meeting and then you are relieved remembering you have already organized several birthday parties for your kids, you have an assimilative attitude.

As an example of assimilation, in studies on expertise some doctors fit an x-ray by default to the closest diagnosis they know while other doctors acknowledge the need for more information when the case is not clear. Some pianists asked to adapt a percussion piece to piano will fit it by default to the closest style they have already mastered, while other will study how to render the percussion effect on piano in innovative ways (Bereiter and Scardamalia 1993, 156–9).

Facing a learning task, at an unconscious and sub-personal level, our cognitive system chooses by default the way of the minimal and less effortful adaptation needed to produce the performance. The cognitive mechanisms involved aim at first finding and then internalizing any easy heuristics and procedures that would work. The search for these easy heuristics is always on during our everyday life, in what cognitive scientists call tacit learning through observational exposure and practice (Reber 1996).

We search through a spontaneous pattern-recognition process that associates recurring situations to strategies that have worked. Be it playing chess, writing, relationship management, or actually anything, we are always unconsciously searching for patterns and heuristics (Gigerenzer and Todd 1999).

Assimilative problem-solving starts at the level of understanding we already have spontaneously available, thanks to past learning. This point is fundamental to the iterative nature of the process. In the long process of skill building, sometimes assimilation will not work. The genuine cognitive effort spent solving those especially difficult problems will be repaid by an increased ability to assimilate further problems, thanks to the new stock of knowledge. It makes sense to use schemas already available, and tacit learning will be as 'intelligent' as the resources available. Effortful cognitive reorganization in itself is the cost our brain is trying to minimize.

For example, as a result of iterative assimilation over a long period, a chess player who happens to observe some Go matches (or practise casually) will unconsciously pick patterns at a higher level than a total beginner in board games. This is because he has already available higher level 'interpretative schema' that happens to be relevant to Go. He could for instance notice that his opponent's opening strategy implies an unbalanced risk reward matrix, meaning that he is taking risk whose reward is modest and possible damage huge.

Assimilative problem-solving is also systematically pursued by formal learning institutions, trying to improve on the efficiency of tacit learning. Things can go faster than when you 'pick up' skills from the environment by effortless exposure or simple practice. A target level of performance being the goal, it is rational to optimize the process by finding ways to learn in two years what used to take four.

This is the very challenge defining most learning institutions: the promise to take you to a specified level of performance applying the easiest pedagogy available. This 'optimization of competence acquisition' philosophy is everywhere. From getting a driving licence to solving equations, the method is drilling the most successful procedures until they become second nature.

But what are the cognitive features of a vast skill set of competence, acquired in the long term under the dire constraints of resource saving? A good metaphor is opposing breadth and depth. In the quest for competence, long experience in a field teaches a lot. This must be granted. In twenty years' work experience as an hotel clerk, your practical habits will have absorbed many distinctions, but the overall structure of your skill set will be disjunctive: you will know that in situation x, you do a, in situation y, you do b, and so on. It is not like learning by heart, because there is some level of organization, but it is very close. The information is not highly organized around interconnected principles and mental schemas. The set of habits is broad but not deep. This is the result of mere exposure or unqualified experience: a taxi driver having the city's map in his head after ten years' service.

Think of different areas of a city before efficient public transport and the internet: a number of largely autonomous zones weakly connected. The neighbourhoods are juxtaposed, you will most likely spend one entire day in a specific zone, according to your needs, instead of freely and quickly circulating from one place to the other. In a sense, you have many different towns. The same is true for a vast competence: it is like the weak unification of different sub-skills that retains substantial autonomy. A measure of unification is still there: you do learn how to switch among sub-skills. But they are not subtly interspersed at a deep level.

Competence is also associated with a specific model of group cooperation, stressing complementarity without emulation. The reason why a large army is powerful is not that every single soldier is good at the same individual skill of fighting. Actually, not everyone will even fight. There is logistics, intelligence, technical support, and so on. Excellence at fighting only emerges at the collective level, in the overall organization.

This has two fundamental consequences: there is no relationship of emulation between higher- and lower-rank individuals. In spite of the fact that certain roles are more sensitive and highly prized than others (the general is valued more highly than a common soldier), the soldier does not have to aim at becoming a general. On the contrary, it may be dangerous that all soldiers be overambitious; the quality of the overall organization depends on every part playing its role well.

Efficiency and specialization are paramount. People are assigned different functions that have to be executed reliably and efficiently. Qualities are needed only if relevant for the task. Continuous striving for individual excellence is not required. It is even possible that collective virtue emerges out of individual vices. Insofar as individuals evolve, it is because they come to be assigned a new function in the overall organizational schema, and have to adapt to the new role.

Of course, groups do often have universal requirements about specific skills, for example, concerning fluency in a language or basic levels of physical fitness, but this only covers few entry-level skills, the general model being built on specialization.

10.3 The Advantages of Mastery

Mastery is not tied to any fixed level of performance. It is defined by the motivation of understanding a field at increasingly higher levels of cognitive complexity, subtlety, and sophistication. This is the case of champions in sport and other competitive domains, as well as scholars. As there is no clear upper limit of reference, the requirement is, as it were, about constant evolvability. There is a craving for challenging novelty, for new problems that would require us to stretch our understanding.

Bereiter and Scardamalia call the process necessary to build mastery 'progressive problem solving' (1993, 96). Time and energy liberated after current problems are solved is constantly reinvested in the search for new challenging problems. A problem is challenging if solving it would promote performance and understanding (the detail and cognitive sophistication of our models) at the same time. As a consequence, performance is not forgotten, because problem-solving ability is enhanced, but not just any progress in performance will be pursued. Mere extension of power within the same conceptual model of a field is not interesting. The best example of this is the way science focuses on anomalies and hard problems whose solution would stretch our understanding and make our models evolve.

In domains defined by progressive problem-solving, experts are requested to get constantly better, to improve all the time, pushing the boundaries of the state of the art.

The most significant difference of the path of mastery with respect to the path of competence is that the information absorbed in the habits gets organized around a more advanced mental model (Bereiter and Scardamalia 1993, 167–75). The cognitive structure of mastery shows deepness and interconnection among sub-skills: in our metaphor, it is like a city deeply interconnected by internet and transportation. This is not surprising: motivationally, mastery aims at thinking and acting at higher levels of complexity. A taste for challenges is cultivated. The consequence is more flexibility, increased capability to transfer knowledge to new domains, and increased likelihood of not being stuck at a plateau of development.

Information relevant to problem-solving must percolate down and get automatized into habits in order to be operational. Habit formation takes time and only happens through practising: simply theorizing about how things should be done is not conducive to real skill. Information internalized in habits can be organized at different levels of cognitive sophistication. Let's say you know how to respond to a specific opening in chess, not making major mistakes up to the third or fourth move. It may be the case that you have learned all the possibilities by heart, which is a zero level of systematization of information, equivalent to learning the phonebook. Or you could recognize in it a sophisticated type of opening, or you may be somewhere in between, recognizing some aspects but not others. This is sophistication built through practical habits, not through rhetoric or intellectual sophistication. You may or may not be capable at making your practical schemas explicit: for sure, you cannot explicate most of them.

The cognitive sophistication of mastery is conducive to more flexibility. There is some irony here, since cognitive sophistication creates a risk of rigidity: being stuck in the same schema and categories as interpretative lenses of reality, unable to see things differently. But, paradoxically, it is competence, which does not prize sophistication, that falls under the burden of rigidity. This is because mastery pushes through whatever temporary plateau of understanding it may have consolidated in the past, solving the problem of rigidity. Whereas competence, not valuing sophistication, is stuck with whatever interpretative schema it has deployed. Competent experts are locked into the mentality that allowed them to reach their level of performance.

This is clear in the phenomenon known in the psychology of expertise as the Einstellung effect (Bilalic, McLeod, and Gobet 2008; Luchins 1942). This is where there is an error only competent practitioners will make in some specific cases, because of their rigid interpretative schema. It is an error of familiarity: the problem will look very familiar to the expert, but is in fact subtly different and requires a different solution. There is extensive experimental literature on Einstellung, especially focusing on chess problems. But errors of false familiarity can be found everywhere, from more mundane cases such as waiters and typists to serious nuclear plant or train accidents (e.g. Hecht and Proffitt 1995). Now, the interesting empirical finding is that both beginner and very high-level experts are immune to these problems: Einstellung is the domain of the competent practitioner (Bilalic, McLeod, and Gobet 2008). Related findings are that 'just good enough' performers adapt with more difficulty to small changes to the rules of a game (Frensch and Sternberg 1991), and that most professionals do not get better with age and experience, being stuck in a plateau (Ericsson 2006). Competence is not flexible.

Learning sciences have shown that performance cannot be simply transferred from one field to another. Habits are dedicated and specialized, so a new field requires new habit formation processes. But existing mental models can be used in the new domain to speed up learning (Bransford and Schwartz 1999). For this reason, having a big toolkit of mental models helps in learning new skills. An expert mathematician will see the simple principle she understands at work in every aspect of reality, whereas a competent learner of complex calculus will just be able to pass the exams. He will only have acquired a highly specialized and almost mindless capacity to solve specific maths problems.

Because an expert is more flexible and capable of transferring knowledge, an expert is also more generative and capable of pushing a field in new directions. At the state of the art in a discipline, pushing through current models is done by finding unexpected applications, which is a form of transfer: seeing how past knowledge is relevant in a new territory.

The craving for challenging novelty is part of human nature, but it must be cultivated as it is not easily sustainable. It goes squarely against cost efficiency and must fight the temptation of assimilative learning. Real-life problems do not force on us the search for richer understanding; they could always be tackled trying to minimize effort. For this reason, progressive problem-solving is best pursed socially, as the norm and modus operandi of what Bereiter and Scardamalia call a community of practice. The isolated seeker is not a conceptual impossibility, but it is not an easily sustainable model.

From the start, activity in a community of practice is participative. In spite of complementarity at the level of specific tasks, everybody is in contact with the main challenges that are pursued. Cleaning the lab floor or making coffee does not count: if even a minimal contribution to the challenge is out of your reach, then you cannot be part of that specific community. PhD candidates are part of research projects alongside senior researchers. Of course, they are not playing the same role, but there is emulation. In the long term, the younger researcher aims at reaching (and maybe overcoming) the level of understanding of the field of the senior. In other words, a community pursuing progressive problem-solving is more like a basketball team than like a modern army. A basketball team is competitive because every single player excels at the same skill of basketball playing. Even taking into account the influence of specialized roles in gameplay and other elements such as team spirit, collective excellence in basketball is heavily dependent on individual excellence, intended as mastery of a large set of fundamentals specific to this sport.

10.4 Why Virtue Should Not Be Modelled on Competence

Thinking of progressively becoming a better person in terms of acquiring moral competence is a terrible analogy for virtue ethics. As I will show, the notion of moral competence implies a radical form of moral cynicism according to which our best moral models—while extremely useful for society—should not be imitated *at all* by normal people, who should aim at basic moral decency. This is exactly the opposite of what Aristotelian virtue ethics has ever tried to show, at least if it is to be taken at face value. Unless, that is, ideas of moral progress and imitation of the wise are entirely to be reduced to 'feel good' motivational talk, and virtue terms such as 'courageous' and 'generous' to badges we attribute to each other to stabilize cooperation and reward good action, with no reference to substantial psychological phenomena.

In this section I will show the radical tension between the psychology of competence and 'core' Aristotelian virtue ethics, and I will give prima facie reasons to consider mastery as a more promising model. Much more needs to be proven in order to accept a specific mastery model of virtue and wisdom, which may turn out to be utopian and have major problems of its own. I will defend my mastery account of wisdom in the last section, after both its architecture based in MacIntyre's philosophy and the substantial implications for education explored by Bereiter and Scardamalia have been fleshed out. Nonetheless, the incompatibility between competence and virtue is a much more general claim that could motivate a new avenue of research for contemporary Aristotelians not persuaded by the specifics of my positive proposal. As such, the claim deserves to be singled out.

The *morally* problematic features of competence are the most general features of competence *as such*, as they would apply to *any* domain. The case against moral competence as virtue does not rest on complex issues of definition of the moral domain as opposed to other normative realms. The social and psychological landscape carved by competence thinking is profoundly anti-Aristotelian in itself. It entails complementarity without emulation: while we all benefit from the existence of a minority of champions, most of us should aim at a decent level; there should be few Olympic athletes and a mass of daily joggers.

Interacting with moral exemplars with the goal of emulating them is a core prescription of virtue ethics, a cornerstone of the Aristotelian conception of moral progress. If you think of moral excellence as a competence, this alienates you from moral models. When awe subsides, you do not really want to become like them, for the same reason a jogger does not want to become a triathlete. There are barriers of motivation and resources. Your motivation to jog half an hour a day has nothing to do with the motivation to become a world-class triathlete: a general sense of admiration for the latter achievement does nothing to rally you to the cause. Your jogging competence is adapted to half-an-hour daily runs, and would not prepare you in the least for a professional triathlon. For all that matters, it would not be more difficult to switch from daily jogger to professional musician. In the end, you will recognize that professional athleticism and recreational sport are two very different things. The fact that society is made so much better by the existence of few champions does not change the situation. The two paths being so different, it is not even clear that any modest amount of imitation would be warranted at all. Leaving aside the motivational boost, a daily jogger has probably nothing substantial to learn from the training routine of Michael Jordan.

In the competence model, when the awe in facing moral heroes subsides, we all just want to be decent persons, the equivalent of the daily jogger. And if we are honest with ourselves, this is already very difficult. We will leave the call to heroism to a small moral elite that we will then admire but not emulate at all, since the path of moral decency and the path of moral excellence have nothing in common. This scenario is as bad for core neo-Aristotelian virtue ethics as it could get. Virtue ethics is reduced to wishful thinking and motivational speeches.

At the psychological level of the individual, things do not look brighter. The rigid context-locked narrowness of moral competence does not square with the subtle and general capacity for moral judgement associated with practical wisdom in a neo-Aristotelian perspective. After all, in recent decades virtue ethics has been invoked to bring rich texture back to moral life, a goal not served by the harsh resource-saving constraints of competence. Moral competence would most certainly fall victim to the situational influences described by social psychology and discussed by philosophers in the last decade.

To better see the danger of the competence account for Aristotelian virtue, let us contrast it with Susan Wolf's attack on perfect moral models in 'Moral Saints' (1982). I will show that the latter is much weaker, as it depends on a narrow and controversial definition of the moral domain that does not fit Aristotelian accounts of virtue in the first place.

According to Wolf, a morally perfect person would tend to be humourless, dull, boring. It is not that morality, at any given level, is incompatible with non-moral qualities, but the overarching commitment to moral perfection would take away the time and energy required to cultivate any non-moral dimension. Morality is only one aspect of life. By endlessly wanting more of it, other dimensions will be suffocated. In fact, we seem to like models that stopped investing in 'even more' morality: 'one prefers the mischievousness and the sense of irony in Chesterton's Father Brown to the innocence and undiscriminating love of St. Francis' (1982, 423).

Accordingly, the same one-sidedness charge would apply to different forms of fanaticism. 'It is shared by the conception of the pure aesthete, by a certain kind of religious ideal, and, somewhat paradoxically, by the model of the thorough-going, self-conscious egoist' (1982, 424).

Wolf thinks that too much morality is undesirable because it would crowd out other human dimensions. But she is eager to stress that forms of human greatness to be admired and sought after do exist: her only contention is with a moralistic account of them. She explicitly defends an intuitionist perfectionist account of human greatness where the character of genuine human models is too complex and rich to be explained by any single evaluative dimension, be it moral, aesthetic, or other. We recognize better persons, but we cannot have a theory of what this superiority is. Any attempt would be reductionist: reduction to moral superiority being a typical temptation.

Wolf's argument trades on the definition of the moral domain as narrow, and by her own admission, it is at its weakest against Aristotelian virtue ethics (1982, 433). Despite recognizing that Aristotle has a very broad notion of morality, Wolf reiterates the point that overdeveloping morality would be one-sided, even in that broad sense of the notion. Intentionally or not, here Wolf is misrepresenting Aristotle. The broad sense of morality Aristotle is talking about encompasses all practical life: there is no part of life that is not relevant to the virtues. Wolf uses morality as something that by definition is opposed to the domain of the non-moral. But this is alien to Aristotle, for whom the moral standpoint is the one from where we can make general sense of practical rationality. A human quality is not an Aristotelian virtue if it is not fundamental from the perspective of how things fit together. Wolf writes as if wisdom or eudaimonia were moralistic notions in a modern sense, but they are not.

Aristotelian virtue ethics is left relatively unscathed by Wolf's arguments, while it appears completely defaced in the competence model of moral skills.

But things look completely different if we model virtue on mastery instead of competence. If moral improvement is the constant search for superior practical understanding, through tackling life problems that would enhance the cognitive sophistication of our moral skills, our take on the difficulty of moral learning changes.

Competence is based on cost-effectiveness: a goal that is too difficult to reach becomes irrational. Excellent moral competences are too difficult to reach and so aiming at them is irrational.

But mastery is a process that does not aim at anything specified in advance. It simultaneously increases understanding and performance, step by step. Being stuck at a plateau is no reason not to push in search of a breakthrough.

Think of science. We do not even know what a perfect theory of physics or biology would look like. Scientists just try to formulate better theories than existing ones and to reach deeper understanding: they push as long as it is needed. In the same way, virtue requires us to act on the level of understanding of practical reality we have, while keeping actively to push through and reach deeper understanding. Progress is not made irrational by being difficult.

As for moral models, if virtue is modelled on mastery then specialization is no longer the enemy of emulation. Think of a research team engaged in progressive problem-solving. Cooperation is both participative and emulative. The youngest researcher is not just making photocopies; his or her insights are useful and vital. At the same time, everybody wants to emulate the level of understanding of the senior researcher, who is the living proof that superior understanding is possible. The relation between apprentice and model is thus both participative and emulative.

Prima facie, mastery seems a more promising starting point to think of virtue and wisdom in terms of skills.

10.5 Practical Wisdom as a Form of Mastery

As I will show across the three remaining sections, the account of virtue developed by Alasdair MacIntyre in *After Virtue* is a surprisingly good fit with the distinction between mastery and competence in psychology, so good that we have a case of interdisciplinary convergence: research programmes in cognitive learning sciences support MacIntyre's ideas.

MacIntyre develops a three-level account of virtue: the first level is composed by social practices, the second level is the narrative history of the individual as it unfolds through participation in several practices, the third level is the notion of a tradition where several practices are coordinated in the long term.

MacIntyre gives the following definition of a practice:

By a 'practice' I am going to mean any coherent and complex form of socially established cooperative human activity through which goods internal to that form of activity are realised in the course of trying to achieve those standards of excellence which are appropriate to, and partially definitive of, that form of activity, with the result that human powers to achieve excellence, and human conceptions of the ends and goods involved, are systematically extended. Tic-tac-toe is not an example of a practice in this sense, nor is throwing a football with skill; but the game of football is, and so is chess. Bricklaying is not a practice; architecture is. Planting turnips is not a practice; farming is. So are the enquiries of physics, chemistry and biology, and so is the work of the historian, and so are painting and music. (1984, 175)

According to MacIntyre, different practices have something in common: several recurring types of problems can be found in most or all of them. These problems are connected with difficulties humans, as the kind of being they are, will typically have in pursuing those quests. For example, in pursuing science one will be confronted with situations requiring intellectual courage and intellectual honesty: otherwise, the scientific quest itself is compromised. In competitive sports, one may need physical courage or loyalty. As a consequence, virtue cultivation is built in any and every practice.

But there is a further level of development. If a single practice is an opportunity to practise virtue, individual cultivation of virtues has to unfold over several practices, in the long term. One will find only a limited set of courage problems in the pursuit of sciences, for example. Courage problems in competitive sports will be different ones. Someone involved in both disciplines will be able to have an inter-practice (and not only intra-practice) take on courage. He or she will understand courage at a deeper level, seeing common aspects and differences between courage in science and sport. Deeper understanding of virtue comes out of practising virtue problem-solving in different settings, and coming to see the underlying unity. Overall, the individual will cultivate various virtues through participation in several practices.

> A quest is always an education both as to the character of that which is sought and in self-knowledge. The virtues therefore are to be understood as those dispositions which will not only sustain practices and enable us to achieve the goods internal to practices, but which will also sustain us in the relevant kind of quest for the good. By enabling us to overcome the harms, dangers, temptations and distractions which we encounter, and which will furnish us with increasing self-knowledge and increasing knowledge of the good. (MacIntyre 1984, 219)

If getting better at life is cultivating practical understanding in many different domains, practical wisdom has the 'meta' function of managing the process itself. As you progressively understand how to be a better scientist, athlete, colleague, or father, you also progressively understand how to solve conflict and interferences within and among first-order learning processes. To use a computer analogy, it is as if the operating system got better at the same time as each individual application improves. Practical wisdom is the progressive understanding of how to solve conflicts within and among local quests of understanding.

As with single virtues, it is useful to distinguish between inter- and intra-practice levels. Wisdom problems are already built into every practice: for example, issues of honesty, courage, and justice may interact in complex ways in scientific research. But a deeper level is reached from an inter-practice perspective, having been confronted with virtue management issues in several domains.

An individual life finds progressively its unity and meaning through extended socialization in a plurality of practices. What is this unity? It is the very realization that different activities express facets of the same notion of human excellence. The plurality of goods one is pursuing is progressively woven together in the narrative of a global quest for understanding: 'the good life for man is the life spent in seeking for the good life for man, and the virtues necessary for the seeking are those which will enable us to understand what more and what else the good life for man is' (MacIntyre 1984, 219).

But there is still a further level. I have been talking of the need to manage different practices at the individual level, as if the issue was just solving conflicts between your career as scientist and musician. But the individual level of practical wisdom cannot be the whole story. Just as you do not invent the practices but you are socialized in them, you are also socialized in typical ways of articulating the interaction among them. This 'politics of practices' is what constitutes a tradition for MacIntyre. Traditions are typically instantiated in institutions such as universities, schools, or hospitals where several practices evolve in interaction. Institutions that express a tradition in this sense are the smallest social unity where virtue cultivation can be autonomously and consistently sustained.

There is a clear similarity between the notion of practice and the knowledge-building communities Bereiter and Scardamalia talk about. We have seen that mastery is the extensive cultivation of practical understanding in communities of practice, each community having its own specific understanding of goals tackled with progressive problem-solving. The examples given in the two cases are by and large the same: scientists, sport, medicine, etc.

But then, if we have a variety of ongoing quests for understanding, mastering virtue cannot be just one among them. This would be thinking in terms of a competence that can be isolated, learned, and then applied. On the contrary, problems of virtues are infused in every practice, so that it makes sense to follow MacIntyre in defining virtue as a solution to typical human weakness in pursuing cooperative understanding.

The individual deepens progressively his understanding of practical life through long-term participation in a variety of practices. As mastery prepares for future learning, the individual on the slow path of wisdom cultivation would become better prepared to further moral learning.

10.6 Implications for Education

Most authors defending the competence vs mastery distinction work in cognitive learning sciences and are interested in reforming school. Today, education is defined by performance goals: students should reach predefined proficiency levels in maths, spelling, grammar, history, etc. The most common complaint is that school fails at its mission, results are getting worse (numeracy or literacy levels going down), and vital competences for modern life are left out of the curriculum.

But the problem may be more radical: emphasizing competences and results, school inculcates the wrong mentality and stops short of the cultivation of practical understanding. How could progressive problem-solving be applied to school? There is a conundrum here, because cultivating practical understanding requires motivation to take seriously and tackle challenging problems. The challenge is relative to the level of the learner, so calibrating the difficulty level should be enough.

The problem is motivation: why should the child be interested in knowing how the cell works? Personal interests vary and school cannot count on pre-existing passions. In communities of practice, people become sensitive to what is considered a real challenge for that community and put effort into advancing towards a solution. But the problem must be a real one, whose solution is unknown, not a mocked or 'staged' problem. Students know both that someone has the right answer of the physics problem, and that they cannot contribute anything to physics at their stage. This is profoundly demotivating: motivation to understand is cultivated though social relevance and participation.

It seems that acquiring competences that give you enough skill eventually to take an active role in some real community of practice is the only way left, and this is what schools do. But this completely misses the point of cultivating practical understanding: if students internalize a competence mentality, the cause of practical understanding is already lost.

A way out of this conundrum would be by applying to education the leagues system of sport. Soccer in the second division does not contribute directly to advance the state of the art of football playing, but it does not lack any social relevance. First, it is connected in interesting ways to the first division, as players may eventually be promoted. Second, it does contribute to developing as much soccer excellence as possible, under more limited constraints and in places where there would be none if only the first division was accorded relevance. The league systems help motivation of beginner and intermediate players. Compared to other forms of awards and reward for beginners, a division has the advantage of being a perfect reproduction of the optimal motivational environment (i.e. participative contribution to the state of the art). Except for pushing the boundaries of the field, anything else that can happen in the first division can happen in the second: great comebacks, exciting rivalry, becoming a hero, and so on.

We are far too obsessed by performance anxiety, the idea that many competences are needed in the modern world. Let us think differently. A student should not be considered as learning neither some nor a lot of biology (competence), but as 'practising biology in the third division'. The motivational difference is huge. The class become a third-division community of scientists developing problems and solutions at their level of understanding, being helped by the teacher as a senior researcher and not being fed the right solution from the top, at least not too early.

While not using the league analogy explicitly, Bereiter and Scardamalia think of school reform in similar terms. Classes are knowledge-building communities with their own internal computer system of communication and publication of results, the equivalent of scientific journals. The results of their efforts really matter: they are accessible for other classes to reference in order for them to have as many real life consequences as possible.

They try to make advances in problems of understanding they really experience, by authentic research activity. But how is this different from asking children to prepare a presentation on dinosaurs? Apart from proper infrastructure and facilitation, the main difference is that 'third-division' research activity must be taken seriously. If it is just a game or a way of speaking, it is worthless: children will acquire neither practical understanding nor competence. In some pilot schools supervised by Bereiter and Scardamalia, the research activity of the children is taken as seriously as possible (1993, 210–16).

The bigger obstacle to extending these pedagogical experiments is social and cultural, not technical. As long as the social demand for school is teaching competences, then any attempts to act as if it was different are doomed. Society should accept that children evolve as little experts in third divisions, and that it will make them more motivated, flexible and capable to adapt and transfer their knowledge to other fields, even if eventually they do not get promoted from the third to the second (or first) division in that particular subject matter.

I have been concerned with the socio-motivational approach of Bereiter and Scardamalia because it is the best fit for a dialogue with virtue ethics, but it should be noticed that many authors in the learning for understanding movement are concerned with techniques to enhance understanding without deep institutional reforms. The techniques are interesting on their own count and may have ethical implications as well.

For example, meta-cognitive strategies literally aim at helping students extract more mental models from experience than they would have done otherwise. When students have enough practice in a sufficiently varied number of relevant situations, their performance increases if they are helped in noticing recurrent patterns and higher-level generalizations. In practice, students must be guided through many instances of a phenomenon (in as many different contexts as possible) and given principles to structure this rich experiential knowledge (Halpern 1998; Gelder 2005).

Deliberate practice is another good example. It is a style of training in which every weakness in the understanding of the student is systematically and repeatedly addressed. This is the opposite of performance-driven learning: instead of producing performance in spite of shortcomings and limitations in the understanding of the student (e.g. executing multiplications correctly, in spite of basic shortcomings about numbers), the very goal of deliberate practice is uncovering and systematically eradicating the misconceptions. Top performers in many fields train following this strategy (Ericsson 2006).

The main limitations of these techniques is that they all require a lot of energy and the source of motivation is left unspecified, whereas Bereiter and Scardamalia tackle the motivational problem upfront.

10.7 Building Wiser Institutions

How could we favour acquisition of virtue and practical wisdom? Here the convergence between Bereiter and Scardamalia and MacIntyre becomes clear again: we should transform school into a knowledge-building community. Better, a set of knowledge-building communities where students practise as little experts in third-division maths, biology, literature, etc. Students should not be prepared to a life starting after school, but rather initiated in the process of understanding the world, from the start. Even if they cannot contribute to the state of the art of any discipline, their research efforts should be taken seriously in and outside school. Those schools would be institutions bearing a tradition in the sense of MacIntyre's third-level account of virtue: institutions where several practices are jointly cultivated in the long term. Their teachers will be guides and role models in research activities that matter. Since their efforts matter, students will confront problems of virtue and wisdom in their endeavours. Those opportunities to exercise virtues and wisdom in the quest for understanding should be brought to focus and discussed by teachers to help students recognize underlying dynamics and develop better mental models.

Here the mastery account of wisdom faces a major objection, a fundamental problem not solved but actually worsened by MacIntyre's account of good institutions. It seems the idea of cultivating virtues and wisdom through several practices in learning communities is only plausible in a strong and radical reading of the kind of 'politics of practice' that would have to knit the community together.

If we are to become wise accumulating virtue lessons through different practices, the process should be as complete and harmonious as possible, the ideal being an institution perfectly organized as a training field of virtue. There must be activities that grow courage, others generosity or justice, and so on. Every facet of any virtue should figure somewhere in the curriculum, as it were. Such a well-rounded cultivation of practical wisdom would indeed be impressive.

Otherwise, if the claim is that we learn *some* ethical lessons in community environments where intrinsic motivation to tackle important goals is encouraged (for example in communities of practices focused on art, mathematics, and music), the sense of moral learning involved seems plausible (we *do* gain those isolated moral insights) but is too diluted to be significant. We would not call this an extensive ethical cultivation. Since it is utopian to reform institutions to match the ideal of a perfect microcosm for virtue training, the mastery account of virtue would seem to lose plausibility as it gains traction.

The theoretical source of this objection is a strong endorsement of the unity of the virtue, of which MacIntyre is guilty (1984, ch. 12). The traditional claim in the Aristotelian tradition is that true virtue is real only if all the virtues are present and act in coordination with practical wisdom. In a more charitable reading, only the central and most important virtues have to be deeply integrated. Now, since moral cultivation is socially embedded, even the latter qualified understanding of the claim makes moral learning extremely fragile outside of perfect conditions. This is the direction MacIntyre is indeed taking. He draws a picture of rare microcosms and niches of virtue in a sea of moral decadence.

But this radical reading of the unity of the virtue cannot be right. Here learning sciences on mastery come to the rescue of ethics. Acquisition of mastery is progressive and goes through stages corresponding to ever-increasing levels of understanding. It is true that higher (as opposed to lower) levels of mastery tend to unify and harmoniously coordinate different aspects of a craft. This is the correct intuition behind the unity of the virtue claim. If a violinist has not yet experimented with staccato or double stops, we expect her to integrate those techniques harmoniously in her playing style at further stages of her development. Mastery does approximate integration in the long term.

But then, the correct implications for the value of intermediate stages of understanding are exactly the opposite of what the unity of virtue is taken to imply. Partial and lacunary stages of understanding are not a wasteland between complete moral decadence and full perfection, they are valuable in their own right.

For cultural or economic reasons, society rewards arbitrary levels of performance. If you study the violin, the first recognition will come when you can impress your friends and family, then nothing until you reach the next reward level, which may be graduating from conservatory, then still nothing until (or if) you start a soloist career. Focusing on performance with a competence mentality creates a huge wasteland of skill levels for which there is no demand.

In the path of competence, stopping in this grey area is irrational, as the additional effort is not repaid by any marginal benefit. If you did not plan to graduate from music school, then stop improving when you manage to impress your friend. But if you pursue understanding in a community of practice, between the moment you can play your first easy Vivaldi sonata and the time you graduate playing Paganini's Caprices you go through several discrete stages of insight in the art of the violin. Each of those stages is valuable in its own right and can be the source of transfer of mental models to other domains. You could stop at those intermediary stages and your learning would have been worth it. After all, even the present state of the art is a temporary stage of understanding to be overcome in the future.

The possibility of a meaningful stop in the pursuit of mastery in a specific domain is very important to stress. It has essential ethical implications for the mastery model of wisdom. In the kind of tradition in cognitive learning sciences I am referring to, stopping in the path of understanding is not so easy to justify, but I think that MacIntyre here comes to the rescue of learning scientists.

As the account stands, a given level of mastery is said to be superior to a corresponding level of competence because mastery is more flexible and generative. Those advantages could pay out in real life and be enough reason to prefer mastering differential calculus instead of passing the exam with the least effort.

But then why would you give up mathematics? Wasn't mastery mainly defined by the intrinsic passion to pursue an ever better understanding? It seems that by stopping one loses the spirit of mastery, if not all the advantages. Worse, by stopping one ends up sustaining the overall logic of competence. As explained above, competence does not pursue further cognitive complexity per se but does exploit opportunistically any cognitive model already available (remember the chess player being able to pick up Go). The insight gained by understanding calculus will be used to build new competences and the effort to 'infuse mastery in the system', as it were, will be lost as a drop of water in the sea.

This line of reasoning explains why we often seem to think that mastery is for lifelong pursuits only: not being sure about the future prospects of your practice (will I still be playing the violin in a few years?) becomes an argument to pursue competence, at least for the time being.

MacIntyre's idea that practices are coordinated by traditions solves this problem, by introducing an overall schema in which pursuit and accumulation of understanding never stops: when a specific pursuit of understanding stops, it is in favour of other pursuits, and mental schemas accumulate through practices instead of being lost back in the sea of competences. So, it is worth understanding calculus because that insight would flow to other mastery pursuits, in a coordinated and cumulative process. This allows for stopping in a specific pursuit while not losing the spirit of mastery.

It is definitely possible to build wiser institutions, where people would develop more advanced levels of practical wisdom. It would be 'intermediate' imperfect wisdom, but still valuable in its own right and a necessary stepping stone for reaching higher levels in future reforms.

In the same way that, in the learning for understanding tradition, strategies to enhance understanding (metacognitive strategies, deliberate practice) should be a complement and not a substitute for institutional reform towards the establishment of knowledge-building communities discussed by Bereiter and Scardamalia, strategies to cultivate practical wisdom as discussed by Athanassoulis (in this volume) should be a complement and not a substitute for serious institutional reform.

For all the merits that dedicated classes of ethics may have, they are best thought of as enhancing the kind of moral learning that takes place spontaneously in the right institutions, not as a substitute for it. Theory helps the one who is already practising in the right way, allowing for clarifications, and the establishment of hidden links. But the student who is not socialized in collective quests for practical and theoretical understanding and is only exposed to classes of ethics could at best develop isolated ethical competences. The narrower the criterion of ethical 'performance' adopted, the better that approach would look. If we aim to prevent specific behaviours such as aggression on campus or cheating at exams, the prospect of success may be reasonable. But no even moderately general form of practical wisdom will ever be generated in this way. Ethical competences are poorly transferable and locked to specific contexts.

Alfano (this volume) makes an important methodological point on theorizing about virtue: the high level of ambition of neo-Aristotelian virtue ethics is no warranty in itself. Utopian theories may lose the pulse of practical life and fare worse than less idealistic approaches in improving society. There may be more indirect benefits in approximating modest real-life moral goals than lofty ambitions. I think he is right: neo-Aristotelian ethics should not prosper out of respect for ancient tradition, but because it actually works. Further research will tell if the mastery account of wisdom I have sketched will meet the challenge.

If it does, we can start thinking how to build better institutions, with the help of virtue ethics and cognitive learning sciences. The only remaining question, which neither Bereiter and Scardamalia nor MacIntyre have answered, would then be how to rally the political willingness to promote this kind of reform.

Works Cited

Annas, Julia. 2011. *Intelligent Virtue*. Oxford: Oxford University Press.
Aristotle. 2002. *Nicomachean Ethics*. Trans. Christopher Rowe. Introduction by Sarah Broadie. Oxford: Oxford University Press.
Bereiter, Carl, and Marlene Scardamalia. 1993. *Surpassing Ourselves*. La Salle: Open Court.
Bilalic, Merim, Peter McLeod, and Fernand Gobet. 2008. Inflexibility of Experts—Reality or Myth? Quantifying the Einstellung Effect in Chess Masters. *Cognitive Psychology* 56 (2): 73–102.
Bransford, John D., and Daniel L. Schwartz. 1999. Rethinking Transfer: A Simple Proposal with Multiple Implications. *Review of Research in Education* 24: 61.
Ericsson, K. Anders. 2006. The Influence of Experience and Deliberate Practice on the Development of Superior Expert Performance. In *The Cambridge Handbook of Expertise and Expert Performance*, ed. K. Anders Ericsson, Neil Charness, Paul J. Feltovich, and Robert R. Hoffman. New York: Cambridge University Press, 683–703.
Frensch, Peter A., and Robert J. Sternberg. 1991. Skill-Related Differences in Game Playing. In *Complex Problem Solving: Principles and Mechanisms*, ed. Robert J. Sternberg and Peter A. Frensch. Hillsdale: Lawrence Erlbaum Associates, 343–81.
Gelder, Tim van. 2005. Teaching Critical Thinking: Some Lessons from Cognitive Science. *College Teaching* 53 (1): 41–8.
Gigerenzer, Gerd, and Peter M. Todd. 1999. *Simple Heuristics That Make Us Smart*. New York: Oxford University Press.
Halpern, D. F. 1998. Teaching Critical Thinking for Transfer across Domains. *American Psychologist* 53 (4): 449–55.
Hecht, Heiko, and Dennis R. Proffitt. 1995. The Price of Expertise: Effects of Experience on the Water-Level Task. *Psychological Science* 6 (2): 90–5.
Hiebert, James, and Thomas P. Carpenter. 1992. Learning and Teaching with Understanding. In *Handbook of Research on Mathematics Teaching and Learning: A Project of the National Council of Teachers of Mathematics*, ed. Douglas A. Grouws. New York: Macmillan, 65–97.
Luchins, Abraham S. 1942. Mechanization in Problem Solving: The Effect of Einstellung. *Psychological Monographs* 54 (6).
MacIntyre, Alasdair. 1984. *After Virtue*. Notre Dame: University of Notre Dame Press.
Reber, Arthur S. 1996. *Implicit Learning and Tacit Knowledge: An Essay on the Cognitive Unconscious*. Oxford: Oxford University Press.
Wolf, Susan. 1982. Moral Saints. *The Journal of Philosophy* 79 (8): 419–39.

Index

n = footnote. *t* = table/diagram.

actions
   (in)consistency with beliefs/attitudes 137–9, 141–3, 145–6
   justification 100
   out of character 65–6, 71
   reasons for 63–78
   responsibility for 71–2
Adams, Robert 191, 194
addiction, treatments of 45
agency 62–78
   counter-normative 71
   dual 74–8
   insufficiency of vocabulary 77
   overdetermination 65, 78
   unified 111–13
aggregation data 168–9
aggression
   amongst children 161, 163, 164–5, 166, 166*n*, 167*t*, 171*n*, 215
   situations appropriate to 47
   see also aggression-reducing drugs
aggression-reducing drugs 44, 47–50, 55
   conditions of use 48–9
   objections to 47–8
Aias (mythical character) 90–1, 92–3, 94, 98–9
alienation 113–14
Allport, Gordon 2–3
Alzheimer's disease 93
anger management therapy 44, 46, 48–9
Annas, Julia 17–18, 39, 190–1
Anscombe, Elizabeth 7, 40, 207–8
aretaic failure 21
Ariely, Dan 218–19
Aristotle 2, 9
   on character formation 7, 39–40, 125, 210, 213
   on friendship 187, 190–1, 190*n*, 200
   on habituation 15, 37, 111, 143*n*, 150
   on morality 242
   theory of virtue 5, 37, 63, 70–1, 134, 146*n*, 186, 211, 221, 225, 239–42, 249
   Nicomachean Ethics 15, 17, 39–40, 186, 187, 190–1
Arpaly, Nomy 85, 123*n*
art and personal necessity 96–8
aspiration 17–18
attitude psychology 141–3, 143*n*, 152
attitudes
   construction 143–5
   (in)stability of 139–41
   strength/weakness of 141–3, 144–5, 149–50
authenticity, of personality 5, 92–5
autonomy, personal 5, 81–2, 86, 87, 92–5
awe (of moral exemplars/sporting heroes) 229–30, 231, 240
Axsom, Danny 143*n*
Ayal, Shahal 218–19

Baier, Annette 64, 66
Bandura, Albert 155*n*, 213
'becoming another person' *see* personality, change of
behavioural dispositions 108–9, 115
   inconsistency with proclaimed views 134–5, 145–6
   situational variations 165–6, 216–17
   in unanticipated situations 144–5, 148
behavioural signatures
   intraindividual 164
   stability of 166
belief(s)
   actions inconsistent with 137–9
   belief–desire pairing, as reasons for actions 63–4
   integration with character 108–9
   unconscious 156–7

Bereiter, Carl 230, 231, 233, 236, 238, 239, 245, 247, 248, 252
Besser-Jones, Lorraine 108–9, 114, 128–9
Block, Jack 168*n*, 175–6
brain
 interventions 56
 medical complaints 93
Bratman, Michael E. 73
Breivik, Anders Behring 98–9
Browning, Robert 203
Buss, Arnold 216–17, 219

capital punishment 53*n*
CAPS *see* cognitive-affective system theory
castration *see* chemical castration
categorical imperative 86
Cervone, Daniel 212
Chalmers, David J. 194, 200
character
 actions not in accordance with 65–6, 71
 consistency 1, 100–1, 212
 definitions 62
 as determinant of behaviour 63–70
 as ethical concept 2–3, 5
 formation 7–8, 14–17, 124–5, 207–25
 impact of punishment on 3–4, 9, 12–14, 24–6, 27–8, 30–1, 32, 42–3
 limits of 81–2
 oversimplified views 56–7, 66–7
 personal responsibility for 15–16
 relationship with will *see* will
 role in liberal order 14–15
 shaping of 14–17
 single phenomenon view 74–8
 and situationism 1, 211–14
 social context 2
 Summary view of 68–9, 72–3, 170, 171
 viewed as unchangeable 56–7
 see also personality; reform; traits
chemical castration 4, 37, 52–6, 58
 arguments for/objections to 53–5
 chemical processes 53
 circumstances appropriate to 55–6
 circumstances of use 52–3
 jurisdictions employing 53
 voluntary acceptance 56
Chesterton, G. K. 241

children, behavioural studies 161, 163, 164–5, 166, 166*n*, 167*t*, 215
choice 15–17, 36–7, 212
 and agency 64–5, 68–9
 (claimed) lack of 21
 deprivation of 49–52, 54–5
 freedom of 20
 moral responsibility for 208
 see also moral choice blindness; prison, availability of choice in
civil society 12–14
 defined 12
 impact of prison sentences on 13, 24–5, 28–9, 30, 32–3
 relationship with liberal order 13–14
 role of personal interaction 28
Clark, Andy 107, 116–20, 121–3, 194, 200
cognitive-affective system theory 5–6, 137–9, 155–80
 aggregation 168–9
 central tenets 159–69
 and character traits 155, 169–74
 critiques 155, 175
 cross-situational consistency 164–6
 diagrammatic representation 177*t*, 178
 'if … then' behaviour contingencies 160–2, 160*n*, 172
 interaction of units 172–3*n*
 intraindividual behavioural signatures 164
 limitations 175–8
 nominal/psychologically salient situational features 162–4
 predictive elements 176*n*
 (problems of) practical application 177, 178, 179–80
 research building on 178–80
 restatement of basic platitudes 155–6, 174–5, 176
 stability of behavioural signatures 166
 units 159–60, 159*n*, 172
competence
 ceasing of efforts on attaining 250–1
 cost-effectiveness 232–3, 242
 as default notion of skill 232–5
 distinguished from mastery 231–2, 251
 education aimed at 246
 as educational goal 246, 247–8, 250

inflexibility 237–8
  as model for virtue 7, 230
    flaws in analogy 230–1, 239–43
    problematic features 240–1
    role of group cooperation 235
constructionism 90
constructivism 74n
control (of implicit bias) 107, 109–30
  direct 110–11, 118
  ecological *see* ecological control
  evaluative 113–14
  forms of 110n
  intervention 115–16, 127–8
  personal vs sub-personal
    mechanisms 118–19
  reflective 111–13, 119–20
  see also self-regulation
Cooper, Joel 143n
coordination, physical 117–18, 119
Corrado, Michael 23–4
cost-effectiveness and skill acquisition
  232–3, 242
courage 55, 244
  failure of 65–6
  nature of 186
Czech Republic, penal system 53

Davidson, Donald 77–8
dementia, among prisoners 57–8
Denmark, penal system 53
Dennett, Daniel 83, 118
DesAutels, Peggy 150n
desensitization, systematic 44
Devine, Patricia 112
diachronic unity 111–12
diminished responsibility 26–7
disease, impact on personality 93
dishonesty *see* honesty
Doris, John 26–7, 38, 90, 100–1, 155,
  193, 207, 210n, 219–20, 225
Dretske, Fred 194
drug use, rehabilitation following 45
  see also aggression-reducing drugs
Duff, Antony 41
duty 86–7

ecological control 116–29
  and character development 128–9
  defined 116–17
  and epistemic conditions 126–7
  and implicit bias 120–9

  and intervention control 127–8
  means of exercising 118–20
  pathways 118
  range of application 117–18
education 6–7, 207–25, 246–52
  aims 208–11, 215–16
  assessment programmes 223–4
  direct/indirect methods 214–15
  management of failure 217–18
  meta-cognitive strategies 248
  over-specification, risks of 210–11
  performance goals 246, 247–8
  practical guidance 209–10
  in practical wisdom 248–52
  role models 224–5
  situational management 216–19
  students' motivations 246
  virtues of good student 210–11
egalitarianism 112, 151–2
Einstellung effect 237–8
eliminativism 67–70, 75–7
  objections to 70–3
environment, care for 39
Epstein, Seymour 168
ethical theory 203
European Court of Human Rights 45n
expectancies 159
expertise, acquisition of 231–2

fanaticism 241
fear, feelings/expressions of 157–8,
  159–60, 163–4, 165–6, 173
Fischer, John 68, 74
Flanagan, Owen 101, 207
Fountains of Wayne 198–9
Frankfurt, Harry 67–8, 73, 89–90
friendliness, distinguished from
  friendship 190
friendship 186–204
  Aristotelian view 187, 190–1
  complexities of 189
  degrees of 192
  distinguished from other virtues 187,
    188–9
  empirical motive 193–4
  evaluative element 192
  externalist motive 194–5
  as model for trustworthiness
    195–202, 203
  modern commentaries 190–1,
    194–5

friendship (*cont.*)
  moral psychological motive 191–2
  motives for 190–5
  relational nature 187–90, 196
  self-awareness of 193–4, 198–9
  as 'thick' concept 191–2, 202
  as virtue/non-virtue 186, 187, 191

Galinsky, A. D. 116*n*
Galston, William 10
Gauguin, Paul 96–8
Geach, Peter 191
generosity 186–7
  degrees of 192
  'factitious' 193–4
Gino, Francesca 218–19
Glasgow, Joshua 108, 109, 114
Goldie, Peter 73, 74*n*
Greenpeace 141–2, 145
Guenther, Lisa 50, 52
guilt, feeling of 157

habituation 15, 37, 51–2, 57, 150, 213–14
  and acquisition of mastery 236–7
  to vice 31
Haney, Craig 24*n*, 25, 29
Harman, Gilbert 155, 193, 207
Hart, H. L. A. 36
Hartshorne, Hugh 207, 214–15, 224
Henderson, Shawn 57–8
hermeneutic phenomena 84
Herrndorf, Wolfgang 93
Hirstein, Bill 44*n*
Hobbes, Thomas 94
homicide, reasons for 43
honesty
  circumstances encouraging/discouraging 222–3, 224
  degrees of 192
  in differing situations 67, 193
  habituation in 37
  vs kindness 38
hope 199–201, 202
Hudson, Stephen D. 63*n*
Huigens, Kyron 40, 42
Hume, David 64, 66, 125
humility, paradox of 194*n*
hunger, feeling of 158
Hurka, Thomas 191
Hursthouse, Rosalind 191

identity, theories of 90
'if … then' situation-behaviour contingencies 160–2, 160*n*
implicit bias 4–5, 106–30
  associative nature 111–12, 115
  consequences 106
  control over *see* control
  defined 106
  and ecological control 120–9
  experiments 135–6, 144–5, 147, 151–2
  holders' alienation from 107–8, 113–14
  holders' unawareness of 129
  means of regulation 112, 121–3, 126–9, 146–52
  moral evaluation 120–1, 126–7, 128
  prevalence 106
  seen as detached from character 107–8, 109–10, 113–14, 124, 125
  seen as integrated with character 108–9, 110, 123–6
  and situational manipulation 134–6
incapacitation, as aim of punishment 54
institutions, building of 248–52
insult, violent response to 43–4
intraindividual behavioural signatures 164
isolation 4, 37, 50–2, 58
  arguments against 52
  conditions 50–1
  prevalence in US jails 50, 52
  psychological impact 50, 51–2

jealousy, expressions of 70–1
Johnson, John 175
justification (of personal decisions) 100

Kamtekar, Rachana 146*n*
Kane, Robert 69, 72
Kant, Immanuel 74*n*, 81, 86–8, 89, 94, 99, 102
kindness vs honesty 38
knowledge, importance of 219–20
Korsgaard, Christine 73, 74*n*, 87–8, 91, 92, 103
Kripke, Saul 194
Kupperman, Joel 17, 20, 207

leadership, gendered qualities 113
Leibniz, Gottfried Wilhelm 86

INDEX 259

Levy, Neil 108, 109, 111–13
Lewis, David 188
Li, Peizhong 112
liberalism
 legal philosophy 10–11, 32
 in pluralist society 11
 relationship with civil society 13–14
Locke, John 90
loss-aversion 197, 198, 199, 201
Louisiana, penal system 53
love, experiences/impacts of 89–90, 95, 103, 198–9
luck 89, 94, 96
Luther, Martin 81, 85, 88, 92, 102
 moral character 82–3
LWOP (life without parole) prison sentences 45–7
 justifications 46–7*n*
 objections 45–6, 49–50
 offenders appropriate to 46

MacIntyre, Alasdair 191, 231, 239, 243–5, 248–50, 251
Malhotra, Deepak 222
mastery
 advantages 236–9
 distinguished from competence 231–2, 251
 Einstellung effect 237–8
 lifelong pursuit of 250–1
 as model for virtue 242–3, 249
 process of acquisition 236–7
May, Mark A. 207, 214–15, 224
McDowell, John 74*n*
McGeer, Victoria 199–200, 201
medroxyprogesterone acetate (MPA) 53, 55–6
mental phenomena, equated with physical 75–6
mental states
 activation 157–8, 172
 clusters 157–8, 166, 172–3, 180
 inactive 156–7
 range of 156
Merritt, Maria 125
Milgram, Stanley 102, 137, 144, 217, 219
 experimental subjects' retrospective comments 136

 manipulation of experimental design 134–5
Mill, John Stuart 67
Millgram, Elijah 195
Mischel, Walter 155, 159–61, 159*n*, 160*nn*, 162*n*, 163*n*, 165, 166, 169–71, 172–3*nn*, 174, 175, 176–9, 176*n*, 211*n*, 215
modesty, paradox of 194*n*
Monteith, M. J. 116*n*
Moody-Adams, Michele 65, 66
moral choice blindness 139–41
moral education, processes of 59
moral improvement
 negative programme of 146–8, 149
 positive programme of 149–52
moral necessity 85–6
'moral schizophrenia' 191
morality 5, 208–11
 enforcement 10–11
 excessive 241–2
 exemplars 220–1, 229, 240
 and implicit bias 120–1
 in individual choices 36–7, 208
 judgements in 223
 obligations of 85–6, 221–2
 personal commitment to 222–3
 and practical understanding 230–1
 role in character education 223–4
 self-respect achieved through 102–3
Morton, Adam 195, 203
Moskowitz, Gordon 112, 116*n*, 122
Murphy, Dominic 26–7
Murphy, Jeffrie 23
music, study/expertise in 250–1

necessity *see* personal necessity; practical necessity
negative emotions, expression of 18
Nehamas, Alexander 187, 195
Nozick, Robert 41, 194

Obama, Barack 147
OCD (obsessive-compulsive disorder) 48

Paganini, Niccolò 250
Parfit, Derek 90
Peake, Philip 166, 211*n*
Peiper, Jochen 26–7
perfection, drawbacks of 203–4, 241

personal necessity 4–5, 21, 81–104
  exceptional nature 101–4
  and interpersonal relationships 95–104
  and limits of character 81–2, 89–90, 93–4, 96–9
  and moral law 82
  and reformability 99–104
  see also practical necessity
Personal Responsibility and Work Opportunity Reconciliation Act 1996 (US) 29
personality
  change of 82, 91, 92–5, 99–104 (*see also* reform)
  development of 93–4
  psychology of 2–3
  studies 178–9, 216–17
  theories of 5–6, 137–9, 175–6 (*see also* cognitive-affective system theory)
  types 178–9
Petersilia, Joan 25
Pettit, Philip 196–7, 199, 201
Plato 87, 146*n*
Poland, penal system 53
Posner, Richard, Judge 36
postmodernism 90
practical necessity 85–8
  balancing of considerations 91–2
  as expression of personality 84–5, 88
  and moral duty 86–7
  and obedience to law 86
practical possibility, limits imposed by 20–1
practical wisdom 7, 243–5
  acquisition 244–5
  means of encouraging 248–9
  social dimension 245
practice, exercise of control via 119–20
practices
  defined 243
  role in acquisition of mastery/virtue 244–5
principles 22, 73
prison 3–4
  availability of choices 37, 51–2, 56, 57–8
  impact on character 13–14, 24–6, 30–1, 32
  life sentences *see* LWOP
  living conditions 24–5, 29–30
  long-term effects 27–8
  personal development programmes 57–8
  range of responses to 28
  repeat offending following release 46–7*n*
  situational nature of experience 26
Pritchard, Duncan 195
problem-solving
  assimiliative 233–4
  progressive 238–9, 242–3
processing dispositions 171–2
psychology
  commonsense assumptions 156–8, 162, 166, 174
  and education 207–8
  experiments in 134–6, 139–43, 144–5, 151–2, 222–4
  external elements 194–5
  of personality 2–3
  relationship with philosophy 1–2, 202–3, 207–8
  studies 215–16
  see also attitude psychology
punishment, criminal 3–4, 9–14, 23–33, 35–58
  aims/rationale 23–4, 42–3
  consequentialist conception 24
  hybrid theory of justification 41
  impact on character 3–4, 9, 12–14, 42–3
  impact on crime rates 54
  justifications 35–6, 40–1
  loss of voting rights following 29
  options 44–9
  problems of reintegration 29, 30–1, 56–7
  stigmatization of offenders 56–7
  see also prison
Putnam, Hilary 194

Quante, Michael 93–4

race relations, CAPS applied to 178
racism, implicit bias towards 107–9, 113–14
  experiments in 135–6, 145–6, 147
  means of regulation 121–2
  'Obama effect' 147
Railton, Peter 120

Ravizza, Mark 74
reductionism 75–6, 78
reform (of personality) 82, 90, 95, 99–104
  see also rehabilitation
rehabilitation
  as aim of punishment 29, 32–3, 35–6, 37, 40, 41–3
  failure of 52
  programmes of 44–5
religion
  and aspirations 229
  relationship with ethical behaviour 222
retribution, as aim of punishment 23–4, 53–4
Rikers Island Prison (NY) 50
Roberts, Robert C. 189, 191
Russell, Daniel 155, 191
Ryan, Charles J. 54

Sartre, Jean-Paul 69
Saul, Jennifer 107, 109, 110, 116*n*
Scardamalia, Marlene 230, 231, 233, 236, 238, 239, 245, 247, 248, 252
Schechtman, Marya 91–2
Schopenhauer, Arthur 67, 70
scientific theory/ies
  compared with moral 242
  criteria 175–6
self-authentification 94–5
self-constitution, theory of 87–8, 104
self-control *see* self-regulation
self-esteem, value of 198–9, 202, 217
self-knowledge 20, 21–2
self-reform *see* reform
self-regulation 127–9
  balanced with self-expression 91–2
  systems/plans 159, 160
self-respect, means to 102–3
sexism, implicit bias towards 107–8, 113, 151–2
Shils, Edward 12*n*
Shoda, Yuichi 155, 160*nn*, 161, 163*n*, 164–5, 166*n*, 168, 172–3*nn*, 174, 177–9, 212
situational manipulation 134–6, 139–40, 216–19
  reduced susceptibility to 151
situationism 1, 6–7, 38, 134, 173, 208, 211–14

situations
  consistency across 164–6
  nominal/psychologically salient features 162–4
  situation-behaviour contingencies 160–2
skill(s) *see* competence
Slote, Michael 191
Smith, Michael 64
snakes, fear of 157–8, 159–60, 163–4, 165–6, 173
Sneddon, Andrew 194
Snow, Nancy 115, 127–8, 155, 191
Socrates 223
soldiers, combat experiences 26–7
solitary confinement *see* isolation
Sophocles, *Aias* 90–1, 92, 94, 98–9
sports
  league systems 246–7
  physical control in 119, 120, 122, 123*n*
State, (lack of) responsibility for character-building 32
stewardship, environmental 39
stimulus values 159–60
Stoic philosophy 146*n*
Strawson, Galen 72
suicide 90–1, 98–9
summer camps, studies of behaviour at 161, 163, 164–5, 166, 166*n*, 167*t*
supermax prisons 51
Sweden, penal system 53
Sykes, Gresham 30, 31

Taylor, Gabriele 31*n*
teachers, as role models 224–5
temperament, role in formation of character 15–16
Thomas, Laurence 196
traits (of character) 1
  causal view 170, 171–4, 171*n*
  and cognitive-affective system theory 155, 169–74
  conditional view 170–1
  habituation in 37, 51–2, 57, 110–11, 150
  morally neutral 209
  and personality psychology 2–3
  situations suited to expression of 215
  summary view 68–9, 170, 171
  and virtue theory 37–40

trust 6
  actions expressive of 70-1
  as component of friendship 195-6
  cunning mechanism 196-7, 202
  friendship as model for 195-202
  hopeful mechanism 199-201, 202
  intrinsic vs factitious 203-4
  relational nature 196-7
  self-concept mechanism 198-9, 202

United Kingdom
  penal system 9, 53
United States
  crime rates/patterns 43
  invasion of Iraq 27
  northern vs southern cultures 43
  penal system 3-4, 9, 25, 29, 40, 45-6, 53, 54
Utøya massacre (2011) 98-9

Van Mechelen, Iven 178-9
Vansteelandt, Kristof 178-9
vice(s)
  circumstances favourable to 30, 31
  perverse pleasure in 21
virtue theory
  Aristotelian 15-16, 37, 63, 70-1, 134, 146n, 186, 211, 221, 225, 239-42, 249-50
  contemporary versions 36-7, 38, 40, 56-7, 193, 201-2, 203-4, 220-5, 252
  and criminal punishment 36-7, 41-3, 54-5, 56-7
  history, to C18 40
  objections to use in criminal context 56-7
virtue(s)
  acquisition of 15-16, 17-18, 39-40, 128-9, 134-5, 211-14, 229-30, 243-5 (see also moral improvement)
  aspiration to 229
  competence model 7
  conflicts between 38
  development strategies 128-9
  distinguished from principles 22
  ethics of 7
  'factitious' 6, 193-4, 203-4
  persons of, as role models 220-1
  punishment as means of encouraging 35-6
  punishment critiqued via theory of 36-7
  range of practices 244
  relationships between 22
  self-awareness of 193-4, 194n
  stability 212
  as 'thick' concept 191
  unity of 249-50
Vivaldi, Antonio 250
vocation and personal necessity 96-8
Voils, C. I. 116n
voting rights, loss of 29

Watson, Gary 22
Webber, Jonathan 38, 43, 69
will 62-78
  character detached from 70-2
  as justification 70-1
  and necessity 89-90
  in opposition with character 70-1
  overlap with character 62, 63, 76
  relationship with character 4-5, 69-70, 74-8
  single phenomenon view 74-8
  as sole function of agency 69
  strength/weakness of 63n
Williams, Bernard 20-1, 68, 76, 76n, 89, 90-1, 94, 96, 98, 102
Wolf, Susan 231, 241-2
word association 135-6
Worms, Diet of 82-3
Wright, Jack 155, 161, 166, 170-1, 174

Yankah, Ekow 42, 56-7, 57n

Zayas, Vivian 160n, 162n, 172n

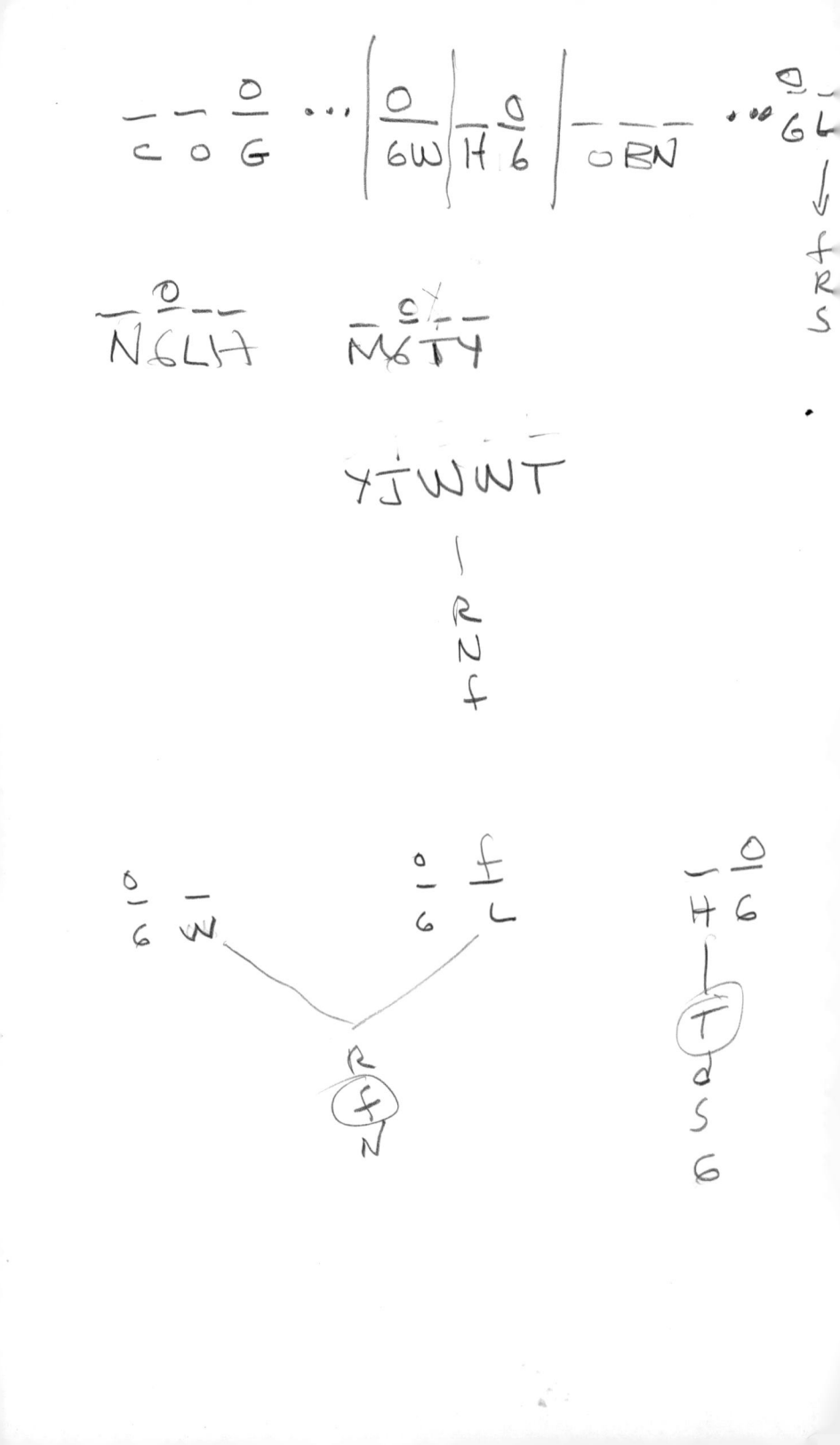

$$\overset{\circ}{\underset{COG}{---}} \cdots \left| \overset{\circ}{\underset{GW}{-}} \right| \overset{\circ}{\underset{H\ 6}{-}} \left| \underset{OBN}{---} \right. \cdots \overset{\circ}{\underset{GL}{-}}$$

$\downarrow$
f
R
S

$$\overset{\circ}{\underset{N6LH}{---}} \qquad \overset{\circ\times}{\underset{M6T4}{---}}$$

$$Y\dot{J}WNT$$
|
R
N
f

$$\overset{\circ}{\underset{6}{-}} \underset{W}{-} \qquad \overset{\circ}{\underset{6}{=}} \overset{f}{\underset{L}{-}} \qquad \overset{\circ}{\underset{H\ 6}{--}}$$

(f)
R
N

(T)
d
S
6